P9-BBO-981

Rudy

MY STORY

LIBRARY OF
WALKER MORNE

Rudy
MY STORY

by DANIEL "RUDY" RUETTIGER

WITH MARK DAGOSTINO

THOMAS NELSON
Since 1798

NASHVILLE   DALLAS   MEXICO CITY   RIO DE JANEIRO

© 2012 by Rudy Ruettiger

All rights reserved. No portion of this book may be reproduced, stored in a retrieval system, or transmitted in any form or by any means—electronic, mechanical, photocopy, recording, scanning, or other—except for brief quotations in critical reviews or articles, without the prior written permission of the publisher.

Published in Nashville, Tennessee, by Thomas Nelson. Thomas Nelson is a registered trademark of Thomas Nelson, Inc.

Thomas Nelson, Inc. titles may be purchased in bulk for educational, business, fund-raising, or sales promotional use. For information, please e-mail SpecialMarkets@ ThomasNelson.com.

Library of Congress Cataloging-in-Publication Data

Ruettiger, Rudy.
Rudy : my story / Daniel "Rudy" Ruettiger with Mark Dagostino.
p. cm.
ISBN 978-0-8499-4839-8 (hardcover)
1. Ruettiger, Rudy. 2. College football players--United States--Biography. 3. Dyslexics--United States--Biography. 4. University of Notre Dame--Football. 5. Notre Dame Fighting Irish (Football team) I. Dagostino, Mark. II. Title.
GV939.R845A3 2012
796.332092--dc23
[B]
2012016188

Printed in the United States of America

12 13 14 15 16 QG 5 4 3 2 1

Introduction

"In life, it's not about how hard you get hit. It's about how many times you get back up and how hard you're willing to keep fighting for your dreams."

It is amazing how a movie can touch your life. I remember watching the powerful film *Rocky* just after I graduated from the University of Notre Dame, followed by *Rocky II* a couple of years after that. I remember that overwhelming feeling of just wanting to go run up some stairs somewhere and throw my hands in the air as I left the theater. That feeling that I could do anything. That I could conquer the world.

The funny thing was, I *had* conquered the world—or at least a small part of it. I had already had a *Rocky* moment in my real life. I had already accomplished more than anyone else ever dreamed I could. Like Rocky Balboa, I had proved all the naysayers wrong. I won. In my own way, on my own path, I won. Me! A stocky, messed-up kid from Joliet, Illinois, whom some people doubted would graduate high school, had gone on to play for the University of Notre Dame football team and to earn myself a top-notch college education.

And I was just getting started.

Watching *Rocky*, and later the outstanding film *Hoosiers*, made me think about my own story of perseverance. Anyone I told my story to was bowled over. "Your life is like a movie!" they'd tell me. I was an insurance agent at the time. I didn't know a thing about Hollywood. But after enough people said it, I started to believe it—and I called on my inner Rocky to see if I could go do something about it.

A few long years and countless struggles later, my life's story became a movie all its own: the 1993 film *Rudy*.

All of a sudden I was invited to give pep talks in locker rooms all over America. Corporate giants brought me into their boardrooms to fire up their sales teams. I was invited to the White House for a private screening. To this day, clips from *Rudy* play during the seventh-inning stretch at Yankee Stadium and at countless sporting events around the world. The film tops lists of the most inspirational movies of all time, and if you turn on your TV, chances are you can find it airing on one cable station or another nearly every week throughout the year.

Rudy became something much bigger than me. Much bigger than I ever dreamed.

Today, nearly twenty years after the film was made, wherever I go, people talk to me about how they call on their "inner Rudy" to find the strength to follow their dreams. People line up at events and appearances to tell me about their own real-life Rudy moments—the way I used to refer to *Rocky* moments in my life, or my own "inner Rocky." It's astounding. My name, *my story*, has become synonymous with inspiration. And over the years, I've asked myself, "Why?"

I wasn't some super-talented kid who rose up from nothing and beat the odds to make it to the Super Bowl. I wasn't some guy with a ninety-mile-per-hour fastball who broke into major league baseball in his forties. I was a lower middle-class kid who suffered through school with undiagnosed dyslexia, who was hard-headed enough to find a side door into the University of Notre Dame to earn my degree and to dress and play for the last twenty-seven seconds of a football game my senior year. Twenty-seven seconds! That's it! And that was the point. A point that became utterly clear to me as the years went by: what Rudy represents isn't some far-fetched Hollywood story. This isn't some impossible, once-in-a-lifetime fantasy that most people can never attain. It's not the story of Michael Jordan or Peyton Manning—individuals with extreme talent they could build upon. The wisdom of age has taught me that the power of my story, the power of the inspiration that so many people feel when they watch the film *Rudy* comes from the fact that at heart, I'm just an "Average Joe." Anyone could accomplish the sort of dream I tackled. The short kid. The fat kid. The smart kid. The struggling kid. The frustrated worker. The bored-to-death business-man. The housewife. The husband. Anyone. The moral of the Rudy story is that anyone with a dream can make that dream a reality—as long as they're willing to put in the hard work and heart it takes to get there.

Some people have the misperception that I was somehow born with more heart, more drive, and more passion to accomplish my dreams than the next guy. What I'm here to tell you is it's just not true. I found my heart, my drive, and my passion one step at a time, simply by growing up, making mistakes, learning from those mistakes, and pressing forward. Heck, I'm *still* making mistakes! In the past few years I made some business decisions that got me in a heap of trouble, but I overcame it and I learned from it and I'll open up about what happened right here in these pages for the very first time, in the hopes that you'll learn from it too. After all, I'm only human. Aren't we all? And we all make mistakes. The difference between those who reach their dreams and those who don't may just be a willingness to look at those mistakes and at all of life's obstacles from a new perspective.

If there's one thing I've learned, it's that life is a journey. A long journey. And the lessons never stop coming. Big accomplishments, big successes, even big bank accounts don't stop that process. Not at all. To learn that life doesn't get easier just because you've reached a certain goal, accomplished a certain dream, or even had a movie made about your life story may be the toughest lesson of all. Life goes on, and so do life's challenges. You simply have to find a way to persevere and push through with all of the determina-tion you can muster.

I don't have all the answers. I don't pretend to have all the answers. If you're looking for a self-help book filled with a lot of hot air, there are plenty of those books on the shelves. Go buy one. Instead, what I offer is the story of my life. A story that's far bigger and more complicated than any two-hour film could cover. (In fact, *Rudy* fans may be surprised to learn just how many of the stories from my life, even the people in my life, were compressed to their essence in order to serve the message and meaning of my journey on film. That's part of the Hollywood magic I'll share in these pages as well.)

What I offer instead is a story focused on a series of triumphs over seemingly insurmountable odds. A story that I hope will inspire you to take the hits and keep moving forward, to triumph over your own obstacles, and to dream bigger. 'Cause once that happens, once you find yourself dreaming bigger than ever before and leading the life you truly want to live, that's when you'll know that you've really dug deep and brought out the "Rudy" in you.

Part I

Growing Up

Part IV: Dream Bigger

Contents

This book is dedicated to my family.

"Rudy's book bursts with timeless truths and principles that, when followed, can help you succeed in anything you do in life. I highly recommend this compelling read to all who are in pursuit of a fulfilling life professionally and personally."

SEAN WOLFINGTON
CHAIRMAN AND CEO OF THE
WOLFINGTON COMPANIES

"*Never give up on your dreams*. That's the message that Rudy shares from his blue collar background to the Notre Dame field and beyond."

DAVE TREMBLEY
MANAGER, BALTIMORE
ORIOLES (2007–2010)

"Rudy is about winning, in the biggest sense of the word. Not just winning on the field, or winning at the box office, or winning in business—but winning in life."

ROB FRIED
PRODUCER

"Just as *Rudy* was a film about so much more than football, this book is about so much more than the life story of Rudy Ruettiger. It's a book about hope. It's a book about inspiration. It's a book that readers can turn back to again and again in the face of life's challenges to remind themselves how to work even harder to turn their own dreams into reality."

STEVE LARSON
CEO, EID PASSPORT

"This isn't the story of one man, one dream, one college, or one football team. It's a story for everyone who's ever had a dream. It's a story of hope. It's a story of perseverance. Rudy is for anyone who ever wanted to know what it's really like to make dreams come true."

REAR ADMIRAL KEVIN DELANEY
UNITED STATES NAVY (RETIRED)

"*Rudy: My Story* is a combination of honesty and heartfelt truths of 'never giving up'. It is a touching rendition of total inspiration."

JON JANNOTTA
CEO, WWW.U-INSPIRE.COM

"If life is all about the journey, then Rudy's story is a journey of hope. I'm thrilled to see him share his full story with the world in this exciting new book."

JOHN E. ADAMS
CEO, CENEGENICS

"In real life, just like the movie, Rudy proves he can take the hits, and keep on coming back."

ANGELO PIZZO
WRITER AND PRODUCER

"As a young kid I had a front row seat for one of the all-time great underdog triumphs. Rudy took me everywhere . . . the locker room, the practice field, the broom closet that served as his dorm room . . . constantly telling me how he would run out of that tunnel one day. When no one else believed, and I mean no one, Rudy did. I was there when he was carried off the field on his teammates' shoulders. Years later, I'm still inspired."

TERRY GANNON
NETWORK SPORTSCASTER
MEMBER OF JIM VALVANO'S
1983 NC STATE NATIONAL
CHAMPIONSHIP TEAM

"The Rudy message never dies. In the lessons of his life, he reminds each of us how possible it is to rise up against all odds."

BRIAN KILMEADE
FOX NEWS, NEW YORK

Praise for *Rudy*

"This book—Rudy's story—is for anyone who has ever been an underdog."

SEAN ASTIN
ACTOR

"Every business leader and entrepreneur in America can learn from Rudy's lessons of persistence and perseverance."

DAN HESSE
CEO, SPRINT

"The power of Rudy isn't just his words or his story. The power of Rudy is his message—a message of selflessness, perseverance, and hope that we all need to hear and remember."

DAVID MONAHAN
PRINCIPLE, COLONY CAPITAL LLC

"I was commissioned to work on *Rudy* in 1993—a date I will never forget because the real Rudy Ruettiger interacted in the making of the movie and shared his passion of never giving up, inspiring all of us. Recently, Rudy reentered my life and came to speak in my class of filmmakers and composers. The energy of his light fulfilling dreams created a memory we will remember forever."

KENNETH HALL
ASSOCIATE PROFESSOR, USC
SCHOOL OF CINEMATIC ARTS

On the Ball

I was ten years old when I got my first glimpse.

I remember the hot vinyl seat searing the back of my legs as I sat toward the back of a school bus full of other young ball players, returning from a Little League field trip to a White Sox game up in Chicago.

The whole day had been amazing. Seeing those players take the field; actually witnessing my first live game; and stepping foot into a major league stadium and feeling the roar of that crowd was electrifying. Of course, every one of us kids from every one of those Joliet teams wore a glove to the game—just hoping and dreaming that we might be lucky enough to snag a foul ball as we sat in the stands. The thought of actually catching, touching, holding on to a major league baseball was about as big a thrill as my ten-year-old mind could imagine.

Then it happened. The wind-up. The pitch. The *clock* of the ball as it cracked off a Louisville Slugger, high and shallow down the left-field line, arcing foul and coming right for us! Every kid stood with his glove in the air. I remember squinting into the sun, doing everything I could to wish that ball directly into my hand. It came close! But I just couldn't reach it. One of the other team's coaches snagged that ball out of the sky as if it were tossed directly to him.

So there we were, rolling back toward Joliet, when that coach stood up and told everyone to quiet down. He stood at the front of the bus with that major league baseball in hand, tossing it and re-catching it a couple of times before holding it high above his head so every one of us could see it. "When we get back," he said, "we're all gonna line up and I'm gonna throw this ball. And whoever gets it can have it."

I nearly fell over. I wanted that ball more than anything I'd wanted in my entire life. The whole ride home, all I did was keep thinking about that ball. *A major league baseball! Mine for the taking!* I couldn't believe my luck.

My knees bounced up and down with anticipation as we pulled into Highland Park. As soon as that bus driver opened the door, we all burst out and ran onto the field. There must have been thirty of us boys all lined up at our home plate, staring out across the baseball diamond to the chest-high wooden fence at the back of the outfield, chomping at the bit to get this ball. Even so, I kept thinking, *That ball's mine.* It *was* mine. I knew it.

That coach got up in front of us on the pitcher's mound while the other coaches and a few of the parents who had come to pick us up corralled us into a straight line so it would be fair to everyone. "Ready?" he said.

"Yeah!" the kids all shouted.

"Are you ready?" he asked again.

"Yeah!" they all screamed louder. But not me. I was silent. I was focused on that ball, watching the red seam stitching go round and round as he turned it in his hand.

Satisfied by the enthusiasm of that final shout, the coach turned around; pulled his right arm back; lifted his left leg; took a big, exaggerated, hard step forward; and launched that ball in a massive arc all the way to the back of the outfield. I never took my eyes off it, even for a split second, even as my feet began to move beneath me. I wasn't conscious of just how fast I was running. I paid no attention to whether I was out in front or far behind those dozens of other competitors. All that mattered to me was that ball, and that ball was all I saw—even as it hit the ground in the neatly trimmed grass, took one hard bounce, and flew right over that fence to land in the overgrown mess of weeds on the other side. I watched that ball the whole way as I blew through the outfield and leaped over that fence like it wasn't even there. I was so focused, I didn't even stop to think about how to get over it—I just did it, as if I had leaped over a thousand fences before and knew exactly what to do. I knew just where that ball had landed. I knew which blades of tall grass and milkweed it landed behind, and I dove right through them, crashing to the ground and feeling that hard, round presence crush into my chest. I pulled my arms in, clutched that ball to me as I rolled over, sprung up from the ground, raised it high above my head and screamed, "I got it!"

Suddenly aware of the world around me, I noticed kids to my right and my left looking in the weeds in all the wrong places; a whole bunch of other players were still on the field or struggling to get over the fence. I left them in the dust. The fact that they were bigger than me, faster than me, and stronger than me didn't matter. I was kind of stunned by it. I remember having flashes of "What just happened?" and "How did I do that?" But what I really remember is the feel of that baseball in my hand. I was bolstered by the knowledge of where that ball came from and the undisputable fact that it now belonged to *me*. Squeezing the leathery weight of it just felt good.

That night, I placed that major league ball on the nightstand beside my bed, where I could see it from my pillow. The last object I would see before I fell off to sleep. I kept it there for years, unknowingly holding on to that feeling. Holding on to that tiny moment when I gave it my all and got exactly what I wanted. A feeling I would someday need to recapture: proof, in the form of a little round ball, that anything—*anything*—is possible.

I misplaced that ball somewhere in my travels through life. I've always hoped that someday it would show back up. But the memory and feeling of that ball will never be forgotten. It's embedded in my thoughts forever.

My mother always made us fold our underwear.

I know that's a strange thing to remember, and probably not one of the first things most people would mention when recalling their child-hood, but I hated it. I hated the very thought of doing it. It made no sense to me. *Why would we waste time folding an article of clothing that we're only going to put in a drawer where no one will see it? Especially considering the fact that it goes on under our clothes!* Don't get me wrong. I'm not against folding underwear if that's what you're into. But to have it forced upon me as a kid seemed like some sort of unjust punishment.

Taking it one step further, my mother actually pressed our underwear before we got dressed for church on Sundays. She refused to let us leave the house without perfectly cleaned and pressed underwear. "Why are you doing that?" we'd ask her, and her reply was always the same: "In case you get in an accident on the way to mass."

I can still picture my mother in the kitchen, clear as day, her tiny frame wielding that heavy iron with ease, standing there in a flower-print shirt, pressing our underwear and the dozens upon dozens of other items that just came off the clothesline—crooning old show tunes to herself while she did it, as if she enjoyed it. The funny thing is, I think she actually did. She had dreams of becoming a singer someday, and I don't think she ever stopped dreaming. You could hear her dream while she hummed, and there was something about putting those clothes in order and tackling that task, one skivvy at a time, that gave her a sense of peace. That inspired me. When she sang a song, she was relaxed and joyful. You could feel her energy and it relaxed our whole household.

In a house full of fourteen children, peace wasn't exactly easy to come by. In fact, my parents believed there was really only one way to find it: through order and discipline. So as far back as I can remember, order and discipline ruled in the Ruettiger house. My mother was in charge, every object had its place, every child had his or her duties, and breaking that sense of order meant you'd find your behind at the receiving end of my dad's big, strong hand—while bent over a hard wooden stool in the kitchen. (Often while mom continued ironing.)

I was the oldest boy in that massive family—my parents had seven boys and seven girls by the time they stopped having children—and let's just say up front that "order" and "discipline" were never my strong suits. My sisters have un-fond memories of me dressing up as a cowboy and bounding down the basement stairs, destroying their quiet attempts to play house by kicking over their makeshift toy kitchen sets. "Mom!" they'd scream. "Danny's doing it again!!" The spanking never deterred me. I'd keep coming back for more.

In fact, that's pretty much the story of my childhood.

My parents, Dan and Betty Ruettiger, married young, and like a lot of people in those days, they started having kids right away. After two back-to-back girls—my older sisters, Jean Ann and Mary Eileen—I came into the world on August 22, 1948. My mother would forget my birthday the very next year and celebrate it on August 23 instead—a date that would stick with me as a sort of pseudo-birthday from that day forward. I'm not sure why she forgot, but it stuck!

I was born Daniel E. Ruettiger (my whole family still calls me "Danny"), at St. Joseph's Hospital. Just like the rest of the clan, I was raised in the town where we were expected to grow old and die, the same town in which both of my parents had also been born and raised: the working-class Chicago suburb of Joliet, Illinois.

Joliet is a good forty-five-minute drive south of the city—far enough to seem like a world away when you're a kid. In fact, I have very few child-hood memories of Chicago at all, despite the fact that it was so close. My memories tend to revolve around a one- or two-mile radius of our house. That was my world. Church. School. The park. The grocery store. The constant sound of train whistles blowing, and the functional, beautyless, hard-worn streets and buildings of America's working class.

My parents' first house at 206 South East Circle Drive had three tiny bedrooms squeezed into less than seven hundred square feet. There was a one-car garage set back and to the side, with our neighbors' houses (all equally small) just a few feet away on either side. As we got older, the little patch of grass under the willow tree out front became a meeting point for those neighbors. It was a spot where we'd play football together. Laugh together. It seemed big then.

It's difficult for me to remember the period before that house was packed full of brothers and sisters. And by full, I mean bursting-at-the-seams full. I was a freshman in high school before we would finally move to a bigger house, and by then there were ten kids in our family. Imagine, just for a moment, trying to squeeze all of that pent-up energy into the four walls of that little yellow box of a post–World War II track home on the edge of a cornfield. One bedroom for the boys, one for the girls; bunk beds crammed together in each. In between sleep and school came what can only be described as resounding (if somewhat controlled) chaos.

The noise was constant. "Quiet, Danny!" "Tim, please!!" My mom did the best she could to keep a lid on it, but if you've ever walked into a grade-school cafeteria at lunchtime, that's pretty much the feeling you'd get if you walked into our house unannounced. After me came Carol, Rosemarie, Betsy, Tim, Francis, Mickey, John, Rita, Norma, Bernie, and Mark. The last few (from John on down) wouldn't be born until we moved into that slightly bigger house my freshman year, but I think after your family exceeds maybe five children, the enormity of the routines remains the same.

My mom loved to cook. Even for that army of kids. Dinners consisted of a lot of spaghetti, bean soup, or chili—stuff that could be prepared in bulk, wasn't too expensive, and would go a long way. In the summers, us kids would sit around shucking thirty bags of sweet corn at a time. We'd all cringe at the thought of liver and onions, but we'd eat it anyway. And occasionally my dad would bring home a live chicken from his parents' chicken farm—chopping the head off and letting it run around 'til it bled out in the backyard before handing it to my mom to pluck, boil, roast, and serve whole for dinner. The weekends usually meant hot dogs and hamburgers, and whatever leftovers there were would get consumed all week long. I don't know how she did it, but it was always delicious. And the smell of that food coming together made us all the more anxious to see dad's car pull into the driveway at the end of each day.

When dad came home, dinner was served at the big table he'd cobbled together by hand, and we all sat around and didn't talk. It was by far the most peaceful time of day in the Ruettiger house. In fact, the only other time I ever remember it being that quiet was each Christmas Eve, when all of us boys would stay up late and freeze in absolute stillness if we heard a noise that might be Old Saint Nick approaching.

At those dinners, for as long as I lived at home, we said our prayers, and if we wanted something we politely asked for it—we never grabbed. Even as kids, we all accepted that it had to be that way. I could see my dad decompressing while we ate. There were times when he fell asleep right there at the table. But I could always see my mom's satisfaction when everything went smoothly. It just made her happy when everything was in order. Even after spending all that time cooking dinner each night, she would take the time to pack all of our lunches for school the next day and line 'em up on the kitchen counter for us. She somehow knew that no family, let alone a family as big as ours, could live in chaos. So she did what she could to get a handle on it—to keep a lid on our antics—every day.

Just think about the logistics of juggling that many kids. I remember one day mom piled us all into the station wagon to go grocery shopping, which was always a bit of an ordeal, and when we got back home to South East Circle Drive, she realized one of the kids was missing! My sister Carol just plain wasn't there. My mom panicked. I'll never forget that look in her eyes, thinking that she had left a child behind, and what if something happened. It was awful to see her like that. But she piled us all back into the car as quickly as possible and raced back to the store. Thank God, there was Carol—my eight-year-old sister—just wandering happy as a clam up and down the aisles wondering where everyone had gone.

From that day forward, my mom counted heads and made us call out our names before she'd put the car into drive, no matter where we went. "Who's in the car?" she'd yell from the driver's seat. "We got eight? Call 'em out!" And we'd run down our names one by one, just to be sure.

Here's the thing that really gets me, though. The thing that seems so impossible in today's world, by today's standards, even though most families don't have half or even a quarter as many kids as my parents did. I mean, my mom's whole life was washing clothes and cooking, right? That alone was more than a full-time job. She didn't really have time to do anything else. Yet she served as the president of the Mother's Club and never missed a Little League game or a school play—for any of her kids. Heck, my dad coached Little League even while holding down three jobs to make ends meet! I think about what a commitment that was. In their eyes, their children always came first: "It's all about the kids." Despite the difficulties and complications that come with having so many children, it's as if that one guiding principle kept both of my parents sane and on track. "We had them; we're responsible for them." Simple.

That's not to say they were perfect parents. Nobody's perfect. Nobody. And I don't particularly agree with how much of their discipline was doled out the old-fashioned way. Just about every report card day, at least a few of us boys would get in line for a spanking over the stool in the kitchen. It wasn't because of our grades. It was over reports that we weren't being respectful to our teachers or were being troublemakers in the classroom. My dad was concerned with honor and respect. So one after the other, *whack!* "Next!"

My brother Francis and I were the main culprits. We were both deemed troublemakers, and we both dealt with the same sort of issues in school. The spankings were so routine that Francis eventually figured a way to get out of it: he'd stuff a couple of thin books down the back of his pants so the hits wouldn't hurt. My dad was so busy going from one kid to the next that he didn't even notice! There were other times when my dad would get so frustrated he'd spank you a second or third time for no apparent reason. I get it. With fourteen crazy kids running around in a little house, all of his worry about fixing the car, and paying the bills, I'd probably want to whack something too. But I wonder what it taught us. Did it keep us in line? Maybe. Would we have turned out for the worse without it? Hard to say. My brothers and sisters and I all grew up to be good people, and I say that without bragging. There are no big mess-ups in the whole family of fourteen. That's pretty extraordinary. Yet I think that's a reflection of the love and support our parents showed more than any hand-to-rear discipline. Even so, it's a tricky game to second-guess and look back with twenty-twenty hindsight. There are no instant replays in life. You get what you get and you have to live with the calls that were made at the time.

Setting corporal punishment aside, I think a lot of parents, teachers, priests, and other authority figures forget just how much influence their words alone can have on a young child. For instance, when we went to the little church attached to our elementary school, St. Mary Magdalene, on Sundays, our family took up two full pews: one for the boys, one for the girls. In order to keep us quiet throughout mass, our parents were strict. They insisted that we never, ever turn around, and my dad told us that if we talked in church, God would punish us and our ears would fall off. What a horrible thing to say! I believed it too—for a very long time. If my dad told it to me, why wouldn't I believe it? I was scared to death to open my mouth 'cause I liked my ears just the way they were—attached to my head!

I'm not sure how old I was when I finally shook off that fear of losing my ears in church. Heck, when I'm under the glow of those stained-glass windows to this day I barely speak—and if I do, I keep my voice down. It's an amazing thing how a parent can fill your head with goofy thoughts like that, and how they can haunt you the rest of your life. They're goofy thoughts that have no good reason to be there, but they are so incredibly difficult to get rid of once they're embedded in your brain.

I don't blame my parents for that kind of stuff. Their intentions were good. They were doing the best they could given their situation, and Lord knows they were learning on the job with no guidebook other than memories of how they had been raised themselves. But that doesn't mean I have to carry on in the same tradition. That certainly doesn't mean I couldn't change. And I would change—quite a few years down the road. Today, I don't dwell on the negative stuff. I hardly even think of it. In fact, if I weren't sitting here writing a book about my life, I might not have brought it up at all. But I want you to get the whole picture. I want you to see that my upbringing wasn't perfect. I didn't have special advantages. I was raised like a lot of other kids in my generation, and I know there were lots of other kids that were raised under entirely different circumstances as well. Circumstances that I can't even imagine.

What I'm driving at here is that where we start in life doesn't define who we will become. If it did, that would pretty much mean we'd never have any kind of progress or evolution in the world, and of course, that's not the case. The only way to move forward is to take what you need from your upbringing. Learn from it—the good and the bad—and apply it to the life you want to lead. When you need a little something to lean on, think back on the good stuff and be thankful for all of that good stuff you had, whatever that good stuff may have been.

What sticks with me the most from those early years, especially as I get older, is knowing how hard my parents worked and how dedicated they were to taking care of this family they created. When I focus on that, all of those other goofy thoughts disappear.

———

Long before I came into the picture, back when my dad was just a kid, the Ruettigers were landowners. My grandparents at one time had more than two hundred head of cattle and enough land for them all to roam on before Joliet grew into a more industrialized town after World War II. Taking care of the farm, the land, and those cattle involved all of the kids as soon as they had the strength to help out, and I'd imagine that's where my dad's old-fashioned bootstrap work ethic began.

If the Ruettigers had held on to those cattle and all that land, my upbringing might have been very different. Unfortunately, that wasn't to be. In a single year, some sort of disease swept through the entire herd, killing every last one of those animals, and when my grandparents couldn't get a loan to replace the herd, the whole operation went belly up. They lost their livelihood. Lost their land. Lost everything.

Thinking of all that, it's easier for me to understand why my dad was who he was.

My father was always covered in grease. He loved fixing things and building things in that Greatest Generation–era, bull-in-a-china-shop mentality of "just get it done." It didn't matter if it was pretty. It just had to work. And it seemed like he could make anything work, from a rusty old lawnmower to our first electric washing machine to the big old Plymouth Fury station wagon with balding tires that managed to cart our entire family around through most of my childhood.

As hard as my father worked, he could never afford a new car with so many mouths to feed. So he brought home junkers and hand-me-downs and kept 'em running on spare parts and duct tape. But we never went without a vehicle.

It's kind of funny now to think about fourteen kids fitting into a single station wagon. Nobody wore seat belts in those days, of course, so we'd pile into the way-back and squeeze ourselves in wherever we could find a spot. It must have looked like a clown car at the circus when the Ruettigers pulled into the church parking lot on Sundays: kid, after kid, after kid, after kid, all piling out of that Plymouth!

Of course, what kid wants his family to be looked at like a bunch of clowns? I'm not sure how old I was the first time I overheard a snide comment about how many kids my parents had. There were times when a co-worker or some old-timer from town would say something directly to my dad: "Why the heck would you want to have so many kids?" But usually it was said off to the side somewhere. "Did you hear? Ruettiger's got another one comin'." "There goes our insurance!" they'd say at work. My mom even got it at the grocery store: "Oh look, poor Betty's got another bun in the oven." It's amazing how hurtful people can be with their words, and especially their tone. *Do you think we can't hear you? Did you ever stop to think how insulting it might be to make fun of someone else's choices in life? Just because they might not be the same choices you'd make doesn't make it right to look down on someone else because of it. And what's so awful about bringing another child into the world, anyway?* I always hated that half-joking voice people used when talking about the size of our family. *Why do you care?* Of course, I never spoke up. I'd just keep those feelings inside—the same way my dad did. I never heard him say anything back to any of those jokers. Not once.

The thing I saw early on was that none of those guys he worked with had any idea just how dedicated my father was to his family. He didn't just work hard at one job in order to support us. He held down a second job, and most of the time a third job in order to provide for us the best way he knew how.

Job number one was at the oil refinery: Union Oil. My dad started working there after the war. He served in the air force as a turret gunner and flew twenty-two missions during World War II, including one in which he froze his foot because the hull of the plane was so cold, which tells you a little about what the conditions were like. It wasn't something he ever really talked about with us kids. I wish I knew more about what he went through. What he saw. What he felt. But when he came home, he found good union wages awaited him at the refinery, and he dug in. Over time, he moved up, eventually leaving the ranks of the union (and losing those guaranteed union benefits) in order to become a superintendent, where he would find himself having to fight the very union that had welcomed him into a job when he came home from the war. He would stay at Union Oil until he retired.

Most nights after he got home from work and ate, he'd go work at his brother's gas station. My uncle Roge, whom dad always called "Whitey," was the youngest of my dad's brothers. He needed the help, and dad needed the money. It was a match made in heaven. And when the time came that my dad had to work nights at the refinery, he'd switch things up and go work at the gas station all day instead. He rarely even took a break on weekends: Saturday morning, he'd rise before the rest of us and head out to work construction with his friend Dan, building houses. Dan was a real creative guy—the type who would design a whole house project on the spot, on a shingle, right at the site, and my dad learned a lot from him. They became very close friends as the years went by. But to swing a hammer after working two other jobs all week must've been brutal on him.

Fatigue and frustration were written on my dad's face for most of those early years. I don't remember seeing him smile very much, and he certainly didn't show much of a sense of humor. In fact, he never really showed his emotions at all. I don't remember him ever hugging me as a kid. He never said the words "I love you." I knew he loved me. I did. But it's almost as if there wasn't enough time in the day for that kind of mush. "Work now, play later," he used to say in that deep voice of his. "If you play now, you'll have to work later, and you won't get to enjoy your life." I didn't understand that. I thought you were *supposed* to play! That's what I did as a kid. I played. But he used to repeat that "work now, play later" mantra to me and my brothers and sisters all the time. Sure, he and my mom would get together with some friends from bridge club once in a while to play some cards and just decompress. They made a point of making a date night once every month or two, just to get a little relief from the family. And dad seemed to get real enjoyment out of fixing the car, or fixing other stuff as a favor to friends. But I can't think of a time in my entire childhood when he did something for himself, or ever showed any real flashes of joy, at all—except when it came to sports.

The New York Yankees, the Green Bay Packers, and Notre Dame football were my dad's escape. As far as I could tell, listening to those games on the radio and watching the recaps on TV on Sunday nights were his one and only form of relaxation. I saw the hope in his eyes, the expression on his face, his bursts of excitement at a really great play. The way he'd stand or shout or pump his fist—or all three!—when one of his teams clinched a win is printed on my memory. It was a whole different side to my dad that sunk in very early on, and whenever I could, I would sit right with him, by his favorite chair in the living room, while he watched and listened to those games.

My dad didn't live through sports. I think sometimes people pour so much attention into their favorite teams that they live through the games. That's not what he did. There's a difference. Sports were his outlet, his relief. He respected and honored those players and those teams, the traditions, and what they stood for. And that certainly rubbed off on me as a kid. I mean, who wouldn't want to be on the receiving end of that kind of admiration and respect?

Not only was I listening to the games, but before long I found myself reading up on the players, memorizing stats. I could run through the whole starting lineup of the Yankees, player by player, dropping their batting averages and RBIs off the top of my head faster than you could find them on the back of their baseball cards. I loved learning about the history of the game, swapping information with friends at school, and then holding my own in conversations with my dad. Bonding with him over the Yankees and eventually trying my best to emulate those great players on the Little League field would make for some of my greatest childhood memories.

Of course, even a young Ruettiger had to learn about work. It seemed that as soon as I had mastered riding a bike, my parents set me up with a paper route. Every kid in the family (girls included) had a paper route; we just handed our route off to the next kid in line when the time came. Everyone got the local paper in those days—which meant I was responsible for delivering something like 160 papers to 160 homes. I wasn't allowed to ride my bike out on the busy main road, so after I was done going back and forth carrying as many papers as I could on two wheels within my own neighborhood, I'd have to walk across the corn fields, even in sub-zero temperatures in the dead of winter, to get to the surrounding areas. I still remember my nose running, and trying to wipe it off with my cold wet mitten only to feel it freezing to my face. Man, it was the worst! But it had to get done. Over time, to make things a little easier, my dad built a custom bike with big baskets on the back end to hold the papers, and a big fat tire on the back to support all that weight. It certainly made it easier not having to go back and forth to reload all the time. Of course, the way my dad built things, the chain never quite fit, and the frame was a little bent, but it worked most of the time. And when it didn't, he'd be right out there fixing it up and sending us back on our way.

Whatever money I made from that route went right back into our household. It wasn't about making money for *me*. It was about making money for the family. And I was okay with that. Heck, I wasn't blind. I saw that other kids' families had nicer things than we could afford, and if I could contribute to making things better, I was all for it. Working toward a goal, making money to buy things, and striving for a better life made sense to me—unlike folding my underwear.

I didn't really understand it at the time, but my parents were striving for a better life too. In fact, that's exactly what they were aiming at when they'd pile us kids into the station wagon for Sunday afternoon drives. My parents would head off in one direction or another just looking at the landscape, checking out land, viewing lakes in the area, dreaming of maybe one day building a house in a peaceful spot where they could retire. And despite the fact that they never made very much money, they did their best to set aside some money every week to go toward that dream. My mother was especially good at saving our pennies. Seemed like she could turn a nickel into a dollar in no time, and she was constantly socking money away for a rainy day or, perhaps, a sunny day.

One of the places that money went was to pay for Catholic school for all of us Ruettiger children. Every last one of us would traipse through the halls of St. Mary Magdalene. I was the first boy, of course, and about the best memory I have from those early years at school is that I was selected to be the milkman. I would pick up the crate of milk by the front door every morning and deliver it to the rest of the kids in my class. Man, you were a big shot if you were the milkman! And I liked that responsibility.

I think people have all kinds of clichéd things to say about their Catholic school upbringings, so I'm not going to dwell on it here. Needless to say, there were plenty of highs and lows to be had at the hand (and rod) of those nuns. For me, the highs lasted all the way through the fourth grade. Classrooms seemed to be about fun and art and dreaming about what our jobs might be or where we might travel as we learned about the world. My fourth-grade teacher in particular was a wonderful, positive person who seemed to want nothing more than to inspire us kids to dream.

Yet something changed within those tan-brick walls when fifth grade came around. I wasn't the strongest student, to begin with. I remember feeling like I was always just a little bit slower, a little bit behind the rest of the kids. But when school was fun, it didn't matter.

Fifth grade was not fun.

The changes in curriculum, the focus on memorization, the rigid approach to math facts and spelling and history got drilled into us over and over again. There was never any context, never any reason given for *why* we had to memorize all that stuff. We just had to do it. And the doing part just didn't sit well with me.

There was one particular assignment that I'll never forget. Our teacher (who shall remain nameless, for the sake of politeness) told us we had to memorize the names of our first five presidents, and that any one of us might get called on the next morning to recite those names in front of the class. I remember thinking, right there in the classroom, *What the heck do I need to know the names of the first five presidents for?* Perhaps if she had made it fun, perhaps if she had given the assignment some context, I might have paid more attention.

That night, I spent my time tuned to a Yankees game on the radio. I sat there envisioning the players on the field, knowing their stats and listening as every moment of it played out in my mind. Before long, it was bedtime. Lights out. Night, night.

Well, wouldn't you know it: the first person that teacher called on the next morning was me. She made me stand in front of the whole class. "Mr. Ruettiger," she said. "Who was our fifth president?" I stood there, silent. "Mr. Ruettiger, answer the question!" I had no answer. I hadn't studied. *How could I study when the Yankees game was on?*

"Mr. Ruettiger, did you study?"

I bowed my head and shook it, "No."

"Why not?"

I shrugged my shoulders.

"With that attitude, Mr. Ruettiger, you will never amount to anything."

Now why would any teacher say something like that to a child? Maybe she thought it was tough love or something. It wasn't. It was just tough. I felt every kid in that classroom staring at me, laughing at me on the inside, thinking I was worthless and useless. And that's exactly how it made me feel.

It wasn't the first time. This particular teacher had no tolerance for the way I struggled with words. No tolerance for the fact that I couldn't finish a test on time. And she let me know it. Often. I was already feeling inadequate. I saw how good my peers could read, standing up in front of the class with a book in their hand, words flowing from the page to their mouths with ease. I couldn't do that. I stopped, I hesitated, I struggled to get the words out, let alone to get them out in a way that sounded good or actually made sense. So to have my teacher make me feel worse instead of trying to help me or encourage me just made me shut down.

It's not like my brain didn't work. I could memorize those Yankee stats like nobody's business. Teachers would always accuse me of not listening, just because I was doodling in my notebook and not staring at them while they lectured. I *was* listening. I tried to tell them. But they'd call me out anyway and punish me in front of the class. *If this is what school is all about,* I thought, *who needs it?* By the end of that year, I pretty much made up my mind that school sucks. And from what I could tell, the school system pretty much made up its mind that I wasn't worth the trouble either. *Forget this,* I thought. *I'd rather focus on sports anyway.*

The first time I showed up for Little League tryouts, I got hit in the head with the ball. Now, I don't care if it's an eight-year-old throw or a professional throw—that hurts! I tried to blame it on the "stupid" glove I was wearing, which didn't really fit my hand and wasn't quite broken in. Gloves in those days were puny and poorly shaped, anyway. In reality, I got hit because I wasn't paying attention. I wasn't focused on what I was supposed to be doing. One hundred percent of my attention should have been on that ball, and I just wasn't a very focused kid. Nothing like a knock in the head to teach you the hard way.

Whether it was because of my dad's interest in the game or just because it's what kids tend to do at that age, baseball became an outlet for me pretty quickly. Learning to catch, to connect with the ball, to run those bases with all of my might as the cool spring air filled up with the promise of summer and the green grass glistened in the sun . . . man, there's nothing better. The really magical thing about baseball was that my parents were always there to support me. I might not have said anything about it at the time, and maybe I didn't even realize it, consciously, but the simple fact that they showed up meant the world to me. To this day, I don't understand how they found the time. But they did. Unless it was utterly impossible for some reason, on some rare occasion, they were right there in those little bleachers at Highland Park, cheering me on. After practice, and especially after the games, my dad would always tell me, "Great job." Even when I didn't do so great. "Just keep playing hard" was his message, over and over—a message I took to heart.

Highland Park, by the way, is one of the more beautiful spots in otherwise industrial Joliet: a wooded park set back from the main road, filled with green grass and a bunch of baseball fields tailored to players of all ages—complete with a flat-roofed, concrete shack of a building that conveniently housed the local bar, where all of the coaches went drinking between games.

I wasn't a natural ball player. I wasn't the tallest kid, or the thinnest kid, or the fastest kid, or the hardest hitter. In fact, the only reason I was any good at catching the ball was because I didn't want it to hit me in the head again!

For a while, though, baseball became the be-all, end-all for me. I played a little harder after that moment when I snagged that major league ball from the White Sox game. I focused more when I played. I did my best to play the best I could. I tried to recapture that feeling I had when I knew that ball was mine. I tried to apply that focus to every hit, every catch, every throw. We had great coaches who talked to us kids like we were all champions in the making. Following their lead, absorbing all of that encouragement, over the course of a couple of years I became the best hitter on the team. I tried to emulate major league players in the way I stood at the plate, the way I wore my hat, the way I dove for the ball without worrying about getting hurt or getting grass stains on my uniform. My mom was always there to wash it for me anyway, drying it on the line so it would be spotless but stiff as a board when I went to put it on the next time. Man, did I love that uniform. I always looked forward to getting a new one, and especially that new hat, every year. That was a big deal.

My hard work and focus paid off, too, when I made the All-Star team. It felt great to actually get rewarded for my efforts. In fact, my memories of playing baseball are almost entirely good ones . . . at least until I was twelve or thirteen. Something happened as we moved up from Little League to PONY League. It became more about the competition and less about the game. Playing on that level, dealing with coaches who yelled at everyone and put you down whenever you messed up, just made the whole thing lose some of its shine. I learned a lesson about the value and importance of building a great team when we were playing for PONY League championship. If we won, we'd go to the PONY League World Series.

I was so pumped up at the possibility, the other team could have put a grown-up major league pitcher on the mound throwing knuckleballs and I *still* would have hit 'em out of the park!

Unfortunately, not everyone shared that passion. I was playing one of my best games ever, but it was down to the final inning and we were down by one with two outs. I found myself on third base, waiting for the chance to run home and tie it up. I knew we could win this thing! My teammate got up to the plate, and I knew all he had to do was hit that ball and I'd score. I thought he had the same passion I did. I thought he saw the glory that was so close you could taste it. I thought wrong. The kid's body language was flat as he pulled the bat up and let it flop, lazily, on his shoulder. His posture said it all. He'd given up hope. He'd lost the fire. That one guy was about to blow it for the whole team. We all cheered him on, yelling, screaming for our chance at the World Series.

It didn't work. When he struck out without even swinging, I cried like a baby.

Assuming everyone on the team shared the same level of passion was a mistake. And seeing my young baseball career end on a down note was certainly not what I had dreamed.

But that's okay. It was glorious while it lasted. And the lessons I learned would serve me well as I headed into high school and turned my attention to another sport: football.

2

Friday Night Lights

Growing up in the Midwest, you start hearing about this place called Notre Dame before you can talk. It's a Catholic thing. You weren't even sure what college really meant, but the idea of it, the myth of it, the legend loomed large: if you were Catholic, you automatically had this dream of Notre Dame planted in your head. And if you went to Notre Dame, you were *somebody*.

The closest we ever got to that exalted place was listening to the voice of Lindsey Nelson as he broadcasted the Notre Dame replays on TV on Sunday mornings during football season. Watching those replays was like a second religion in my family, and for my dad, his passion for the Blue & Gold ran deeper than even his love of the Yankees. My dad always loved the underdog, and when you look at the kids who went to Notre Dame, they were ethnic kids like us—the Germans and Polish and Irish who were raised at a time when that simple ethnic distinction made them underdogs in America, no matter how gifted or talented they were. Those were the guys who played there. Black-and-white visions of that stadium filled my head as a kid, as did images of "Touchdown Jesus," the infamous, giant, skyscraper-size mural of Our Lord Jesus Christ with his arms held up toward heaven in a near-perfect reflection of a ref's touchdown signal, which went up in 1964. It was always visible in the distance over that stadium wall, above the tunnel through which those gods of the gridiron ran out onto the field for each game. They really did seem like gods too. They were bigger and faster than normal guys, and they showed more finesse and expertise with the ball than any normal human being had a right to.

In my mind, Notre Dame seemed like a far-off kingdom. As far away as heaven. The very idea of it was lofty and illustrious, almost mystical, certainly mysterious. For all of those reasons, the school and the football team resonated more like a fairy tale than something that could be found here on earth.

Because of my interest in football, and partially because my dad was so excited to finally have a boy old enough to play, I wound up attending the very same high school my dad went to. I could have gone to the brand-spanking-new Catholic school, Providence High (where all of my younger siblings would go), that had just been built across town, but when dad found out they were offering soccer instead of a football program, he marched me right in to see the priests at Joliet Catholic, housed in a big old brick building that used to be called De La Salle High School back when my dad attended.

Football was a major part of Joliet culture, in that "Friday Night Lights" way. High school teams played every Friday during the season (yes, under the lights) at Joliet Memorial Stadium on West Jefferson Street, the main road through town that's otherwise dotted with car dealerships and shopping centers. Traffic would back up with all the spectators trying to get in. And when our team won, Joliet Catholic would shine a light in the school's tower, basically the highest point in all of Joliet, since the school sits atop The Hill district. You could see that beacon for miles.

As the district name suggests, that old, somewhat ornate brick school was located at the crest of a hill right up off the west bank of the Joliet River, a stinky, polluted body of water that cut along the edge of downtown, which itself was sliced up by the overlapping, intersecting railroad tracks that dominate the landscape, some sweeping people in and out of Joliet Union Station and some carrying freight and coal. As we got older, we'd go cruising in that downtown area just past the school grounds, checking out all of the girls who seemed perfectly happy to walk around and be checked out. When we were fortunate enough to have saved some money from a car-washing job or mowing lawns (a dollar a day, if we were lucky), maybe we'd buy a movie ticket and catch a show at the beautiful old Rialto Theater, diagonally across from the library where we'd sometimes come to study. And, of course, every kid dreamed that someday they might have their name and picture painted on the side of the big train trestle, which someone turned into a "wall of fame" for Joliet athletes. (Interestingly enough, flashing forward a few decades, my brother Francis's picture is up there. He became a renowned weight-lifting champ. My picture is not. I'm not a champion athlete at all. And I'm okay with that. I'm great with it, actually! More on that later . . .)

Like any big town divided by tracks, there was a good side of the tracks and a bad side of the tracks in Joliet. It's something that persists to this day. The south side is some pretty rough territory, ripe with crime and poverty. And it's down past that bad side of town, just over the line into the town of Rockdale, where the power plants rise up like concrete cities, looming over the landscape, letting young men know there's a job waiting right there when they get out of school.

School for me didn't get any easier as I entered high school. In fact, I pushed back against learning even more than I had as a young kid, with good reason. Before I was enrolled, the school's principal, an educated Carmelite priest who was widely respected in Joliet and beyond, took one look at my entrance exams and told my father, "We've got to put your son in slower learning classes. Your son's not that smart." He said it in the office while I sat right there, and he said it in such a way that it sounded to me like an unalterable fact. To tell my parents in private would have been one thing, but to say it in front of me like that? It hurt. It made me angry. And when you're told you're "not that smart" by an authority figure with that much power and influence, why wouldn't you believe it? It's no different than my father telling me my ears would fall off in church. When someone you look up to speaks, you tend to listen. You tend to take it in. And that can cause a whole world of hurt, which those authority figures may not even realize they're laying on you.

I don't blame that priest; in the same way I don't blame my parents. They weren't purposefully trying to hurt me. He wasn't doing it to be mean-spirited (at least I don't think he was). There simply wasn't the same sort of awareness of kids' feelings in those days that we have today, and speaking frankly about the rigors and expectations of education right in front of the child in question was just the way things were done in those schools.

The real problem comes after those words are spoken and a plan is put into action. Then the hurt gets worse. They put you in the slow classes, which leads to you getting picked on and made fun of, which leads to all kinds of self-esteem problems. Heck, I'd carry a science book in my hands on the way to wood shop so the other kids wouldn't know where I was going. I never understood this whole elite system of learning that teachers professed. How could I have any kind of a self-image when teachers all made it clear that the smart kids went to college? It confused me. No one ever pointed out the fact that we need good woodworkers, good electricians, good mechanics. It was downright embarrassing to be placed in shop class while everyone else studied science and math and set their sights on various universities. Why couldn't they have focused on my strengths? Focused on the stuff I knew how to do? Showed me how to make a career out of that? How to be inspired to learn more, rather than forced to learn less? I would sit there and cry my eyes out at times. "Why can't I learn?" It would just destroy me. And what does that lead to? Nothing but problems.

I wound up hanging with a tough crowd in high school—a group of guys who were reckless, who liked to get into fights. It gave me a sense of belonging, in that other students looked up to me, or feared me. I was one of the "bad boys" who would head down the hill by the Joliet River after school and get into a brawl with some kids from another school, usually from the south side of the tracks. There were probably only two handfuls of real fights I participated in, but two handfuls is a lot in four years!

Amazingly, my fighting rarely got me into trouble. I was scrappy and usually won. I came home looking no more beat up than I might have after a hard football practice. A black eye. Swollen knuckles. Yes, I played that hard! Football was an outlet for my pent-up aggressions, just like fighting. So mom and dad never noticed.

Strangely enough, the one time my dad intervened, he saved my life.

The guys I hung around with the most were named George and Ralph. Ralph was probably my best friend. We were both short and shared a similar sense of humor. I could pick on him, and he could pick on me, and it didn't mean anything 'cause we were so much alike. It was the essence of great camaraderie. I liked his family too, and so did my mother, who rightly didn't approve of too many of my friends in those days. Of course, none of them realized what a risk-taker Ralph was. He was just a real reckless guy, especially when it came to driving.

There was this one kid we hung around with junior year, a guy we all called Big Nick. And Big Nick got into a lot more fights than I did. Probably for many of the same reasons: he was a smart guy, but had problems. He didn't fit in. He wasn't a good student. It's the same cycle with almost every one of these types of kids, right?

One day Big Nick got drawn into a fight with a gang from another school. The whole thing was set up ahead of time, and he wanted me to come join him. "Come on! Let's go fight these guys! I'll pick you up!" he said. I couldn't tell my dad I was going out to get in a gang fight, of course, so I tried to sneak out of the house that particular night, and my dad caught me coming out of the window. For some reason, he happened to be right outside my window fixing something on the house when I stuck my butt out there.

"Where are you going?" he said.

"Nowhere," I answered.

"Get yourself back in that house, right now!"

Big Nick went ahead without me. I remember sitting in school the next day when word started to get around. Somewhere in the middle of that brawl, another kid hit Nick in the head with a rock. Nick was dead. I sat there stunned, not only in sadness at the thought that this guy I palled around with—and was just hanging out with the day before—was gone. Actually *gone*. But I was also stunned by the simple fact that it could have been me. I could have died too. If my dad hadn't been in the right place at the right time, my life could have ended right there. All because I was sneaking around and doing stuff I knew darn well I shouldn't have been doing in the first place.

If a sudden death isn't enough to stop you in your tracks, I'm not sure what is. But it didn't stop me. I kept hanging around the same crowd. I'd still go out cruising with George and Ralph, getting into whatever trouble we could find. By trouble, I mean like the time we got caught egging George's girlfriend's house. It was pretty innocent stuff for the most part. They were both good guys from good families. They really were. But we were all just filled with so much of that teenage angst, or whatever you want to call it. I guess it's to be expected. I wasn't old enough or experienced enough to pay attention to the signs that God was putting right in front of me.

Since my freshman year, my family had been living in a much bigger (close to 1,200 square-foot) split-level house that my dad and his partners built at 808 South Brigg—less than a mile up the road from the St. Mary Magdalene school, which made for an easier walk for my younger brothers and sisters than I had in my early years. It was a modest house with enough room for all of us kids to stretch out a bit. But it existed in a constant state of construction for many years—there were no doors or windows when we first moved in. That's just how my dad operated. All the boys hunkered down in the specially built bunk room on the lower level. The noise, the craziness, the quiet dinners—everything we had established in our previous house continued as it had, but just a little bit bigger. With more than an acre of land to ourselves, we were able to stretch our activities outside more than ever before, including great pick-up baseball games and home-run derbies that dad would organize off on the side lawn. (A side lawn! Imagine that!)

With fourteen kids, there was always something nefarious going on. My mother was always catching my older sisters sneaking in or out of the house, so she was pretty well practiced before she turned that same attention to my brothers and me.

Money was still tight, so when it came to things like haircuts, my dad would just line us all up in the kitchen, hold our heads down, and buzz it all off. He wasn't exactly a gentle man when it came to working with tools, including that barber's trimmer, so we all wound up with nicks and cuts all over our heads and would wear baseball caps for days just to cover the ugliness.

My mom would shop for our suits at Sears & Roebuck, and we'd be lucky to get a new comb and a tube of Vitalis for Christmas. We'd get new underwear for Christmas too, which always turned into a challenge: all of us brothers would wind up losing our underwear or running out, not having a pair when we needed it, so we'd steal each other's perfectly pressed and folded skivvies when no one was looking. It became a regular routine. I'd go to put a pair on and they'd get stuck going up my leg because somehow I wound up with one of my little brothers' drawers in my drawer! It was a pain.

All those growing boys in the house also made food a big challenge. My mom continued to cook big meals, but we were never satisfied. We were always hungry and always snacking, which drove mom nuts. In fact, she wound up hiding food in her bedroom closet just so us boys wouldn't steal it.

The challenge of handling all of us Ruettiger boys extended beyond home as well. In school, teachers started losing track of who was who from year to year. As time went on, they just seemed to give up. They'd just call us by our last name: "Hey, Ruettiger!" Then even that seemed to be too much of a verbal burden, so our teachers, our peers, our coaches—everyone—just shortened our name down to "Rudy." All seven of us, for the rest of our lives, would be "Rudy" to just about everyone outside of family.

Oddly enough, within our family, we came up with a different shared nickname for each other: "coach." I'm not sure how or why that started, but I call my brothers coach, I called my dad coach, and they call me coach whenever we pick up the phone or if we're gathered around at one of their houses. "Hey coach, grab me another beer will you?" Whichever brother it's directed at, they respond to it. I like to think of it as a sign of respect. After all, you're supposed to respect a coach, right?

My dad had funny nicknames for everyone too. Mine was "wise guy."

For a lot of those years, I always had a comeback or an argument or a complaint about everything my dad ever suggested. I always put up a verbal fight or gave him a little lip. Like a lot of teens, I thought I had all the answers, always thought I knew better. So he just started calling me "wise guy," and it stuck for many, many years.

One night during senior year, I had plans to hit the town with my buddies Ralph and George. Ralph was driving, and he was always late, but I remember sitting there waiting and waiting on him, a lot longer than usual that night. I finally called Ralph's house to see if anyone knew what was taking him so long, and his dad picked up. "You haven't heard, have you, Rudy?" he said. His voice was real shaky.

"Heard what?" I asked.

"Ralph is dead."

I lost my breath.

"What?" I asked.

I couldn't believe it.

He'd been in a car accident on the way to my house. He apparently had tried to pass another car in a no-passing zone, the same kind of reckless stuff he'd done ever since he got his license. We'd be in the car and he'd be swerving back and forth across the yellow line, and we'd tell him, "You're gonna get killed someday, man!"

This was that someday.

I may have missed the sign from God that first time around, but this time it hit me like a bullet in the back. After two big warnings, it finally registered: *I gotta change. I gotta get away from this. I'm hanging around with the wrong people. I'm not focused on the right stuff in life.* Not that George or Ralph or Big Nick were bad guys. They weren't. Not at all. They were good friends. All of them. Good people. They had just spent too much time drowning in the negativity of a school system that neglects kids who don't fit the perfect mold, and the boatloads of other pressures society puts on its youth—the exact same way I had. For some reason, I'd managed to survive. I was thankful. I was hurt. I was shocked. I didn't understand it. But when I got off the phone with Ralph's dad, I knew I was done with that life.

Going to Ralph's funeral was the most surreal and profound moment of my life up to that point. It felt almost like it wasn't happening. I still felt like Ralph was walking around somewhere. I could still hear his voice. It was freaky.

There were no more fights for me after that. Whatever anger and frustration I had been releasing through my fists got stuffed back down inside, where it belonged.

Funny thing, though: even then, at that still-young age, I had a feeling it would find another way out.

━

Football really was my salvation in high school. For some kids it's art. For some it's music. For me, it was strapping on those pads, yanking that helmet over my head, and getting out there with the team. I was relentless on the field, especially my senior year. My teachers always complained that I was untrainable or uncoachable in my academic pursuits because I refused to do things their way; in fact, I wasn't capable of doing things their way, and yet out on that football field the coaches usually loved me because I got out there and played as hard as I could. Head coach Gordon Gillespie made every player feel like he was a part of the team. I looked up to him in a big way. He made every one of us believe we could accomplish great things on that field. He inspired me to put it all on the line in every practice and every game. It's as if all of my aggression was channeled into playing. I took hits like no one else. I got the sense some of the big guys wanted to see how hard of a hit I could take, and there was never a hit that kept me down. I always came back for more. Same way I did in those fights down by the river. Always. My drive went right back to what my dad told me on the baseball field: "Just keep playing hard." That made sense to me. We were all in this together, and there was no way I would allow myself to be a weak link in any other players' eyes.

Football is different from baseball. You're not alone at any point, never standing at a plate with the pressure solely on you. You're truly a part of something, from start to finish. Wherever your effort ends, someone else's begins. It's a game full of moving parts; all of those parts have to work together, and every part of the machine is equally important (despite what some quarterbacks think). Every single person has a role to play, and you have to play it well if you ever want a shot at winning.

I liked that.

I also have to admit I liked that feeling of being out there under the lights on Friday nights. All those people cheering. You were somebody when you were on that team. A big shot. People paid attention. And to a kid who wasn't used to being paid much attention to in school, that filled me with a sense of pride.

It didn't seem to matter that I wasn't the tallest (I stopped growing at just around five feet six inches) or the fastest or the strongest on the team. As long as I played hard and played my part, I basked in the glory of those wins just as much as every other player. As much as I floundered in school, I excelled on the field and was rewarded accordingly. I was All-Conference Guard and All-Conference Linebacker. Nothing could stop me!

I loved the game so much. I'd go practice or join in pick-up games even when I wasn't supposed to. One time, I convinced my mom to let me borrow her car. She kept saving those nickels and finally had a car of her own, a Buick Skylark, and she wouldn't let anyone else drive it. But on this day, I convinced her that I really, really needed to go downtown to the library to study—and she gave in. Imagine her surprise when I called her a few hours later from the hospital with a broken collarbone. "I thought you were at the library!" she yelled. I couldn't drive back. She had to arrange to have a friend bring her to the hospital so she could take me (and her car) back home. Well, by the time we got there, my dad was home from work and had heard the whole story. My little brothers still recall the fear they had for me as I walked into that living room to face him. He was so mad! I felt like a fool, of course, for lying. But I wanted to play football every chance I got. On this occasion, I took a shot and lost.

Of course, my hardheaded attitude—the one that kept me coming back for more even after being spanked as a child—was still in full effect. A few weeks later, on the very day I got my cast taken off and was told by the doctor, very specifically, to take it easy, not to do anything but rest and relax for a couple of weeks, I went down the street and wound up playing touch football with our neighbors. Giving it my all, I snatched the ball on a long throw, took a hard fall, and *crack!* Broke that collarbone all over again.

I hobbled back to my dad, who was in the driveway changing the tires on the station wagon. He was always changing those tires, from bald tires to nearly bald tires that he'd grab for free from his brother's gas station. I'll never forget the look on his face when he saw me. That look of frustration and disappointment. That look of, "How am I ever going to get through to this kid!" He was so hurt and let down to think that I would go right out and hurt myself playing football after being told so specifically not to do so!

I hated that look. I remember thinking, *I never want to see that look in his eyes again. Ever.*

I knew there was no future for me in football, of course. Maybe that's why I tried to play so often. When would I ever get a chance to play after high school? I wasn't going to college, and no matter how good it made me feel or how good I thought I was, it was clear as day to me that I could never play professionally. I knew I would never play with the gods of Notre Dame, so I didn't even fantasize about stuff like that. It just couldn't happen. It was something I did for fun, and for me that was enough.

Like I said, I didn't even realize where Notre Dame was. It felt like a far-off fairytale land. That is, it felt far-off all the way up until late my senior year, when I went along on a religious retreat with the rest of my class to the Fatima Retreat Center . . . in South Bend, Indiana. Right on the edge of the Notre Dame campus.

I was shocked that the trip was so short. It felt as if we'd barely left, what with all the carousing and joking that goes on in the back of any school bus. In reality, it was only about a ninety-minute trip from Joliet. Ninety minutes and we were there. That far-off place was real. That seemingly unknowable place was close.

Fatima House was a low-slung brick building surrounded by beautiful green lawns, and as soon as we got off the bus at the top of the circular drive, the priests divided us into two groups: one group would go take a tour of the Notre Dame campus, the other would head inside and get started with our spiritual exercises. I was pumped up to see Notre Dame, so I immediately went toward that group, until one of the priests stopped me. "Rudy," he said, "this is for college-bound students. Not you."

I don't blame that priest for stopping me. He was right. I wasn't college-bound. He was trying to be nice and save me some embarrassment, I think. After all, you had to get all As, maybe a few Bs; you had to be in the top percentile; you had to test well; you had to be one of the elite to attend Notre Dame. I knew all that. I had heard it my whole life. But I also knew then and there that those priests would be hard-pressed to keep me from seeing that campus now that I was standing right on the edge of it. And the thing I really wanted to see was the stadium. I wanted to get up close to that world of Notre Dame football I'd heard about, watched on TV, and dreamed about all my life. I could hardly believe I was standing so close to that place that always seemed so impossibly far away.

Late that afternoon, during some down time when we were supposed to hang out in our rooms, I convinced a buddy of mine to break away from the group and go exploring. We snuck out the back of the building and hurried across the lawn toward a beautiful lake, which I would later learn is called Saint Mary's Lake. If the priests had caught us, they'd have hung us by our toes! But I had to see that campus. I couldn't resist.

The lake was stunning, speckled with the warm glow of afternoon sunlight, surrounded by a gravel path dotted with joggers and smiling students walking by with their book bags. Two or three minutes down that path, we rounded a corner past a big old tree and there it was—the Golden Dome—the gorgeous crest of the campus, rising over the landscape at the top of a hill, topping the Main Building with an immense statue of Mary. I had glimpsed it on TV. In person, shining in the sky right in front of me, it was much, much more magnificent.

As we came around that corner and approached the campus's heart, I was surprised by the stillness. It felt as if I had crossed into some other world. The tumbling branches of a giant old willow tree bristled to the left. Swans glided gracefully over the surface of the lake to the right. We crossed a little roadway and set foot on a path marked by beds of pink flowers on either side, like a runway guiding us toward a strange glowing light up ahead. With each step, the light became clearer. It wasn't one light; it was the light of many—candles, hundreds of them. White candles in glass holders, glowing side-by-side on black wrought-iron pedestals, their flickering glow reflected in the earth-colored stone of the shallow cave that surrounded it all.

Without any intention, without any map, we had found the Grotto of Our Lady of Lourdes—that sacred space on the Notre Dame campus where hundreds upon hundreds of men and women, for decades now, have come to seek solace and guidance in prayer; to light a candle for loved ones lost or struggling; to kneel before the beauty of this outdoor space as a simple white statue of the Virgin Mary looks down from a prominent spot on the rocks just above. It seemed timeless, like something you'd see in a history book from centuries ago in some far-off land.

It was beautiful.

We continued up the pathway to the right of that hallowed spot, wrapping around behind the Basilica of the Sacred Heart, between great stone buildings that, again, seemed like pictures from a storybook or somewhere in Europe—certainly not a short bus ride from the hard-worn streets of Joliet. The Golden Dome then revealed itself again. This time we were right under it, walking out in front of the Main Building, turning around on the lush green lawn, staring up at its shining top and then at the golden cross at the top of the Basilica's steeple next door. There was something about the landscape, the architecture, something I couldn't put my finger on that kept drawing my eyes up toward heaven. And despite being forced to listen to years of Catholic mass through my well-attached ears, and despite serving as an altar boy for a little while in my youth, I thought, for the very first time, *So this is what people mean by a "religious experience."* It was breathtaking.

Finally, as I pulled my eyes back down to earth, I saw something more enlightening than anything I had laid eyes on so far that day: I saw students. Everywhere. Reclining in the grass, sitting on benches, swinging on a porch swing in front of one of those dorms, walking the pathways, descending the steps under the Golden Dome. Students who didn't look like those Notre Dame football players I'd seen on TV. Students who weren't hulking gods. Students who didn't look like some other breed, some other group of elite, privileged people of which I knew nothing. I saw students who looked, for lack of a better description, like me! Just regular-looking kids. Short, stocky, smiling, easygoing, casually dressed, everyday-looking guys and gals who seemed to be the sort of people I might be able to talk to.

These kids walking around with book bags over their shoulders looked nothing like the perfect, untouchable students I always imagined attended college. Nothing like the lofty, snobby, good-at-everything type of people I thought you had to be to go to Notre Dame.

I couldn't get over it. I talked to my buddy about how cool it seemed as we continued toward the library and turned to see Touchdown Jesus, that immense, colorful, gold-tinted mural, looking out over a reflecting pool to the lawn and Notre Dame Stadium. There it was. The home of the Fighting Irish. The battlefield on which all of those games played out. The place where all my Sunday radio and TV memories originated. The vaunted home of one of my dad's few great passions.

The bells of the Basilica rang out as we ran across the lawn toward that north end-zone entrance that led right into the tunnel that opened onto the field. The light shone through the end of that tunnel, casting long shadows in our direction. We heard voices, echoing from around a corner somewhere, and all of a sudden the Notre Dame football team was walking down the sidewalk right in front of us! They were all beat up, battered, and grass stained, just coming back from a practice; and as they all piled into the locker-room entrance just off to one side of the tunnel, my buddy and I got swept up in the group and just followed them right on inside.

I couldn't believe the size of these guys. They really were as big as they seemed on TV. Bigger! As they headed into the locker room, my buddy and I saw faces we recognized and kept nudging each other: "That's Alan Page!"—the defensive end who helped bring the team to the championship the year before. (He would go on to play for the Vikings and the Bears before getting elected to the Supreme Court in Minnesota.) We got so swept up in the excitement of the whole thing that we just went with the flow. I couldn't believe we were in the locker room! It was awesome. Our eyes must've been as big as saucers as we started chatting some of the guys up. "Oh, it's so great to be here, to see you guys. Yeah, we're just visiting from Joliet, and you guys are awesome!" We must've sounded like giddy fans. We were.

The thing that really surprised me, though, was just how many players were in that locker room. Dozens of guys. I never realized how deep the team roster went. This wasn't like high school. And they weren't all hulking six-foot-five giants like Page. The fact is, there were plenty of guys on that team who looked like me! Over the smell of that sweat and the noise of everyone talking over one another in a post-practice, pumped-up excitement, it hit me like another slap in the face: not only were there students here who looked like me, there were guys wearing Notre Dame uniforms and playing on this team who looked like me too! They were on the shorter side. Stocky. I never saw these guys on TV. Never saw them on the field. But there they were, in the very same locker room as the big guys.

"Hey! Who are you guys? What are you doing in here?" The voice came booming from the doorway. We turned, knowing we'd been caught, only to see that the man behind the voice was Ara Parseghian, the greatest coach Notre Dame had seen since Knute Rockne. He had just led Notre Dame to the National Championship in 1966. I was awestruck. I didn't know what to say. Then a string of words just came shooting out of my mouth: "I'm gonna play football for Notre Dame!" I shouted. I have no idea why I said that. It made no sense.

"Well, not today, you're not. Get out of here!" he said. We apologetically slipped outside into the glowing late-afternoon sun bouncing off the walls through the end of that famous tunnel. We looked at each other and just laughed. We were so excited, so pumped! We couldn't believe it! We were inside the Notre Dame locker room and got yelled at by Coach Parseghian!

Figuring we'd pushed our luck far enough and seen just about as much as we could for one day, we ran all the way back to Fatima House, snuck back inside just in time for dinner, and were thankful no one noticed we had gone.

I didn't think a whole lot more about Notre Dame in the days and weeks after that afternoon. I was glad I had seen it, of course, but I had no reason to dwell on it. I went back to the retreat, we read our Bible verses, and we took that quiet time that our priests asked us to take to reflect on ourselves, our lives, and how far we had come in our high school careers. That was all good. I enjoyed that time. But it didn't move me.

As time went by and I thought back on that day, the feeling I got from taking a walk on that campus is what moved me. The feeling I got from stepping inside that locker room moved me. For some reason, as we walked around that lush, beautiful campus, I didn't feel like an outsider. I felt as if I belonged there. It was almost a cleansing feeling—clearing away some of the negativity that had clouded my mind. I had resigned myself to what I thought was an unalterable fact, of course: I was not a "college-bound" guy. And yet, when I look back now, I can see that a seed was planted. That seed would grow even when I wasn't tending to it or paying attention to it at all.

I made it through the end of my senior year without any real fights, any real drama, or any real passion. I graduated third in my class . . . from the bottom. My GPA was 1.73. I partied. I celebrated the fact that I was done with those twelve years of crap and agony. And that was that.

For a moment, I didn't worry about what lay ahead. I didn't stop to think about what was to come. I didn't bother thinking about anything, period.

Sea Change

Have you ever felt as if you were in a place where life just sort of happens to you? Like you're not in control? As if someone punched the autopilot button and you're strapped to your seat inside this contraption, helplessly headed wherever it takes you? As if you have no choice? As if you're stuck fulfilling the expectations of what other people put upon you, and you don't have any expectations that are truly your own?

That's exactly where I was after high school—still living at home, still stuck in Joliet. My mom still packed my lunch each night, right along with the rest of the kids', only now I was taking that lunch to a place of work instead of a place of learning. I took a job at the local coal-fired power plant. Why? Because my dad had an in with a supervisor there, the job was available, and that's what you do. My mom really wanted me to be a priest. She had been pressing that career path since I was a kid. But for years I had told her, "Mom, I don't want to be a priest. I want to go out with girls!" When the power plant job took hold, my mom was the one who drove me in and dropped me off every morning until I finally earned enough money to buy a used '66 Mustang.

In a lot of ways it felt like nothing had changed. I had a locker. I had a lunch break. Only I felt like a freshman again, enduring the hazing and teasing that goes on with any new guy in a tough environment like that. I remember a superior yelling at me, "Rudy! Go get a bucket of steam! Bring me a bucket of steam, right now!" I went running around like a fool, asking everyone where I would get a bucket of steam. Of course, everyone was in on the joke, so they'd say, "Oh, go ask that guy. He'll help you!" Half an hour went by before I finally realized it was all a big joke.

I was busy all day doing stuff I didn't care about, and it didn't take long for me to pour as much heart and soul into my work as I did into school. (In other words, not very much!) There were days when I'd skip work entirely. I didn't care.

Autopilot. Living a life filled with other people's expectations, other people's plans, other people's ideas of what my life was supposed to be.

If it weren't for the war, that going-through-the-motions may well have been my path for life.

By 1969, Vietnam had seeped its way into every corner of our country. Talk of it saturated nearly every conversation everywhere you went. The load of it was heavy on everyone's shoulders, and perhaps none more than recent non–college-bound high school graduates like me who were eligible for the draft.

I had never been a gambler. I never saw the point. Tempting fate on the roll of the dice just wasn't my thing, and the heavier the weight of that draft piled on me, the less inclined I was to let some lottery decide my future. I didn't want to die in some jungle somewhere. I knew I didn't have the grades or skills it would take to become an officer or a pilot or to get a desk job back home while my peers went off to fight on the front lines of this terrible war—a war that seemed to be doing more damage to the American psyche than any of our bombs were doing to the Viet Cong. I knew that I was the type of guy who would be sent directly to the front lines.

When life and death are on the line, it spurs you to think a little differently, maybe the way we should be thinking all the time, or at least most of the time. Especially when it comes to the big decisions such as where we're headed in life, what we do for work, who we're gonna marry, and so on.

So I decided to do the only thing I could to take the power away from the roll of the dice. I decided to take fate into my own hands.

I didn't let anyone know I was headed to the navy recruiting office. Not my family. Not a friend. I didn't want anyone to deter me. I didn't want anyone or anything to change my mind. It was what I wanted to do, what I felt I had to do, and I did it.

The way I saw it, the navy was the safest choice I could make. I didn't want to die. Plus, there were perks. I had never been on a boat. I had never seen the ocean. I had certainly never seen the world. Like I said, the one- or two-mile radius around my house was it, except for the occasional baseball game in Chicago or field trip to a neighboring city or state. I had no idea what I was in for. It didn't matter. Something inside told me it was what I needed to do. So I did it.

When I shared the news with my family, they were shocked, of course. But they also understood. They wished the best for me and even threw me a going-away party before I headed off to training camp. I think my dad was surprised I manned up and made a big decision like that all on my own. Maybe it was just that he knew what I was about to go through, having served himself, but on the day I left, he had a different sort of look in his eye than I'd ever seen before.

I didn't hop a train to some exotic locale in the murky swamps and searing temperatures of the Deep South for my boot camp, the way you see in a lot of movies or read about in books. No sir. I traveled forty-five minutes north of my house to a freezing cold training facility in Chicago. Still, it didn't take long for me to realize I was about as far from home as a young man could be.

As we filed into the facility, the first thing they did was shave our heads. I was used to that, of course, only these guys did a gentler job of it than my dad. I remember looking around at all of these other faces as they lost the identity of their long '60s hair in an instant. There were guys there from all over. All walks of life. All ethnicities. There were some guys with lice falling out of their hair as their locks hit the ground. It certainly wasn't high school anymore. It certainly wasn't the workplace either. And it set in very quickly that this wasn't just a quick jaunt from Joliet; there would be no going home.

"Get this through your head, men: you're not going home to your mother. I'm your new mother, and this is how it's gonna be!" These drill sergeants were dead serious, screaming at us, shouting directions on where to go, where to stand, which line to get in, to stand up straight. Boom! There was no transition. This was it. This was how it's gonna be.

The first time I got yelled at I wondered if the guy was picking on me. But then he went right over and yelled to the next guy, and the next, and it dawned on me that we were all gonna be treated equally here. This wasn't school. I wasn't being called out and sent to the back of the class. We were all being called out and told to forget everything we thought we knew. No baggage. No goofy thoughts. "Clear your heads!" A sort of brand-new, start-from-scratch reality. They were breaking us down in order to build us up. I liked that.

I also liked the fact that they took away our civilian clothes and issued us a brand-new uniform. They even stamped my name into my underwear. What a relief to know I'd have underwear of my own! After all those years of having my brothers steal every clean pair of underwear I ever had, I was now the proud owner of my very own hand-stamped skivvies. Plus, my very own socks, my very own shirt, none of which would be grabbed away when I wasn't looking or passed down to someone else. Coming from a family that seemed to thrive on its relative shortage of new clothes, I immediately saw my uniform as a privilege. After all those years at home, I appreciated the little things.

The harsh reality that I couldn't go home also set a certain instinct in motion: the survival instinct. You'd better start doing what they say. There are no outs. There is no room for rebellion.

"You can't go home to your mama!"

Next thing I knew, they were marching us into our barracks.

"Hey! . . . Raawwr! . . . This is where you sleep. . . . This is how we want your lockers. . . . This is how you fold your clothes and make your bed."

Funny enough, the biggest part of my surviving in those barracks would come down to the discipline I had already learned at home. The navy is about structure. And who taught you structure? Your family. Your mom and dad. All those years my parents had been instilling in me the simple fact that your character is more important than having a new car. Your character is more important than having new clothes. You're a part of this household and you will contribute to your family. Hello! That's the navy in a nutshell! Suddenly, everyone is wearing the same clothes: same pants, same underwear, same socks, same shoes. And we learned real quick that we'd better have those shoes shined, that everything had better be in order, that our lockers had better be in shape. A lot of guys struggled with that at first. But not me. I had to make my bed before I left for school every day. I had to pick up my clothes. I had to keep my things organized from the very beginning back under my parents' roof in Joliet. And I certainly knew how to fold every part of my uniform, including that brand-new underwear of mine.

It occurred to me, very quickly on that very first day, that there was something much deeper than chaos-control behind my parents' insistence on discipline. The reason they wanted us to know how to do all of these things was so we would be able to handle them when we faced real life. My dad had been through the War. He was quietly preparing his kids for what he had faced, should we ever have to face it. I couldn't have understood that at the time. And he couldn't have explained it, in part because there just wasn't time to explain it, and in part because a kid wouldn't understand the explanation anyway. What was he going to say to me: "This will be good for you when you go to boot camp"? I wouldn't have believed that in a million years! I never thought for even one second that I would go to boot camp, until just before I walked down to that recruiting office and enlisted. It was never in the plan! So even if he tried, I would have rejected my dad's explanation completely.

Now, this was life. It was real. And I got it.

The drill sergeant at our barracks was a big, gruff guy with a husky voice, who smoked cigarettes; he was right out of Central Casting. The very first time he came through for an inspection, he tore into my shipmates—we were all called "shipmates" even though we were still on dry land—for every little detail left undone: the corners on the blankets, the sloppy lockers, the wrinkled shirts. When he got to me, he looked at my locker, took one look at my uniform, took one look at my perfectly folded underwear, and said really loud, so everyone could hear, "That's good, sailor. Show your other shipmates how to do that."

Whoa.

"Yes, sir!" I said.

That was big. *Show your other shipmates how to do that?* That's not the kind of thing someone usually says to the dumbest kid in class.

He didn't ask me where I had learned that skill, which until that moment I had never considered a skill whatsoever. He didn't have to. He saw my character. He knew I had good habits just by looking at the results. Looking back on it, I realize that's what good people see in all walks of life. What true leaders see. As gruff as he was, I immediately knew I was in the presence of a guy I could respect. And it dawned on me: with that one, confidence-boosting, encouraging statement in front of the rest of my shipmates, he instantly turned me into a bit of a leader too.

That was a first.

That gave me confidence.

That flipped a switch in me.

The fact that I could do something so seemingly insignificant, something so routine as folding my underwear, and have it mean a lot in this new environment started me down a path of believing in myself. I realized that doing the best at whatever I could do was, in fact, worthwhile. It was, in some ways, like playing my part on the football team, except this was real life in the real world.

I'm pretty sure that's when a new thought began to take hold for me: *I don't have to be a star to be somebody.*

Working within the forced limitations of the structure of the navy's teamwork brought out my individuality. My purpose. My heart. As tough as it was, that do-or-die mentality of the navy's leadership that's exhibited by empowering the team over individuals worked like magic for me. It works for lots of young guys. There's a reason why our military has such a great history of creating leaders—the system just works.

It was not easy. For nine full weeks we were drilled. Constantly. We watched kids break down in body, mind, and spirit. Remember, this was wartime. Vietnam was raging. They had to test us because we were heading out into a world where those tests would truly matter. We weren't headed into the jungles, but when you go on ship you've got to be disciplined and structured. When they call general quarters, you have to know what to do and you can't panic. They need you to react as you're told—almost like a robot. "Don't worry about what's going on, just do your job." For most people in a time of crisis, if they stop to think about what's going on, they freeze. The military can't have you thinking like that. It's the same on the football field. That's why there's so much repetition in football practices: as soon as you start worrying about that opponent, you're done. Worry about your job and how you're going to execute your job. *Don't worry about the play. Execute.* Having that football background and the ability to see the correlation definitely helped me get through it. A lot of guys don't learn that mentality because they have the talent, so they can get away with not fully paying attention to the amount of teamwork it takes to win a game on the field. Me? I wasn't talented. I had to work hard for every inch of accomplishment, and that was certainly still the case in my first days with the navy.

In fact, as I opened my eyes to reveille before dawn every morning, through countless moments of physical agony and exhaustion over the course of each and every day, and as I collapsed onto my bed each night, I found myself questioning whether or not I could make it: *I don't know if I can do this. Can I do this? Can I get through this?*

I had never faced anything so physically and emotionally demanding in all my life. But every time I questioned myself, I fell back to the very same thought: *I've gotta do this! I've gotta! I can't quit! I can't!*

Guess what?

I did it.

So did every other kid. From every walk of life. Of every size and shape. Not one of the shipmates in my barracks dropped out. Not one of them failed. And that got me thinking, *This isn't like school at all*. They pushed us hard, sure. But they actually wanted us to succeed. Every one of us. And we did.

On graduation day, I stood with them, proudly, shoulder to shoulder. I looked out at my parents and my brothers and sisters in the audience, and I swear they were looking at me with more pride than I'd ever known. As if I were *somebody*. A big shot. Especially my dad. He had a look in his eyes. When I walked over after the ceremonies, he walked right toward me with the sort of excitement he'd show while listening to the Yankees game, or watching Notre Dame highlights on Sunday nights. He put his arm out, shook my hand, and grabbed my shoulder . . . with that look. The polar opposite of the look he gave me back when I broke—and then re-broke—my collarbone. I think he recognized that I had changed. That was awesome for him.

"I'm proud of you, Danny," he said as he looked me in the eye and squeezed my hand tight.

That was something.

I have to admit, I was pretty proud of myself too. This was bigger than anything I had ever accomplished. Scary, yes. Nerve-wracking, sure. Tough? You bet. Yet I did it. All on my own. I emerged, standing on my own two feet, ready to tackle the world.

Of course, the big question that looms the moment you graduate from training camp is, "Where in the world am I going?" And when they hand you that envelope with your deployment orders in it, there is nothing like that feeling. This thin, sealed, folded piece of paper is all that separates you and your fate. It's amazing how much weight a little envelope can hold!

I was shaking when I tore mine open. *Where am I going? What will I be doing?* I read as fast as I could, as my new fate emerged in black and white: I would be shipping out to Boston, where I would serve as a yeoman on the USS *North Hampton* (CC-1)—a communication command ship that was fully capable of serving as a command center for the president of the United States in case of a national emergency or disaster. Heady stuff. It was dry-docked at the Charlestown Navy Yard in Boston, Massachusetts.

Holy cow! I was going to Boston! I'd never been to Boston. I'd heard about it, of course: Paul Revere. The Red Sox. The Boston Celtics. It's hard to describe the feeling, knowing you're about to leave on this great adventure to a brand-new city all the way on the East Coast when you've never traveled much farther than the forty-five-minute trip to Chicago your entire life.

I remember hitting the airport in my navy blues; feeling good and proud to wear that uniform but scared at the same time; landing at Logan airport and trying to navigate my way around; making my way to the navy yard thinking I had some idea what I was getting into . . . until I laid eyes on that ship. It was huge! I had never seen anything so big. Towering like a skyscraper, stretching out longer than the street I grew up on. Like a floating city. A floating factory. I was nervous. I remember walking up the gangway onto that great ship thinking, *Wow! This is cool! This is my real station now! No more of that yelling and screaming they did at boot camp!* Knowing I would now be charged with actually carrying out everything I had been taught in boot camp, I reached the top of the ramp and fumbled in front of the officer who was there to greet me.

"Hello, sir. Seaman Ruettiger, sir." I messed up! I was supposed to say, "Permission to come aboard!"

"Sailor, relax," the officer said to me. "Say it again."

"Permission to come aboard, sir. Seaman Ruettiger."

So far, so good. He didn't yell at me. Just as I suspected, this whole thing was going to be more about respect, teamwork, and getting the job done. Moments later they dropped me down a hatch and told me to report to the master at arms, the guy who would tell me where to go and where my quarters would be and what my role would be on the ship. Well, he and I didn't get along right away. He was smoking a cigar when I got on board, and the stink of it made me sick. He saw that and, well, let's just say he didn't go out of his way to avoid blowing smoke in my face. The boot camp mentality was still there for us newbies. I quickly found that lots of the older sailors, the lifers especially, liked to pepper the new recruits that way. I tried not to let it bother me. After boot camp, I figured, this would be a piece of cake. Heck, anything would be a piece of cake!

They took me down these little gangways and hallways, and the whole thing felt like a maze with no landmarks. I kept thinking, *How am I gonna find my way back?* Then it was down another hatch and I'm dropped into a room full of all kinds of bunks on top of each other and next to each other, filled with dozens of new shipmates. "This is where you sleep, this is your living quarters, and we'll see you back up at such-and-such an hour." That's it! I felt like I wanted to hide out in my bunk for days; I was so scared I was gonna get lost trying to find my way back out. Of course, asking the rest of the crew won't get you anywhere. They know you're a new guy, and they tease you and play with you.

The hazing, if that's what you'd call it, was pretty tame in those days, but there were certainly a few traditions. Once I was told by someone of higher rank, "Go drain the I-beam and bring me the bucket of water!" How the heck do you drain an I-beam? I started asking around only to realize it was a joke. It was no different than that "bucket of steam" trick I'd endured back at the power plant. *Hardy, har, har.* Very funny, guys. Everyone goes through that stuff. Every one of those guys went through it themselves. So in the end, as long as you don't take it too seriously, it's harmless. It's pretty funny actually. It wasn't the sort of hazing meant to knock guys out and make 'em quit. I never got that sense at all. In fact, the way everyone shared in it added to the sense of camaraderie and support I felt very quickly on that ship.

Before long I found my way back through the maze and reported to the master at arms for my duty: I joined the maintenance data collections office, where I would basically act as a glorified secretary. There's a master chief in that office and they control all the maintenance data, which means if there's maintenance being done anywhere on that ship, it was our job to record it. The navy needed to know how long it'd take a team to do certain jobs, such as how long it would take to pull a certain pump out of commission. I wrote it all down. The point, the way I understood it, was if they ever decided to decommission the ship, they would know approximately how many hours it would take to remove that pump and put a new one in; they could estimate the time and costs, and so on. It was not exactly rocket science but important work nonetheless. And that's what I did.

The USS *North Hampton* was dry-docked in Boston for a solid six months, and that allowed all of us to get a chance to know the city. After our daily duties were done, we were basically allowed to do whatever we wanted. For most guys that meant carousing and partying, but for myself and a few others, it meant a chance to go out and earn some extra money. I wound up finding work as a dishwasher and bus boy at the Harvard Alumni Club, where the who's who of that elite, Ivy League school came to mingle and dine with their peers—people like Ted Kennedy, the brother of President John F. Kennedy, and his more recently assassinated brother, Bobby Kennedy. I wound up serving guys like that, although I didn't really know too much about them, and didn't really care. The other wait staff would point someone out to me every once in a while and I'd say, "Oh, that's nice." I guess if Joe DiMaggio had walked in, it would have been a different story, but the elite academics and politicians didn't float my boat.

I have to say, though, exploring Boston was wonderful. Having lived a life of school, home, practice, school, home, church, home . . . only to be followed by a life of work, home, work, home, church, work, and more work—all within two or three miles of my house—it felt fantastic to walk around and see the sites in a new city. It's a small city and pretty easy to walk from Southie all the way to the Italian restaurants of the North End if you want. We even scored tickets to Red Sox games. I can't tell you what a thrill it was to see the Yankees play the Red Sox in Fenway Park. A dream come true! To sink my teeth into a Fenway Frank? It was awesome. Truly awesome.

The thing I quickly felt was that the world was so much bigger than I ever imagined. New possibilities started to open up for me more and more every day, mostly right inside my own head. I started to dream bigger. I started to think about what I might want to do with my life and where I might want to go. I had never really thought about living anywhere other than Joliet, and here I was living in Boston (for the time being). I could live anywhere, couldn't I? There seemed to be worlds of possibilities around every corner, possibilities that expanded far beyond my father's point of view, or my mother's point of view, or my peers' points of view back in Joliet. Even working at a place like the Harvard Club took down a certain wall I had imagined existed my whole life. It didn't feel strange to be in that elite company. It was just like anywhere else. I had a job to do. I did it. Didn't matter if that job was being performed for a Kennedy or Joe Schmo off the street; I did my job, and usually did it well, and that was all that mattered.

That might not seem like a big realization to some people. But to me? It was.

Just when I thought my worldview had expanded as far as it could, the USS *North Hampton* finished up its dry-dock and we all left town for a little shakedown cruise. Our destination? Guantanamo Bay, Cuba.

This may sound ridiculous to you, but growing up in Illinois, I truly had no idea how much water there was in the world. Two-thirds of the earth is covered by the stuff! I also had no idea how my stomach would react to being out on that water, and it turns out my stomach didn't like it one bit. I got seasick the moment we pulled out of Charlestown, and that seasickness lasted the whole ride down to Cuba . . . and beyond.

If you've never experienced seasickness, imagine you have a stomach flu and you just can't shake it. For days on end. You don't have a fever, but you might as well because your head hurts, and you can't see straight, and the continuous rocking and rocking and rolling of the boat just makes it worse and worse, like you've got a case of the spins after drinking too much, except the room really *is* spinning, the horizon gets lost, you can't get your bearings, and you hurl and hurl and hurl 'til there's nothing but thick, clear liquid and the taste of bile in your mouth, 'cause you just can't swallow any food.

It's enough to make you question whether or not you're going to make it. It's enough to make some men think of jumping overboard and ending it right there. But you know why I never got to that point? You know why I made it through? Because the guy next to me was just as sick. *If he can do it, I can. He's sick; I'm sick. He's not giving up; I'm not giving up.* That's what I learned out on the water with the navy. That's what's wonderful about the military. *I don't even know who this guy is, but he's sicker than a dog and he's just as sick as me, maybe sicker, 'cause he's lying in his puke and*

I'm not. Poor guy, he's not giving up. Still fighting. That's the spirit I like. I need to be like that too. Never give up. We can do this.

When I talk about camaraderie, that's what I'm talking about. We were all in it together. All two thousand or so of us on the 664-foot vessel were a team. Every one of us, together. Never did that shine brighter than when we had to do a refueling and every single person on that boat chipped in. First-class, second-class, yeoman—didn't matter. You could wind up pulling a line while your superior officer pulled that same line right beside you.

That impressed me.

I found myself wishing that school had been that way. I found myself thinking that every sports team needed to be that way. Every company. Every workplace. I found myself dreaming of how great the world would be if everyone's boss came down off their high horse to tow the line with his workers now and then. How great would America be if it modeled itself after this sort of military brotherhood?

The lush, green, windswept, sandy shores of Cuba were unlike anything I had ever seen on this earth. The shimmering, crystal-blue water looked like something out of a movie. It all happened so fast; it was hard to imagine this was my life. That this was, in fact, my chosen destination. I had taken the steps that had led me to this place. I had chosen to do this. Me. I made this happen.

For most of the guys on the ship, Guantanamo Bay was a gateway to ecstasy: the fun, the booze, everything lay ahead just beyond that gate, a ride on the cattle truck into town. But for me? Guantanamo Bay was ecstasy. I went out with the guys a couple of times, but for the most part, when I wasn't working, I stayed right there, enjoying the shore, taking runs around the base, and lifting weights. I was getting in shape. Training. For what? I wasn't sure. But something. I felt like I was preparing for something, for whatever came next. I didn't know what it would be. I didn't have a plan. Just a feeling.

From Guantanamo we came back to Portsmouth, Virginia, where the navy decided to decommission the ship. Everything was going to nuclear power at the time, and while the ship was decommissioned they had to keep a skeleton crew on board. Because of my position in maintenance data collection, I was forced to be part of that skeleton crew while the bulk of my shipmates were reassigned. Because they kept us around so long, they told us, "When we finish this decommissioning, you can have your dream cruise. You can go anywhere you want. So pick out where you want to go." That was our reward!

I knew what I wanted. With that feeling that life was opening up to me, I wanted to see the world, so I chose a Mediterranean cruise. Maybe I should have been a little more careful about the way I worded it, though, because while they gave me the chance to see the world, they put me on a tiny little destroyer escort: the USS *Robert L. Wilson* (DD-847), to be exact. "You'll see the world now, sailor!"

It was a purposeful move on the part of the navy. The guy who made up the orders said, "If I put you on an aircraft carrier, you'd get lost. You belong on a destroyer." He knew my personality. Because it was small, with only three hundred shipmates, he knew I'd have a better shot at developing relationships and experiencing the camaraderie and teamwork I loved.

The whole thing sounded amazing to me: we would be escorting the USS *Enterprise* (CVN-65) across the North Atlantic into the heart of the Mediterranean.

Imagine that! Me, Danny Ruettiger, one of the Rudys from Joliet, going to Europe!

The thought of it seemed too good to be true, but next thing I knew, I was throwing my duffle bag onto my bunk in the belly of the little cork of a boat. I say "cork" because that's exactly how it floated on the water. Like a cork. Bobbing and dipping and tipping on every single wave. I didn't even know the meaning of seasickness before I wound up on the *Robert L. Wilson*. I was sick as a dog! The whole trip across the North Atlantic I was cursing myself for not telling the navy I'd rather stay ashore and build them a new boat! *Why oh why did I put myself onto this tiny motion-sickness machine?*

It didn't make matters easier when we hit stormy seas on a night when I was on duty, alternating between watch on deck and coming into the bridge to take a turn steering the ship. With such a small crew, we all took turns doing everything. If I had felt better, I would have found that duty pretty exciting. How many people get the opportunity to steer a vessel of that size in their whole life? But I was puking too much for it to matter.

I was reporting directly to a young lieutenant that night as I stood at the helm. I liked this particular lieutenant a lot. He seemed like a real down-to-earth guy, and he was a great leader. He treated his men well, even as he pushed us to get what he wanted and what the ship needed. I was so sick, I wasn't exactly doing a great job of keeping that ship on course, but I did my best to follow his orders: "Sailor, come right ten degrees rudder."

"Sir, come right ten degrees rudder, sir!" I'd respond.

"Correct," he'd say, so I'd pull off ten degrees rudder. It's all very systematic. If I wasn't puking between orders, perhaps the ship wouldn't have zigzagged through the open sea quite as much. But I did my best nonetheless, and in between following orders and puking, I noticed something I had never noticed before on that young lieutenant's hand.

"Sir, you have *ND* on your ring. What does that stand for, sir?"

"Notre Dame University," he said.

Wow! I had never seen a Notre Dame ring before. I had never stood next to a Notre Dame man in my life. Despite what I had noticed about the bulk of the student body when I snuck onto campus during that retreat day in my senior year of high school, I still had this vision of Notre Dame graduates being larger than life. Yet here I was taking orders from one, right now!

"Wow, you went to Notre Dame, sir?"

"Yeah," he said. "Just steer the ship, sailor."

"Yes, sir," I replied, but I just couldn't stop myself.

"Sir," I said, "do you think someday I could go to Notre Dame?"

"Sailor," he said to me, "absolutely. Absolutely you can. Now stay on this course!"

Maybe he was just trying to appease me. Maybe he just wanted me to shut up and steer the ship! But I didn't take it that way. Not at all. For the first time in my entire life, he planted a little seed in my brain that the untouchable "not for me" world of Notre Dame might not be so untouchable after all.

"Absolutely," he had said.

He could have said, "Not in a million years, sailor!" He could have said, "Heck no! Not the way you're steering!" or ignored me completely and just kept firing off orders. But he didn't. He gave me that little encouraging word: "'Absolutely.'"

It's hard to get something that's the polar opposite of what you've been told your entire life out of your head. "Notre Dame isn't for kids like you . . . You're not college-bound . . . You don't have the grades . . . You don't have the money . . . Notre Dame's for the best of the best. The elite!" It suddenly occurred to me that none of the people who put those thoughts in my head had actually gone to Notre Dame. Most of them had probably never stepped foot on the campus or had any real idea what the admission requirements were. It's funny—and a little disturbing, actually—how easy it is for us to believe the stuff we hear, whether it's the truth or not.

As I stood there on the bridge setting a rough and rocky course for Europe, I found it astounding that a brand-new question was rattling around my seasick head: Could I maybe, someday, go to Notre Dame? Followed by an unexpected answer: *Absolutely*.

While the sickness continued (exacerbated by yet another cigar-smoking superior who loved to blow that smoke in my face), the doubts I had about choosing that course washed away the moment we hit the Mediterranean sunshine. Never in my life had I imagined I would ever find myself in a place so beautiful.

Italy, Spain, Malta, Greece—we hit a different port every three days. It was a dream! Think of what I was doing just a few months earlier: waking up, leaving for work, coming home. Now? *I'm seeing the world, and they're paying me! Paying me to see this!* Our captain was a great guy who really let us experience it all too. We pulled into Crete and he ordered a "Swim Call," where all of us jumped off the boat into that bath-warm turquoise water; a couple of guys stayed on deck with rifles, watching for sharks. (Luckily none came.)

Feeling that sun, that water washing over me, that's when I really started dreaming. I met a lot of good guys on that ship, and I started hearing their stories, these sea-going sailors who'd been in the navy for many years. I saw their skin, with that sea-salt look, the hard skin of true sailors, man. The real deal. They'd lived, truly lived. Then in the back of the poop deck in the evening, when it was calm and all I heard and smelled was the ocean, my mind seemed to wander, almost escape itself, as I stared up into a star-filled sky and realized the possibilities were endless. Endless!

It was during those nights when my thoughts turned to Notre Dame. I know it sounds crazy that a single conversation, a few seconds with that young lieutenant on that stormy night, could set my mind on a brand-new course, but it's true. I found myself running around that ship, staying in shape, sweating in that scorching sun, dreaming of what it would feel like to go to Notre Dame. I didn't know how I could get in. It's not like my grades had magically improved just because I joined the navy. It's not like I made enough money to cover tuition. Still, the thought that it was *possible* just would not leave my brain. That one conversation changed the thought of Notre Dame from a fantasy to a dream, the difference being that a fantasy is untouchable, unattainable, and unreachable; a dream is something you can work toward, something you can envision, something you can feel beckoning you from right in front of you.

I started to see myself as one of those Notre Dame students and felt like I was suddenly becoming a student of the world.

In Athens I decided to see the sites. How could I not? And I quickly discovered the camaraderie and bonding that can happen between different cultures on the other side of the world. My buddy and I wound up chatting with a Greek family who offered to show us around. The doctor and his wife and kids took us to the Acropolis, and some amazing historic ruins that were in the process of being dug up. It was beautiful. That family fed us and they were honored to have Americans at their house. We got to Rome and the same sort of thing happened. And at every stop we made, I decided, I'm gonna go tour. I'm not gonna get drunk or chase women like the other guys. This is awesome! That's just what I did. My mind-set was that I wanted to see everything I could. Plenty of shipmates spent their time getting wild and crazy, but I just couldn't pass up this opportunity to take the world in. Who knew if I'd ever be back? I didn't want to regret missing any of it, and I tried to make sure that wouldn't happen. I still took time to work out. Lifting weights became a ritual to me. I took time to run. I even made time to take training courses back at the ship, in whatever subjects they had to offer, just to improve my study skills and to prove to myself that I might be able to make it in a class-room after all. Those Notre Dame dreams kept kicking in my gut. And somehow my travels and my sightseeing were feeding me in a way I had never felt in any classroom. I wanted to learn about everything. I wanted to know more about the world.

You hear about the Coliseum, the Pantheon, the cathedrals, and now here I was seeing them all firsthand. It was awesome. How can you not be moved seeing Michelangelo's work? Staring up at the ceiling of the Sistine Chapel, seeing that image of man touching God, imagining that artist lying flat on his back on scaffolding for months at a time, you can't help but think, *Wow. How'd he do that?*

It's inspiring. It makes you want to do great things yourself. Or at least put in some extra effort.

How could it not?

I even saw the pope as he stepped out onto his balcony to bless the crowd in front of St. Peter's Basilica at the Vatican. What an awesome sight. All of those people. No matter what you believe, there's a power-ful spiritual presence in that place that you can feel in your bones. And to think of the reach of the Catholic church! I thought back to our little church in Joliet. I thought, once again, of Notre Dame, and the beauty of that campus, and the overwhelming spirituality I felt while standing on that plush green lawn as the golden statue of Mary smiled down upon me.

On a daily basis that Notre Dame dream kept growing. Everywhere I went, I'd find something that reminded me of the possibility. It wasn't a dream of going to college. No other school would do. It was the dream of being a part of that campus. Of capturing and living out that spiritual feeling I had when I looked up at that Golden Dome, and over at the cross at the top of the Basilica. Of fitting in with that student body and open-ing the doors to an education that could help to make me more than who I was today. More than what my parents and peers expected me to be. More than what I had allowed myself to even fantasize about.

With all the working out and bulking up I was doing in the navy, maybe I'd even have a shot at playing football at Notre Dame! Okay, so that still seemed really far-fetched, but I recall having the thought. More than once. After all, if I could dream about going to that top-notch school, why couldn't I dream about playing for their top-notch team?

It wasn't just a fantasy anymore. As I've said, it was a dream. That's a big difference. And that dream seemed closer and closer, even though I had no idea how I would ever make it come true.

As our Mediterranean tour came to an end, so did the nonstop escalation of the war in Vietnam. The emotional toll of that war was one thing. The financial toll was another. The government was cutting back on military spending, and as part of the deal, they decided to allow servicemen like me who had eighteen months in uniform to opt out early.

There wasn't even a question for me: I was sick of being seasick. I knew I wasn't cut out to be one of those salty-skinned lifelong sailors. Plus, the navy had already done more for me than I had ever imagined it could. I had seen the world, and I had grown stronger in every way imaginable.

I had a new dream to pursue now. I didn't know how I was going to do it, didn't have a clue, but I knew it was time to go home.

Reading the Signs

I'm not exactly sure when it started to sink in—
that gnawing feeling that I was in danger of giving up. I think it was
almost a year after I came back from the navy when it started to spiral.
I felt that my life was quickly tracking backward, falling into routines,
in danger of running on autopilot again toward a destination that wasn't
my own.

I had traded my bunk in the belly of a ship for a room in my parents' house, back on Briggs Ave. (My own room, thankfully. I was finally
allowed out of the basement bunkhouse and into a solo bedroom now that
both of my older sisters had moved out.)

I had traded my important work on a communications ship fit for
the president to go back to the power plant. It was a higher-paid position,
in maintenance, with more responsibilities. I was thankful for that. But
still . . . I had traded "swim calls" in the Mediterranean for sitting in the
stands under the lights on Friday nights, watching high school football with
old buddies from Joliet Catholic, then reliving our glory days over beers.

I had traded walks in the stunning streets of Athens and Rome for a daily commute down dusty Patterson Road, on the bad side of the tracks, past run-down houses with overgrown yards, a car lot bragging "We Buy Junk!" on its big, old, faded sign, and right through the chain-link gates that led to those skyscraper-sized smokestacks and train-car loads of black coal piled up like mini mountain ranges.

This wasn't my life. This was more like my father's life. The life of a Union Oil man who did what he had to do to support his big family. A proud life, sure. An honorable one. A good one! But it wasn't mine. I knew it. I knew where I wanted to be. I just didn't know how to get there, and for a good long time, life—with its bills, its expectations, its routines, and its too-easy-to-be-trapped-in patterns—seemed to get the best of me.

I managed to stay in shape, just as I had in the navy, by running and lifting weights. My younger brother Francis had set up quite a little gym in my parents' garage, and it served me well.

When I'd run, I'd run all the way to Providence High on the other side of town to work out on their fields, and when I caught wind that they had finally started a football program, I volunteered and started coaching. I loved the game as much as ever, and coaching seemed to be the only way for a twentysomething guy to stay involved. I was a terrible coach. I yelled at the kids and did all the things I would eventually realize a coach really shouldn't do. But I had fun with it. And I pushed those kids to get faster and stronger and to play their hardest, not just at the games but at every single practice. "Give it your all! Teamwork, teamwork, teamwork!" All that stuff that was reinforced in my gut by the navy.

I was still dreaming. Dreaming big. Dreaming of Notre Dame. Especially when I'd run, when I'd work out, when I'd be alone with just my thoughts. I even had the confidence to tell other people about it. At work, someone would be talking about the game, and I'd say, "I'm gonna go to Notre Dame someday." Guys would laugh. Chuckle. Give a little sneer, like I didn't know what I was talking about. Occasionally they'd give me some grief about it, and there were a couple of times when that old pent-up anger got the best of me and I'd wind up in a fistfight coming out of the elevator.

I'd bring it up at home, to my dad, and he'd say the most practical things he knew to say: "Well, how're you gonna get in if you don't have the grades for it, Danny?" or "How you gonna pay for that? It's a lot of rich kids go to Notre Dame."

It's hard not to let that kind of stuff get you down.

But then there were a couple of guys who reacted very differently to my Notre Dame dreams. A couple of buddies from work. Older guys. Guys I decided to pay attention to, for some reason, more than I ever paid attention to the naysayers.

The first was George. George was a drunk. He admitted he was a drunk. He knew he had basically given up on life, given up on any dreams he might have had when he was younger, and resigned himself to the fact that he'd work at the plant until they forced him to retire, drowning any sorrows in cans of beer in the meantime. What was amazing to me is that he seemed totally at peace with that decision. One of the ways he made peace with himself, I think, was to stay connected to dreamers like me. I'd meet George at a bar after work, or sometimes stop by his house for dinner, and he'd pepper me with questions about my travels in the navy. He was an ex-navy man himself, and we swapped a lot of navy stories whenever we hung out together. He also asked me to imagine and describe what I thought life would be like at Notre Dame once I got there.

He liked to dream right along with me, and that inspired me.

Then there was Siskel. Siskel was a stocky guy, like me, but in his fifties. Real quiet kind of guy. He was very good at his job, which I admired. And he saw that I was having a hard time with some of the other guys. So one day at lunch we struck up a conversation. I could tell he was really listening to me, not dismissing my ideas as crazy or naive. The very first time we really talked about it, he told me, "You go do your dream, Rudy. You're young enough, you got nothing to regret." The more we talked, the more I put the pieces of his own story together. He had been at the power plant for more than thirty years. Thirty! The thing was, he had a dream once just like me. He wanted to go to school. He wanted to become a doctor. But instead, he married young, started a family, and felt he had to work to support that family. He needed a job with security. At least, that's what he convinced himself he needed. Next thing he knew, thirty years had gone by. And without saying too much, he made it very clear that he regretted the fact that he didn't pursue his dream. "Go do it, Rudy!" he'd say whenever I brought up the Notre Dame idea. "Who's stopping you? You can go to Notre Dame. Why not?"

Why not? I kept asking myself that question. Asking and asking. Was I too scared to take that risk? Maybe. Would I make a fool of myself? Quite possibly. *What if I give it a shot and I fail? That would be terrible!*

It's amazing how strong our voices can be when we're talking ourselves out of something: *I should be happy to have a good job. This life isn't so bad, is it? I have security and safety, and I'm saving some money. I don't need to go to Notre Dame. People lead really good lives without going to Notre Dame.*

But Siskel's words, George's words, and that young lieutenant's initial encouragement on that stormy sea on our journey across the Atlantic kept bouncing around my head and bringing me back to that much simpler thought of *Why not?* Then, one day, I finally got a glimpse of what I thought might possibly be my answer.

I had dated a couple of girls in town after I got back from the navy. One of them I didn't even really like that much, but her father was a Notre Dame graduate and I just wanted to be around him. How's that for dedication to my dream?

I was with the second girl, though, when an opportunity dropped right into my lap: a fellow Joliet Catholic grad who was a year behind me had two tickets to a Notre Dame football game that he couldn't use and he asked me if I wanted them. "Are you kidding?! Yeah!" So my girlfriend and I took off in my Mustang and made the trip east on I-80 to South Bend, Indiana. I was so excited to see that stadium again. I was so pumped to step foot on that campus again, period. But as we drove into town and headed to campus, something caught my eye that completely turned me around.

I saw a sign by the side of the road for something called Holy Cross Community College. I looked over and saw a few modest little brick buildings, which I assumed were all part of that school. We were just down the street from Fatima House, where I came for that retreat my senior year of high school. It was basically right across the street from Notre Dame. *What is that place?* I got chills.

"You see that little school over there?" I said to my girlfriend. "I think that's my answer to Notre Dame."

"What are you, nuts?" she said. Like everyone else, it seemed, she was tired of hearing me talk about this Notre Dame dream of mine. I guess you can only listen to people talk about something for so long before you just don't want to hear it anymore. We all get that feeling, right? Like, *Do something about it or shut up already!*

"No, I think that's it," I said to her. "Look at it. It's right there! There's gotta be a connection. What if that's my way in?"

She didn't get it. My mind kept racing through the whole game. *What was Holy Cross? Was it part of Notre Dame?* I had heard of community colleges but knew nothing about them. None of my teachers or counselors or anyone had ever suggested to me that it might be an option. *This community college is right here! Practically on campus! Could it be a way in? Could I go there?*

It was all I could think about, even as we stepped into that stadium, took our seats on those little wooden bleachers, and watched the Fighting Irish come out of that tunnel with Touchdown Jesus standing tall in the background.

By the time we walked back to the car, my girlfriend was mad at me 'cause I was so distant and distracted. I didn't blame her. In my mind I was already moving on. I was thinking about what it would be like to be here, going to that little school across the street, and coming to these football games whenever I wanted—with or without her by my side.

I always imagined there would be something remarkable about the most important day of my life. Maybe we all do that. You'd think there would be a certain sense of foreboding, a feeling in the air when you get out of bed. Something to tell you, "Hey, watch out. Big accident coming today." Or, "Pay attention, Rudy. This day's a biggie!"

But life's not like that. Things happen. Boom! No warning.

When I think back on it, the only thing that stood out about that Saturday as I headed into work at the power plant was that nothing stood out. Nothing. Not even the weather. The skies were gray. Overcast. Typical. Bland. That's it.

Compared to the weekdays, Saturdays at the plant were kind of quiet. The demand for electricity never stops, of course, so the actual mechanisms that deliver the power were just as loud as ever: the constant whoosh of pressurized steam, the pounding metal and resounding thud of feeder chutes opening and closing in sequence as they drop their heavy loads of coal onto the conveyor belts and the powerful crunch of pulverizing rock as all that coal moved steadily through the crusher. Yet on Saturdays and Sundays, the managers and crew were somehow more relaxed. A little less urgent. That pent-up energy of waiting for the weekend was gone, and for guys stuck on the weekend shift, I guess there was a sense of resignation. A sense that the work just had to get done, period. So even in the lunchroom, where things were rowdy on a Thursday or Friday, it wasn't. It was quiet.

I ate lunch with Siskel that day. I sat across from him and we pulled our packed sandwiches from metal lunch pails just as you'd expect guys like us to be eating from, just as we did every other day. I don't even remember what we talked about. It simply wasn't a standout conversation. It wasn't one of those times that he listened to me talk about dreaming of going to Notre Dame, or when he backed me up and told me to stop talking and go do it. A month had passed since I had first laid eyes on Holy Cross, and I hadn't really done anything about it. I had just fallen back into the same old routine of work, home, work, home, work. It wasn't one of those times when Siskel opened up either, wishing out loud that he'd become that doctor like he knew he could have. No. Siskel didn't really talk much anyway, unless I said something to him first. So it was just an everyday, run-of-the-mill conversation. No significance.

After lunch, we all went back to what we were doing. I was an equipment attendant at that time. It was up to me to check all the equipment, make sure everything was oiled and running right. If there was a problem, it was up to me to shut things down, if necessary, so the electrician or

mechanic could get in there and fix it. There was a procedure to everything, a sequence, so no one would get hurt. And it was a big, big deal that
we take things one step at a time.

Siskel was a mechanic, so we'd wind up working together often. After
I'd shut something down, I'd watch him work, and I'd always bug him
with questions because he was so good at what he did. I always admired
his work ethic. He knew what he was doing. After all those years on the
job, whatever he did, he did it well.

On this particular afternoon, after lunch was over, I was adding
hydrogen to a low-pressure unit, a process that takes about twenty minutes to complete. There's a lot of waiting around at a power plant job, and
this was one of the classic cases. I stood there waiting and waiting for the
unit to fill, daydreaming a little bit, when all of a sudden I got a call on
my radio from the control operator.

"Rudy, C1 tunnel, got a trip. You and Siskel need to get out there and
see what's up."

A "trip" meant the conveyor had shut down. Maybe something was
jammed. Could have been anything really. But we needed to get it going
again.

I was almost done adding hydrogen and couldn't stop with the job
incomplete, so I hopped on the radio right away to Siskel: "Just give me a
minute. I'll meet you out there."

He replied in the affirmative.

A minute or so later, I had wrapped up the job and was headed out
to the C1 tunnel. It was maybe three hundred yards away, but it didn't
take long to walk over there. With the turbines and furnace going, it was
hot. You couldn't hear yourself talk over the whoosh of steam in there.
And yet, as I walked out, I could hear the conveyor belt running. I could
hear the feeders. I could hear the crusher. It sure didn't sound like there'd
been a trip. The system wasn't stopped at all. I remember thinking, just
for a second, *That's strange. Why's it running?* And that's when I saw him:
Siskel. Motionless. Lying flat on his back on top of the conveyor, passing
under the feeders and being carried toward the crusher.

I ran over as fast as I could and pulled him off. His body was limp and heavy. I radioed for help. "I've got a man down! Help! I need help!" I followed our training and safety procedures and started giving him mouth to mouth. Another worker, an ex-marine, ran up seconds later and started giving him chest compressions. I just kept breathing into his mouth, which was covered with blood.

I'll never forget that taste. That smell.

I had never seen a dead body before. Ever. Here I was touching one. Smelling one. Trying to breathe life back into one. Trying to breathe life back into my friend. And that life was gone. Just gone.

I stood up. Woozy. A bunch of the other guys gathered around and we all shared that horrible feeling of knowing there was nothing we could do. My co-worker kept at it, over and over. He refused to give up. "Stop," I finally said. "He's gone."

Just then, almost miraculously fast it seemed, the paramedics arrived and took over. I remember standing back in a daze and watching the whole scene unfold. Of course, everybody was trying to figure out what happened. There were about five different feeder chutes, about a foot off the belt. And from the best we could figure, Siskel must've come in and seen whatever the problem was right away and thought it was an easy fix. So he hopped up there to take care of it himself rather than wait for me. Taking that shortcut is probably what cost him his life. If I had been there, I would have shut the whole thing down, electrically, to avoid any chance that the system could start up unexpectedly. I would have stood by and waited until the fix was made and any men were clear before turning everything back on. That was my job. But I never had a chance to do my job. The system must have called for fuel while Siskel was up there, and the belt must've started with a jump. That knocked him off his feet and before he could get his bearings the belt pulled him forward. His head smashed right into the first two feeders—one, two—and broke his neck.

Now here he was. My friend. On the floor. The paramedics tried and tried, but then they stopped too. There was nothing they could do. They lifted Siskel onto a gurney and we followed them out as they wheeled him toward the ambulance. Before I knew it, the doors had closed and he was gone. I watched as the ambulance pulled away.

I stood there covered in Siskel's blood and stared up into that gray sky. *Why, God? Why? I was just talking to him. He was right there. Now he's gone? Why, God? Why? Tell me. Tell me what to do!*

It all happened so fast. Just like that, his life was over. I couldn't believe it. I couldn't stop thinking about it. One minute he's there, next minute he's not? *Why didn't he wait for me? Why did he jump up there? Why did this happen? What was he thinking? What did he die for? What am I doing here?*

That last question was the one that got me. What *was* I doing there? I didn't want to work at that plant. I certainly didn't want to die at that plant. What was I doing?

Call it whatever you want: Instinct. A gut feeling. The voice of God. Whatever it was, I heard it. I felt it. Right then. Right there.

Leave.

It wasn't fear. It wasn't anger. Okay, maybe it was a little anger. Anger at the unfairness of it all and how awful it was. But it wasn't rage. It wasn't irrational. It was honest. The purest, most honest feeling I'd ever had. That voice in my head, in my heart, in my soul kept telling me, "Go!"

So I did. I stood at my locker at the end of the shift and stuffed all of my things into my bag. Emptied the whole thing out.

"Rudy, what are you doing?" a couple of guys asked.

"I'm leaving," I said.

It was more than a feeling now. I had said it out loud. It was real.

All those times Siskel had told me, "Get out of here. You don't belong here. What good is security if you're not happy?" And this is what it took for me to finally listen?

Go for the dream. That was the message. A message that now came loud and clear.

When I walked out the door that afternoon, that was it. I didn't officially quit that day. I didn't say anything to my supervisor. But I knew: I was done. I would do exactly what Siskel had been telling me to do all this time. I would do what I knew I wanted to do, for all this time, but simply hadn't found the courage to do on my own. Siskel's accident somehow gave me that courage—the courage to walk away. It was the courage to not do the safe thing, the easy thing, the acceptable, "normal," proper thing that any man with a steady, good-paying job is supposed to do. The courage to stop worrying about failing and to just get out there and *try*. To try! Why are so many of us afraid to even *try*?

When I got home that night, I didn't tell my parents I was going to quit. I didn't want to hear their complaints. I didn't want to hear any second thoughts or doubts or fears about what I was doing. Instead, I started to make a plan. I had my first clue already: Holy Cross College. I knew that somehow Holy Cross would be my way in.

But how?

Over the course of the next twenty-four hours, my mind did a complete one-eighty. I stopped thinking about all those reasons why I *couldn't* go to Notre Dame, and instead started focusing on how I *could*. I started to put a plan into motion, even though I had no idea how that plan would unfold. And for the first time in my life, that fear of the unknown didn't seem scary at all. You know what seemed scary? Dying without trying. A lot of people have a dream, but they're afraid to go for it, too afraid they'll fail. Suddenly, after that fateful Saturday, all I kept thinking was, *Who cares if I fail?* After you've seen a life end that quickly, it puts it all in perspective. I wasn't going to ask for other people's advice now. I wasn't going to give anyone in my life the chance to stop me from doing what I needed to do. I already had the answer I needed. God gave me that answer. My gut gave me that answer.

One day later, I hopped into my car in the morning and peeled out of the driveway without telling anyone. I pulled onto I-80 and headed east . . . toward South Bend, Indiana.

I had no idea what I was going to do once I got there. I just knew I needed to find out what the connection was (if any) between Holy Cross and Notre Dame. I needed to figure out some way to get my foot in the door. Maybe no one would listen to me. Maybe no one would help me. Maybe the whole thing was stupid and I was about to make a gigantic fool out of myself.

You know what? I didn't care.

Part II

Blue & Gold

Holy Cross

An amazing thing happens when you take a leap of faith. A stunning thing. I must've heard about it a hundred times in those old Catholic masses, but it never sunk in. I had to live it to understand it. I had to go through it to be able to look back on it and see how it all fell into place.

What happens when you take that bold first step in the direction of your dreams without any knowledge or forethought or assurance about how it's going to turn out, without any particular light to guide you other than that feeling in your gut, without the ability even to see whether that step is secure or safe or just a hole in the ground that you're about to fall into—what happens is that the path to your destination suddenly appears before you, one stone at a time. The path might seem strange. It might take you in a different direction than the one you intended. But you'll get to the destination that's meant for you. All you've got to do is keep walking, and those stones keep appearing. The further you go, the further you'll trust the process until you're walking forward without even thinking about the unknowable path ahead. You're just trusting, just going with it, confident that the path will be there.

That's faith. That's belief. And that's powerful.

I pulled my car into the back parking lot behind this little beige-brick building at Holy Cross and stepped inside to find a simple tiled floor, a silver cross on the wall, sparse decorations, and a bulletin board full of notices. It felt like a school, but with something extra: a little fireplace set in a sunken area just a step down and to the right, with a few wooden chairs and couches with thick brown cushions. A gathering spot. Almost like a living room. There were a couple of students lounging there, reading books. It felt comfortable.

A sign pointed me to the office, which was just a few steps to the left. A woman greeted me with a warm smile and asked if she could help me. She said it as if she meant it too—not like one of those gatekeeper secretaries you meet in some offices, whose only job is to keep you from getting to the important people in the back.

I said my name was Rudy and that I was interested in learning a little bit about this school. She said "Brother John" would likely be able to help me, and she asked me to take a seat. Couldn't have been a minute later when Brother John Driscoll stepped out, shook my hand with a big, warm smile, and asked me to come join him in his office.

Brother John Driscoll was the head of the school; he was a little balding guy who chain-smoked cigarettes like they were going out of style. He was the man who founded Holy Cross in the mid-1960s. Somehow, just by walking through the door, I had reached the man at the top. It felt great!

Within about ten seconds, he answered my biggest question: yes, Holy Cross is affiliated with Notre Dame. The Brothers of Holy Cross— the same Catholic order that founded Notre Dame University—ran the school. And yes, the Brothers would recommend that a certain number of students from Holy Cross transfer over to Notre Dame each year, if their grades were solid and they had shown the abilities and skills and passion it takes to make it. As a two-year community college, one of its primary goals was to take good students and make them great, to prepare them to move on to fine universities, Notre Dame included, he told me.

That made me nervous. I knew for a fact that I wasn't a "good" student. My record would show that. But I went ahead and told Brother John my whole backstory anyway: how I'd been blown away the first time I ever stepped foot on the Notre Dame campus, and how something about it felt just welcoming to me—almost like a home, if that makes sense. I told him about my time in the navy, and about Siskel and the terrible thing that happened just two days earlier, and why it was so important to me to come to Holy Cross and to fulfill my dream of going to Notre Dame.

After listening to everything I had to say, Brother John explained that there were a few things he would need to see—transcripts, a recommendation or two—but that after all I'd said and the initiative I had shown by driving all the way to see him that day, he didn't see any reason why I couldn't enroll at Holy Cross for the fall semester. "We'd love to have you, Rudy."

I could hardly believe my ears. My old self wondered, *Is this guy for real?* I didn't know that a place of higher education could be so welcoming.

Until that moment, I don't think I truly believed that that kind of grace and acceptance was real.

I hopped back in my car and drove toward Joliet with my mind spinning. I left there not with a hope of applying, not with a thought that I might get rejected, but with what amounted to an all-out acceptance. "We'd love to have you." All I had to do was complete the necessary steps. How to complete those steps was a mystery to me, but on that drive home the answers started to come. I knew where I could find someone to help.

Of course, I didn't tell my parents where I had been. Telling them wasn't an option yet. I needed to take the next steps. I needed to make it real enough to make sense to them. Real enough that they wouldn't bring up the doubts and fears that parents raise when trying to protect their kids from failure, including the big question of how I was going to pay for tuition. I hadn't even asked Brother John how much the school cost!

I didn't care. I knew I'd figure out a way to pay for it. Somehow. I wasn't going to let that stand in my way. I didn't want anything to stand in my way. *But how?*

I hoped that a man name Pat Sullivan would have some answers for me. I had met Pat at Providence High when I was coaching football. I knew that he served as a college counselor, among other things. I had a feeling he would know about this stuff—how to get my transcripts and what kind of recommendations I would need, and all of the things Brother John said were required of me. So as soon as I got the chance, I ran over to see him.

Pat was just as warm and accepting of the whole idea of me going to Holy Cross as Brother John was. He saw my passion and excitement and didn't seem to doubt for one second that I could not only get in but do well at that school. And he fully supported my dream of using Holy Cross as a stepping-stone to Notre Dame. He said he thought it was a smart thing to do—*Me? Smart?*—since the affiliation would give me a leg up that I might not have if I attended Joliet Community College, or any other good community college for that matter. He was thrilled that I had the courage to go for it, and he offered to do anything he could to help. He even hopped on the phone to Holy Cross right then and there, as I sat in his office, and spoke to Brother John about the requirements. All of a sudden, the ball was rolling.

Pat was also the guy who revealed a major miracle to me: my tuition would be paid by the navy. I had never heard of the GI Bill when I enlisted. Or, if I had heard of it, I wasn't paying attention and had no idea what it was all about. The reason I enlisted was to secure my fate, to save my life, as it were. But I had no idea that the navy was going to save my life in so many ways. The simple fact that I had served in the navy meant that they would pay my tuition under the GI Bill. They would even cover the heavy expense of Notre Dame tuition once I made the transfer from Holy Cross. (Assuming I could make it.)

I felt like I had won the lottery. A lottery I didn't even realize I had played.

I went back to Holy Cross a few times that summer to drop off the various portions of my application and to figure out all the logistics. There were times when I'd pile a couple of my little brothers in the car just to have some company on the long drive, and I'd wind up leaving them sitting there with the windows cracked open for what seemed like hours while I sorted everything out. They still rib me about it to this day.

The provisions of the GI Bill didn't cover room and board, and I got scared for a moment that I wouldn't be able to afford a place to live while going to school full-time. But Brother John took my worry in stride and sent me over to see a man named Father Bayness. Father Bayness ran St. Joseph's Hall, which everyone called St. Joe's. It was a dormitory run by the Brothers of Holy Cross that housed a mixture of Holy Cross and Notre Dame students and seminarians, situated right on the Notre Dame campus. The place was a well-kept secret that I felt privileged to discover. Father Bayness asked if I would be willing to do some maintenance, mowing the lawn and keeping the place looking good, in order to earn my stay. "Mind? I would love to!" I told him.

That was that. I had my tuition covered. I had a place to stay. All that was left was to tell my family and to finally, officially, quit my job at the power plant.

As you can imagine, my parents were shocked. They asked the questions I anticipated they would ask: How could I get in with my grades, and how was I going to afford it? Boy, were they surprised when I had all the answers. Going into the navy was one thing, but to think that one of their kids was heading off to college—it was something they hadn't dared to dream. I was the first one ever in my family to go to college. They were proud and happy and nervous and a little confused at the same time about how I managed to pull it all off.

The guys at work were shocked too. Co-workers tried to shoot it down. "What's Holy Cross? You're not going to Notre Dame after all!" *Just wait, buddy.* Supervisors tried to keep me there. "Why do you want to leave? You have a bright future here, Rudy. You're a good worker." *Because I'm going to Notre Dame!* I didn't argue with anyone. I didn't want to get in a fight. I didn't want to put any of those guys down, and I didn't have any right to. This was my dream. My life. That's all. So I said as little as possible and just got the heck out of there. I was ready to go. I had been preparing to go for all this time. Finally, my time had come.

I had no space in my mind or my heart for anyone to tell me I was being ridiculous for going to school at an age when most of my peers would have already graduated. I had no room for anyone to tell me I couldn't do it or wouldn't make it. I had graduated boot camp. I had already been through the navy. I had been through the toughest part of life, in many ways, and had overcome obstacles greater than I ever thought I could. So this whole decision—it was *nothing*. Now that the ball was rolling, it didn't feel like a huge challenge to me at all. There weren't nearly as many obstacles as I thought there would be in order to get into Holy Cross, and those obstacles were easily surmountable. I knew this was what I wanted, and there was no reason I couldn't have it. *Why not me? You can't take this from me. I know what I can do now. I know what I'm capable of. I've still got a long way to go, and I know I've got to earn my way through. I've got to get the grades and work hard and prove myself if I'm going to move from Holy Cross to Notre Dame.* I understood all of that. And I would earn it. I just knew it.

In fact, I knew even more than that. I was so set on getting into Notre Dame that I didn't doubt it anymore. It was going to happen. I believed it with everything in my being. It's as if I was willing that dream to happen. I believed it so much that I started to will a whole new dream to happen too.

Every trip to Notre Dame's beautiful campus that summer brought me back to 1966, to those first few moments of discovery during that senior retreat and that feeling that I belonged at Notre Dame. Sometimes I arrived early in the morning, before the Holy Cross office was even open, just so I could walk around that campus in the peace and quiet, letting it sink in that this was real. This was my new home.

The more real it felt, the more often my mind wandered back to that moment at the stadium when my buddy and I wandered into the locker room with the football team. I thought about all those guys you never saw on TV, all those guys whose names I had never heard on the radio, all those third- and fourth-string guys who were shorter and stockier than those giant first- and second-team players who would go on to professional football careers. I thought about Coach Parseghian and that ridiculous line I blurted out to him about wanting to come play football for Notre Dame someday. Only now, it didn't feel so ridiculous anymore. It felt like the truth. I *did* want to play for Notre Dame. I was *going* to Notre Dame. I was right here on campus. Coach Parseghian was the first coach in Notre Dame history to actually encourage walk-on players to try out for the team. There was no reason I couldn't make it happen.

Moving into St. Joe's that fall felt almost as big as walking up the gangway of the USS *North Hampton*. *This is my new home.*

St. Joe's was an old-fashioned four-story, beige-brick dorm house filled with lots of little boarding rooms and a few communal bathrooms for maximum efficiency. It slept about 140 students on its top three floors. The main floor had a dining room, a communal area, and a chapel, which I quickly found to be a perfect, quiet place to study without being disturbed, where no one would come knocking on my door to chat or to try to convince me to go out carousing.

I started out in room 224, without much of a view, but to me the view didn't matter. I was here. I was on the Notre Dame campus! I could step out my door and walk right down to St. Joseph's Lake, follow the winding path off to the right through the beautiful woods, which led me to everything I ever dreamed of: turn right and follow the path along St. Mary's Lake, up past Fatima House to Holy Cross; or down around and off to the left where I'd wind up right in the spot where I first discovered the glowing candles of the Grotto on that senior retreat back in high school. It was my personal gateway to the Basilica and those beautiful lawns under the watchful eye of Mother Mary atop the Golden Dome. It was all right there.

I could hear the bells from the Basilica without so much as stepping a foot outside.

My room was so narrow I could almost reach my arms across from one wall to the other. My bed was like a military cot, with a metal frame and a mattress with no box spring sitting on top of a set of spring-like wires.

There was a lamp on a little utilitarian wooden desk by the single window, a closet with room for a few hangers and a set of wobbly drawers. That's it.

Some kids might have a hard time adjusting to that. To me? It was much more than I ever had to myself growing up in a shared room with six brothers, and far more comfortable than my sardine-packed quarters in the belly of a navy destroyer escort. Heck, it had a door that I could close whenever I wanted. It even locked!

To me, it was more than enough. I was grateful for every inch of it.

The first person I met in that dorm was a student named Freddy. I was so excited to be there, I introduced myself about as boldly as a guy could: "My name's Rudy. I'm gonna go to Notre Dame to play football. And I was in the navy!" He was a sophomore at Notre Dame, and it turned out that Freddy and I were both dreamers. He had his eyes set on the law, maybe becoming a judge someday, and he loved that I made such a bold statement as soon as I met him. We both had money issues, and we had both agreed to mow lawns and keep the place clean in order to pay for our room and board, which meant that we'd wind up spending a lot of time together. Thankfully we hit it off. In fact, the two of us became fast friends almost immediately, and Freddy would soon help me in ways I never imagined a fellow student ever could.

My very first class at Holy Cross was math. I dreaded it. I was nervous. I had visions of repeating my high school experience all over again—visions of that fifth-grade humiliation in front of all of these smart college kids.

It took about ten seconds for all of that fear to fly out the window. Our professor, a little Holy Cross Brother named Pedro, stood in front of the fifteen or so students in one of the school's eight classrooms and said, "How many of you guys want to go to Notre Dame?" All of us raised our hands. Maybe one guy didn't. Clearly I'd have my work cut out for me competing against all of these guys for a spot, I figured.

"Good," Brother Pedro said. "That's good. You all know what you need to do to get to Notre Dame: you all took basic math in high school."

I spoke up. "I didn't have any algebra. I wasn't smart enough," I said.

"You're smart enough," he countered. "Here's the deal. This course is parallel with the math they teach at Notre Dame, and it counts as the math credit. So if you pass this, you won't have to take any more math at Notre Dame."

Wow. That sounded pretty good to me. I just hoped I could pass.

"As of this moment, you've all got an A, so don't worry about it," he said.

We all have an A? What did he mean by that?

"Here's what you need to do to keep that A: you need to follow the plan. The plan is: Show up every day. Do your homework. If you don't know how to do it, ask your friend."

Did he just say all we need to do to get an A is to show up and do our homework? In a heartbeat he took the pressure off the grade, the grade being one of the big obstacles I dreaded. Do you know how exciting that was? I kept writing down everything he said. *Ask your friend. You mean I can ask a friend for help if I don't know the answer? In high school that was called cheating! This is awesome!*

It certainly seemed like a plan I could follow, unlike the plans they tried to lay out for us all in high school, where I (like everyone else) had been told that in order to become a "college-bound" student I would need to take trigonometry and all kinds of advanced math. Brother Pedro insisted that wasn't true.

Why didn't anybody tell me this sooner?! If I hadn't been so excited about it, I might have been angry. Why had I been told time and time again that there was only one way to get to college when here I was, in the middle of my first college class, hearing an entirely different truth? I wanted to run back and bust open the doors at my high school to tell everyone, as if it were some kind of secret I'd uncovered. *Why on earth would anyone keep this a secret?*

Some of the other Brothers were a little more rigid. They seemed more like regular teachers to me. But none of them put me down. None of them put anyone down. It seemed like they really wanted us all to succeed. That was new. Some were even fun! I'll never forget Brother Larry's biology class. We laughed so much, it didn't even feel like we were learning. But we were. And even in the more rigid classes (Brother John's psychology class, for instance) I took that easygoing attitude Brother Pedro preached about and applied it liberally—asking my friends for help whenever I didn't understand something, and not feeling guilty for asking for that help, which was such a relief to me.

Even so, I still found myself struggling. A few weeks in, that old grade-school frustration kicked into overdrive. I wasn't keeping up the way I wanted. I didn't do well on my first assignments. I failed my first two quizzes in English and psychology. It wasn't anywhere near the kind of work I needed to do to get into Notre Dame.

Back at the dorm one night, I complained about it to Freddy. I remember saying to him, flat out, "I'm just not a smart guy." He looked at me as if I were talking nonsense, and his immediate response was a generous one: "Let me help ya," he said.

Freddy was smart. That's just the plain truth. He had dreams of becoming a judge someday, and it was clear to me that he had the brains and the drive to get there. The fact that he would open up and offer to share some of his knowledge with me was a gift.

The first time he looked at my notebooks he said, "Geez, how come you take all these notes?" I was shocked. I thought everyone took notes that way. I told him I just take down every word the professor says, so I can go over it all once I'm back home. "Well, that's your first problem," Freddy said. "You're so busy writing, you're not listening. You gotta listen! You're not listening if you're taking all these notes."

No one had ever mentioned that before. I asked him how to do it right, and he just started teaching me. He made it seem simple.

Another time I said to him, "How am I gonna pass Spanish?" Well, he *was* Spanish! He was happy to help me with that too. "This is all you need to know. Here's how you pass your test." He explained to me that most teachers try to teach you too much, and you need to pick through it and remember the most important stuff so you don't get overwhelmed. Not only did I take too many notes, I studied too much, he said. Plain and simple. Studying everything made it too overwhelming. What I needed to do was learn how to study the *right* stuff. He even stepped in when I was tired to make sure I went to take a nap. "You're not going to learn anything if you're barely awake. Go to sleep, then come knock on my door and I'll help you," he'd say.

Once I learned Freddy's techniques, it started getting easier. My tests improved greatly. I wound up doing better on homework assignments.

All they did in high school was let me know how stupid I was. Why didn't anyone sit me down and show me a different way to study? Or how to study, period? Why didn't anyone ever consider the fact that I might have a learning disorder?

It was shocking to me when my Holy Cross English teacher, Mrs. Shane, first brought that news up. No one talked of dyslexia in those days, though that's clearly what I was facing. She simply noticed that I had trouble concentrating, trouble absorbing whatever I was reading. She and Brother John worked together to get me tested—not as a way to single me out but as a way to help me. They let me know that there wasn't a cure for these sorts of things and that there didn't need to be. It just may take a little work to figure out how to help me learn better, they said, since I processed things a little differently than a lot of other kids. They made it all seem like a very normal, helpful process. They shared examples of some really famous people who had learning disorders, including Albert Einstein. It was shocking. *Why hadn't anybody told me? Why didn't anybody try to help before now?*

In fact, there's a great quote from Einstein that seems fitting to share here: "Everybody is a genius. But if you judge a fish by its ability to climb a tree, it will live its whole life believing that it is stupid." For my whole life, I'm pretty sure I was that fish!

When it came to reading, which was the biggest problem for me, Mrs. Shane tried to get me to slow down and read each line with purpose. I didn't want to do it. It took forever. It drove me nuts to read slowly. Then one day, she suggested that I try listening to soft music while I read—classical music, ideally—just to calm my brain down a bit. Well guess what? It worked. Listening to a little peaceful music allowed me to understand what I was reading. It worked like magic. I have no idea where she got the insight to be able to suggest something like that. It was just clear to her that I had a learning disability, and rather than using that as an excuse to let me slide, or an excuse to give up on me, she did what she could to help me. Between Mrs. Shane, Brother John, and the major help I was getting from Freddy, I got a handle on it. I turned my study habits around. I turned my whole relationship with learning around.

Before I knew it, my first semester at Holy Cross was over. I was surprised how quickly it flew by. College classes were more intense than high school courses, but they were also short-lived. I liked that you could see the end just a few months out and wouldn't be stuck doing the same stuff for an entire year. It made sense to me. There was a goal you could see. A finish line. An end zone.

I had never had so much as a B all through school, yet my first college-level report card was all Bs and a couple of As. It felt awesome. Those were the kind of grades I had always been told I needed in order to be "college bound." Funny that I had to actually go to college before anyone would help me figure out how to get those grades in the first place.

Kneeling at the Grotto

Despite my good grades, Brother John was very clear to me: the only way I could get to Notre Dame was to complete four semesters at Holy Cross. Applying early wouldn't do me any good.

I didn't listen.

Who could blame me? I was excited. My GPA was through the roof (by my own personal standards, at least). My study habits were improving; heck, I *had* study habits for the first time in my life. Walking across that campus every day, interacting with other students, getting out there at St. Joe's just to mow the lawn and keep the place looking good, got me more and more excited about being a Notre Dame student. So with that very first report card in hand, I filled out my application to transfer and dropped it off in the admissions office in the Main Building, under the Golden Dome.

The building itself is daunting. The massive granite staircase leading up to the entrance seems to put the whole place on a high pedestal. The doors are massive. The entry hall is massive, and the weight of the thick, dark-wood moldings gives the interior a sense of history. The hall is covered with magnificent old paintings of Christopher Columbus. Back in those days no one questioned the Columbus legacy or whether it was right or wrong that the Europeans came in and basically took the land from the Native Americans. When the paintings were done in the late 1880s, Columbus was seen as a saint: a Catholic Italian who risked everything, who did the impossible, who sailed across the vast ocean when everyone said it couldn't be done and discovered America in the process. (Talk about a leap of faith!) Luigi Gregori, a Vatican portrait artist whom Notre Dame's founders brought over to work some artistic magic in the Basilica, did the paintings. Gregori took on the Columbus murals after the original main building burned down in 1879. They were almost one hundred years old as I walked past them with my application in hand. I couldn't help but feel like I was a part of that history, as daunting as it was. The feeling of elitism, of implied greatness, permeates the walls at Notre Dame. It's the polar opposite of the warm embrace of Holy Cross. I could feel it in that building, and it still made me feel like I was a bit of an outsider. *But not for long!* I kept telling myself.

I dropped the application in the appropriate slot. Then I waited. I checked my mailbox every day. I started living like I was a Notre Dame student. I put a Notre Dame stamp on my Holy Cross ID and ate in the South Dining Hall whenever I wanted, with its high, vaulted, church-like ceilings and large, wooden communal tables. I fed off the energy of all of those students. I wore a Notre Dame jacket and acted like a Notre Dame student in every way possible. I got involved with student government, attended student council meetings, helped influence and make decisions that would affect the Notre Dame student body. No one asked to see my ID. No one knew the difference! No harm, no foul, right?

One day, I checked my mailbox at St. Joe's and found a letter with the Notre Dame insignia in the upper left-hand corner. The envelope was thin. I tore it open right there in front of my little mailbox slot and read those words no one ever wants to read: "We regret to inform you . . ."

I took a deep breath and leaned back against the wall. It stung. I was living the dream so thoroughly that I couldn't imagine it not coming true.

Part of me also expected it, of course. I knew I had applied too soon. I knew I had to prove myself. I *was* proving myself. I was just a little impatient is all. So I tried to shake it off.

Calling my parents with the news wasn't fun. I don't think it made a difference to them if I didn't get into Notre Dame. They were blown away by the fact that I got into Holy Cross. But they were sad to hear the disappointment in my voice and concerned that maybe I had gotten my hopes up too high. I didn't want them to feel bad for me, but they did. I guess that's what parents are supposed to do. They worry about their kids. They don't want to see their kids get hurt. And I didn't want to see them get hurt!

The thing was, I wasn't really *hurt*. I knew I had applied too soon. Whatever frustration and loss I felt in that moment just sunk down into my gut, where it became a new batch of kindling. *By the end of this first year*, I told myself, *my progress will be so undeniable that Notre Dame will have to let me in!* It didn't take me long to get fired up all over again.

In fact, from that day on, I think it's pretty accurate to say I worked twice as hard: acing tests, slaying assignments, listening to and absorbing lessons, shunning the parties and girl-chasing that my younger peers were embracing and instead hiding away in the vestibule of St. Joe's peaceful white-painted chapel and concentrating, intently, on my studies. My schoolwork came first—day in, day out—almost without fail.

Don't get me wrong; I wasn't a saint, and I wasn't some stiff either. Freddy and I would go out to Corby's, a little Irish dive bar a few blocks south of campus, once in a while to blow off some steam. For someone so smart, Freddy had no idea how to talk to girls. He was super shy about it. So I helped him in that department, which was a little payback for all of his tutoring and academic help. I could talk to girls easily, mainly because I wasn't a threat. I didn't want anything from them, and they sensed that, so I became their friend. They knew they could trust me. I'm not sure why, exactly, other than that I was a little older, a little wiser in that department. I had done just enough running around after high school and in the navy, and I knew that I wanted to focus on what was important to me: my academics, getting into Notre Dame, and getting a spot on

Ara Parseghian's football team. I think girls sensed that focus right away. That allowed them to talk to me without putting their guard up. I also found that girls at Notre Dame's sister school, St. Mary's, were more than willing to help me with my homework, which meant I wound up hanging around girls' dorms all the time. That's a pretty easy spot to meet girls—a whole building full of them. Whenever I could, I would set Freddy up.

We hit the town now and then with a guy I met in class at Holy Cross: Dennis McGowan, whom everyone affectionately calls "D-Bob." D-Bob and I hit it off immediately. He's a real big guy with a life-of-the-party look about him. He's the kind of guy who could wear a Hawaiian shirt to a formal affair and get away with it. Not anything like the buttoned-up college students I expected to see at Holy Cross. At heart he was a comedian. "Class clown" barely touches the surface of just how funny this guy was. And he was funny in the context of a class on business law! So just imagine how he could make you laugh when we were at a bar.

D-Bob had enrolled at Holy Cross for the most practical reason imaginable: he wanted to learn more about business to improve the business he was already in. He and his family lived right there in South Bend, where D-Bob owned a sporting goods store. It was a total mess of a store. Customers would walk into the place and not know what to think. It looked like a tornado had passed through! But if you asked him for a certain running shoe in a certain size, he always knew exactly where it was, and he could recommend four other shoes that you might like even better. Because of that, his customers kept coming back. He was a fantastic salesman and a fantastic businessman in many ways; he was just completely unconventional and a little dysfunctional. As dysfunctional as D-Bob was in his store, his family was not. He was a little older than I was, married with kids. His family was fantastic, and he was fantastic with his family. They would come to embrace me as one of their own, just as I would embrace them as my second family outside of Joliet.

D-Bob and I helped each other. We supported each other through the ups and downs of daily life. We started making T-shirts together and selling them around campus to make some extra money. But most of all, we laughed. I needed that. Desperately. I had been putting too much pressure on myself. I needed a D-Bob in my life to give me a sense of humor, and I needed a Freddy to put me on the straight course. You can't have it all one way. You've gotta have a balance in life. Those two friends balanced me out like no others ever had. They balanced each other in a way too.

Unlike Freddy, D-Bob could have gotten any girl he wanted—and he did before he was married. He just had a way of talking that would turn girls woozy. It's a gift. A gift that makes it tough to stay in one relationship very long, that's for sure, but a gift nonetheless. So between the two of us, we'd wind up finding dates for Freddy all the time.

One last thing to note here about D-Bob: he was a big drinker. A little too big, if you know what I mean. And he knew it too. It's something we would address later on.

While I continued to press forward on the academic and friendship fronts, I also did whatever I could to stay focused on the football portion of my Notre Dame dream. The best way to do that was the same way I had in the navy and in between all those days at the power plant back in Joliet: by working out. I ran all over that campus every day. I also made my way into the weight room at the athletic civic center (the ACC) and bulked up.

The second way was to get as close to the team as I could. I couldn't get tickets to most games. They were all sold out. (So much for that "going to games whenever I want" dream I had when I first set eyes on Holy Cross.) So I picked up an extra job on the stadium maintenance crew. I couldn't believe how easy it was: I just walked up to the stadium one quiet afternoon when there was a crew out there working on the grass, I asked who was in charge, and someone pointed the man out. I told him I was at Holy Cross and wanted to get into Notre Dame, maybe even get onto the football team, and he hired me on the spot. It was the kind of work some people would call "grunt work"—picking up the ocean of garbage left behind in the bleachers, painting railings, trimming and edging the grass. But it sure didn't feel like grunt work. It felt like I was a part of history, helping to shape the beauty of that stadium where thousands of people, millions if you count TV, would watch the Fighting Irish play those Saturday home games.

One day I happened to notice a crew in the locker room painting the players' helmets, so I joined in. It was a group of Notre Dame football managers, the folks who take care of the uniforms and helmets and day-to-day logistical stuff for the team, and no one seemed to care that I wasn't a student. Once again, no one asked. I have to say, holding those game-ready helmets in my hand was a real treat. I liked that feeling of helping prep the team. Did you know they use real gold flakes in the paint? I learned that firsthand. I wasn't supposed to be doing it. Heck, I wasn't supposed to enter the locker room, that place where all the greats had stood, where the legendary Notre Dame coaches had given pep talks and speeches that would make their way into movies and onto records that kids all over America would memorize and play over and over in their bedrooms. I remember thinking, *I could be standing in the very same spot where Knute Rockne once stood!* I mean, you get to thinking about the history, the Four Horsemen, all of it. How could anyone keep me out of that place!

I never let the fear of getting caught get in my way. I felt like an integral part of the Notre Dame community and I just kept doing things as if I were a student. That's how confident I was in my ability to break down that wall and make my dream a reality. Nothing could stop me.

The third way I kept my head in the game was to actually get out there and play some football. Turns out Notre Dame has a massive interhall football league. We're not talking flag football. We're talking full-on, intramural tackle football. It's one of two colleges in the whole country where it happens; the other is the United States Military Academy at West Point. It's truly a dream for guys who thought their football careers were over after high school.

"Wait a second," you may say. "What does Notre Dame's interhall league have to do with you, Rudy? You weren't at Notre Dame yet. You were at Holy Cross." Well, the interhall teams were divided by dormitory. Our dormitory, St. Joe's, was on the Notre Dame campus. And when it came time to sign up, no one asked if we were Notre Dame students. Our hall designation was all anyone seemed to care about, so I signed up with a bunch of my fellow Holy Cross/St. Joe peers, and started practicing.

Man, did it feel good to strap on those pads and pull on that helmet after all those years. I think the league had fifteen teams in all, and with so many great athletes—I saw a statistic once that said one out of every five students at Notre Dame was a varsity captain of one sport or another in high school—the competition was serious. To this day the Notre Dame newspaper, *The Student Observer*, covers all of the interhall games, and the championship is held in Notre Dame Stadium! It's awesome.

I alternated between middle linebacker and fullback at our first practice. After all that working out in the navy, I was about as solid as a guy could get at that point in my life. So solid that I didn't think any of these guys would be able to tackle me. I was feeling pretty cocky! On the third play, the quarterback handed me the ball and I pushed through the line when a long-haired hippy-looking kid nailed me around the ankle and flipped me right over. That taught me a lesson in humility, that's for sure. The guy who tackled me was named Bo Potter, and he was a Holy Cross student with his eyes set on Notre Dame, just like me. We became friends after that moment. Funny how that sort of thing on the football field can bond people! He wasn't the only strong player either. Notre Dame defensive coordinator Joe Yonto's kids were on the team. At some other college, some of these guys might have been varsity players. Not at Notre Dame. Guys like George Gulyas and Fred Rodgers, Mike Flynn; all of 'em had big dreams and big goals, and they were walking through Holy Cross as a stepping-stone to bright futures.

None of us took the game too seriously, though. It was fun. It was kind of like baseball was in my younger days. We all played hard, but we enjoyed ourselves. In fact, there were times when I'd purposely try to make the guys laugh as a form of strategy. I'll never forget there was one varsity player on the Notre Dame team at that time who I considered a bit of a hero: Andy Huff, the fullback. The guy was a lot faster than me and more agile, but he was built like me. Stocky. Watching him play, just seeing that physicality on the field helped me envision myself on that team.

So there were times when I'd get the ball in one of our interhall practices and yell, "Andy Huff coming through! Get out of my way! Here comes Andy Huff!" It would crack the guys up. They would laugh so hard they *couldn't* tackle me.

Those practices and those games were a great way to blow off some steam, and I had plenty of steam to blow off. It was frustrating having to wait, having to be patient. Assimilating into the Notre Dame world and yet constantly living under the threat of getting caught somewhere doing something I wasn't supposed to be doing wasn't all that fun, believe me. I just wanted to be at Notre Dame! I still harbored a lot of pent-up anger and frustration about the past too. About school. About my learning disorder. I mean, why did God want me to work twice as long and twice as hard as everyone else to get the grades I needed? I didn't understand it. As much as I tried to hide it and just enjoy every day at school, that frustration was definitely building.

One day, when I was out cleaning the aisles between the bleachers in the stadium, D-Bob came to find me. I was done with the work and had walked up high, to the very top seats in the southeast corner. I did that sometimes—just sat there looking out over the field, dreaming of what it would be like to play football for Notre Dame. I was in a fairly down mood, letting myself feed off of all of that frustration, when D-Bob came walking up.

"What's up? What're you doin' up here?" he asked.

He sat down next to me, and I tried to turn my attitude around.

"I'm gonna play football down there someday," I said to him.

D-Bob looked at me and shook his head. He could tell I wasn't kidding around. He could tell I meant it.

"The day you play football for Notre Dame is the day I quit drinking!" he said to me.

I couldn't believe he would say something like that. To agree to quit drinking was a big, big deal to him. I knew it. I felt it.

"That's a bet," I said, and we shook hands, high above the glorious Notre Dame field that solemn afternoon, with Touchdown Jesus looking right at us the whole time.

The fact is, I took D-Bob's promise seriously, and I let him know I would hold him to it. There was no way I'd let him squirm out of it when it happened. And it was gonna happen. I knew it. I just knew.

———

I ended my first full year at Holy Cross with all As and a couple of Bs. You should have seen the looks on my parents' faces when I got home to Joliet and handed them that report card. They were floored. So was my brother Francis, who was still struggling through school and getting into all kinds of trouble, just like I used to. I think the fact that I had gone to college and improved so much had a real effect on him. Made him think about focusing on his future a little more, you know? I was glad for that.

I went home and took a construction job for the summer that my dad hooked me up with. It was hard work, for good pay. Working-class heaven. I didn't want to do it, but I needed the money.

I was living at home when I received my second letter in the mail from Notre Dame. Despite Brother John's insistence, my impatience and stubbornness (let's call it "determination") got the best of me: I had applied once more to the school of my dreams, two semesters early.

I had good reason, I mean, *Did you see my report card?*

"Danny, there's a letter for you from Notre Dame," my mom said when I got home that night. It was already well past dinnertime. The sun was just about down. I stepped into the kitchen and saw that letter lying on the counter, right where she used to put my lunchbox—and it sunk my heart. The envelope was just as thin as the first one. I didn't even need to open it to know what it said. But I opened it anyway.

This time, reading those words didn't make me sad. It made me angry.

I told my parents I didn't get in, and they tried to console me a bit. They could see how upset I was. They knew how badly I wanted it. They tried to say those protective things parents say, about how I should be proud of what I'd accomplished, and that I shouldn't let it bother me. I didn't want to hear any of it.

"I want to know why," I said. "I want answers!"

I stormed out of the house and hopped in my dad's car with that letter in my hand. I had sold my Mustang to help pay for some of my school expenses. I didn't know that my dad's car had a faulty steering mechanism at the time, and that he would worry to death the whole time I was gone. But it held out just fine and nothing happened. Thankfully.

I squealed out of the driveway and hopped on I-80 East. I drove under a star-filled sky, cursing out loud, angry at the world. *Why? What else do I have to do? Haven't I done everything I need to do? What more can I do?* I wanted answers, right that second.

As I drove toward South Bend, I started to think about the extra layer of disappointment my failure must've been causing my dad. A lot of his co-workers at Union Oil knew I had gone to Holy Cross with the intent of getting into Notre Dame. And for that whole year of waiting, those co-workers gave my dad crap. "Your son still going to that community college? . . . Why don't you tell Rudy to quit dreaming and get a real job like the rest of us. . . . Can you imagine a Ruettiger at Notre Dame? Ha!" All that kind of crap. He hated it. He never spoke up, but he hated it, just like he hated the chatter about how big his family was and how all those kids were going to drive up everyone else's insurance rates. I could see it in his eyes. I could read it in his face. And every once in a while he would actually say something to me about it.

The whole thing made my blood boil.

By the time I parked on campus it must've been eleven o'clock. I grabbed that letter off the passenger seat and stormed over to Corby Hall, where all of the administrators lived. I was mad as a hornet when I walked up the steps onto the porch and knocked on that old wood door.

I was surprised when Father John Cavanaugh opened the door. He was the retired former president of Notre Dame and was quite elderly. His presence diffused my anger a little. I felt as if I had to dial it back a bit, out of respect. Even so, I was still in quite a state. "Father, I'm sorry to bother you so late, but I'd like to speak with Father Hesburgh." Father Hesburgh was the current president of the University, and Cavanaugh immediately let me know that wouldn't be possible. It just wasn't proper to wake Father

Hesburgh at this hour. "But I'm a student over at Holy Cross, and I want to come here more than anything. I'm ready. I want to know what I have to do," I insisted.

He smiled and invited me inside. He asked me to take a seat. "I'm glad you came, my son," he said to me. "We're always looking for good priests."

What? For some reason he assumed I had shown up in my emotional state in some sort of existential crisis, looking to join the seminary! Holy Cross Seminary. "No, no, no, Father. I don't want to be a priest. I just want to know why I can't get into Notre Dame. I've got the grades. I've worked hard. I want to go here more than anything else."

He seemed very confused.

"I'm not sure what to do with you," he said. "Let me get Father Tom. He'll help."

Father Cavanaugh hopped on the phone to Father Tom McNally. I knew Father McNally. He lived at St. Joe's. He came riding over on his bicycle at that late hour and sat with me for a few minutes. He felt my frustration and said the only one who could really answer my questions was Father Burtchaell, the University Provost.

"I want to see him," I said. "Right now."

"Right now?" he asked.

I insisted. So he called him, reluctantly. "Okay, Rudy. He'll meet you in his office, over at the Golden Dome."

I thanked him and walked over, up those great steps, where Father Burtchaell stood waiting at the top of stairs, glaring at me with a look of, *What seems to be the problem, son? What's going on that couldn't wait until some decent hour?*

He didn't say a word as I approached.

"I need answers, Father," I said. He was reluctant, but he still had that priestly way about him, as if he knew it was his duty to listen to a young man in pain. He asked me to come inside and we walked up to his office on the second floor, amongst all of that dark-wood molding and those fifteen-foot ceilings. Taking me into that space felt almost like a form of intimidation. But once we sat down, he listened. He listened to my whole story, of how far I'd come, how hard I had worked, how I had all As and Bs now, how I wanted to do this to prove to myself that I could, to prove to all those people back in Joliet who said it was impossible, to prove to all of those Union Oil guys who busted my dad's chops that Daniel Ruettiger's oldest son actually made it to Notre Dame. I wanted to show my brothers and sisters that *anything* is possible if you set your mind to it and work hard. Wasn't that the truth, after all? Was I asking too much? I felt all along as if I were following God's will, I said. Could I be fooling myself?

"You know, son, Notre Dame's not for everyone," he said.

I didn't know how to respond to that.

I told him all about my grades again, and how well I was doing. He actually seemed impressed. "You're doing everything right, Rudy," he said. "But it's a very, very rare occasion that we accept first-year transfers. We often turn down first-year transfers with perfect 4.0 averages. It's about the experience as much as it's about the grades. Didn't anyone explain to you that based on your previous record you'll need to complete four semesters before applying for transfer?"

I put my head down. "Yes. I just . . . I want this more than anything!"

"I understand, Rudy. But there are no shortcuts here. Have patience."

No shortcuts. Right. I should know that.

I sighed. There was no denying that he was right. I knew I was being impatient. Sometimes patience is the hardest of all virtues to grasp, isn't it?

"Is there anything I haven't done, Father? Is there anything more I can do?"

He thought about this. "I think you're doing everything you can," he said. "But in the end, it's not entirely up to you, is it?"

The moment he said those words, I understood what he meant. I thanked him for his time and apologized for showing up in the middle of the night. He said it was okay. He actually called Father Tom again and asked him to set me up in one of the dorms. He didn't want me driving all the way back to Joliet at that hour. He wished me luck.

It was well after midnight as I exited that great building and descended those steps, still carrying that rejection letter in my hand. I stuffed it into my pocket, turned right, and followed the winding path behind the Basilica, descending the steps to the Grotto. There wasn't a soul around— just me and the flickering glow of those white candles in the darkness. I lit one . . . then another . . . and another. I knelt before that beautiful shrine and prayed for guidance. I prayed for strength. I prayed for patience. I prayed for understanding.

It occurred to me as I meditated there, for hours, that I had no backup plan. Maybe that was good. A backup might be an excuse to quit. But I hadn't let the thought of *not* getting into Notre Dame enter my mind. *What would I do if it didn't happen?*

I prayed a little harder. I did everything I could to banish that thought from my mind. I had to trust my gut. I had to trust in God. I had to trust that the path would appear beneath my feet, even in this, what felt like my darkest hour.

The way I saw it, I only had one choice: I had to keep moving forward.

I never wound up going to the dorm that night. I stayed up all night at the Grotto. As the sun came up, I just started wandering around the campus. I decided to walk over by the ACC, the big building just east of the football stadium that held the basketball courts, the hockey rinks, the weight rooms, and all of the athletic offices for the Notre Dame sports program at the time. After staying up all night, I had this burning desire to stop into Coach Parseghian's office to let him know that I wanted to play football for him. He was such a commanding presence, I respected him so much, and I admired him so much that I was a little scared to do it, but it seemed like a fear worth facing. That whole summer I felt like I was firing on all cylinders. I was so pumped up about what was happening, so pumped up about my future, that I convinced myself I should just go see him and say what I had to say. *Why not?* Every time I had taken a bold step and spoken up so far, the result had been positive. So I went for it.

Remember now, it was really early. The door to the building was locked. I didn't want to give up, though, so I just hung around a little while . . . until I saw Parseghian's car pull up. I was embarrassed! I didn't want him to see me hanging around. I wanted it to seem more casual. I don't know what I was thinking exactly, but I ducked behind some bushes near the entrance and watched in secret as he let himself in and headed to his office.

I paced around for a minute, just gathering my thoughts, regaining my courage. Then I grabbed the cold metal handle of that door, swung it open, and stepped inside.

As I came around the corner, I saw Parseghian at his desk through the window. There was no secretary out front. There was no one else in the building. I took a deep breath and stepped in.

"Coach?" I said.

He looked up. "Yeah?"

I don't remember my exact words, but it went something like this: "Sorry to bother you, Coach. My name's Rudy. Rudy Ruettiger. And I want to play football for Notre Dame."

"You a student here?" he said.

I was struck at that moment by the way Coach Parseghian reminded me of my father. He was firm. To the point. Commanding, but approachable in his own way.

"Not yet," I said. "But I will be. I'm enrolled at Holy Cross. I've been a Notre Dame fan for as long as I can remember, and I just want to let you know that when I get here, there's nothing I want more than to play for you. I promise I'll give you everything I've got."

Parseghian looked at me. He could see I was about half the size of his best players. He had every right to laugh at me or to tell me to get lost. But he didn't. Instead, he gave me a little nod.

"I bet you will, son," he said. "I bet you will. You come see me when you get in."

He looked back down at his desk, back down at whatever he was doing before I burst in, and I took that as my cue. I had said enough. "Thank you, Coach!" I said. He looked up and nodded.

I walked down the hallway, threw that door open, and stepped out into the early morning sun with a smile on my face so broad it could have cracked my cheeks. "I bet you will," Coach Parseghian said to me. If he had told me to get lost, to forget about it—anything that would have dissuaded me—I might have shriveled up and given up on that dream right then and there. But he didn't. He did just the opposite. He didn't even question whether I had what it took to get into Notre Dame. He didn't say, Come see me "if" you get in. He said "when." He gave me hope.

I bet you will.

As I stood outside of the ACC, I suddenly felt embarrassed. *Was that a mistake? Did I just make a fool out of myself in front of Coach Parseghian?* It's normal to have doubts after making a bold move, I think. Luckily for me, a few familiar faces suddenly popped up on the path outside. Joe Yonto's son, Tony, and a group of hockey campers came walking along. "Rudy! Hey, what're you doing here?"

I didn't know what to say. So I faked it. "I'm up here looking for a job," I said.

Lo and behold, I just happened to say the right thing. "Really? One of our camp counselors just left. Would you like to be a camp counselor?" Tony asked me.

Ummm, "Yes!"

He took me upstairs in the ACC to meet Joe Sassano, the guy who headed up the ACC and who ran the hockey program. Sassano liked me and gave me the job as a hockey camp counselor for the summer.

When I took my dad's car back later that morning, my mom came right out the front door yelling at me at how upset my dad was. "You could've killed yourself!" she said, telling me all about the car's steering being broken, and how mad she was that she had to let my dad take her car to work. I apologized left and right but told her it had to be done. I explained that I'd been up all night praying, and that I got a new job: I'd be living and working on the Notre Dame campus for the rest of the summer.

"I'm just glad you're alive," she said.

Me too! I thought. It still frightens me to think that the steering on that old Plymouth could have gone out on me anytime during that 180-mile roundtrip excursion. A mechanical failure could've derailed my whole mission—or worse. Luckily it didn't. Or maybe it's more than luck.

I wonder about that sometimes. I wonder about those moments, when we're carried through.

By the time my dad came home, he was more concerned with my new job situation than the fact that I had taken his car without asking. "How much are they paying you?" he asked. I sheepishly told him it was about half as much pay as I had been making at my summer construction job. But it didn't matter. It was important for me to be on campus. I felt it, in my gut. Sometimes that gut feeling is all you've got. And you've gotta trust it.

In the Ring

Between my frantic midnight visit and my work at the hockey camp that summer, the administrators and a whole bunch of other people at Notre Dame got to know my name. I could say hello to some of those leaders when we passed on a pathway by the lake, and they would recognize me. Ara Parseghian had a son who worked at the hockey camp. I was already friends with Joe Yonto's kids. I didn't seek them out, and I never thought once about using those friendships as some sort of a connection to give me a leg up to their dads, but it's funny how people come into your life when you're open to it, when you're pursuing your dreams without question. As embarrassing as my audacity of knocking on the administrators' doors at midnight might have seemed from the outside, it was exactly my audacity that got me noticed.

When the fall semester began, I moved up to the fourth floor in St. Joe's. My room was in the back this time, with a perfect, unobstructed view over the treetops to the Golden Dome across the lake. I took inspiration from that every time I sat at my little desk. And yet, despite that view, and despite a series of late-night Grotto prayer sessions, I still had plenty of bottled-up anxiety and frustration heading into my second year. All the same old stuff: the worry, the doubt, the fear, the impatience, combined with the lingering high school and grade-school memories—all of it sat just below the surface ready to bust out at any moment.

I also learned that the odds were stacked against me even further that year: Notre Dame merged with St. Mary's and began admitting women for the first time in its history. It seems amazing today to think that such a prestigious school *wouldn't* have allowed women all the way up until 1972. But that's the way it was. Don't get me wrong: it was great having all those young women on campus! What guy wouldn't love that? It just meant that I would have to compete against an even wider field of candidates for the few transfer slots that would open up the following year.

All of it made me work harder. I had no choice. I had no backup plan. It also made me spend even more time on campus, developing relationships with everyone I could, so when it came time to make an admissions decision, they would be sure to think of me, to remember me, and to think about how badly I wanted to be there. When they saw my name, they would think of me always being on campus, always working hard. That goes a long way, believe me. Never underestimate the power of a personal relationship. Those relationships mean everything, especially when you don't have the money, talent, or other connections to get you where you want to go in life. Sometimes a relationship is all you've got! So I worked it. What was I going to do if I didn't go to Notre Dame? Go back to Joliet? Back to the power plant? No way! Wouldn't happen. I had to go to Notre Dame because it was the only future I could see. The only future I *wanted* to see. And increasingly—despite the improbability—that future for me included envisioning myself on the Notre Dame football team.

I poured myself back into interhall football that fall. Running that ball and taking those hits was still one of the best ways I knew to blow off some steam. Our equipment was all hand-me-down stuff from the varsity team: a bunch of beat-up gold helmets and tattered uniforms. I decided to pour some pride into those uniforms and wound up designing a whole new get-up, with white shirts (similar to Notre Dame's away uniforms) that I ordered at a discount through D-Bob. We also painted the helmets navy blue, and one guy in the dorm painted a fancy *SJ* in orange on the side of each one—*SJ* for St. Joe's. I loved the idea of making the team look good. There's pride in that. There's a feeling that you want to live up to the uniform, to your teammates, to the spirit of what you're doing.

The whole experience kept me bonded to my housemates at St. Joe's, including the guys who weren't on the team. There was something about the energy and camaraderie of the game that increased the camaraderie of the whole sophomore-year experience. It's like all of us were part of the same team off the field. In fact, there were about fifteen of us Holy Cross guys who were gaming to get into Notre Dame, and we wound up labeling ourselves the Rat Pack. One of our buddies even had a logo designed, and we all wore shirts with this drawing of an ugly rat lifting barbells on it.

We were all dreamers. We were all reaching for something more, all following our hearts. I couldn't wait to see where we'd all wind up. Interhall football helped me focus on all of that: Coming off the field with that glow that came from the pumped-up feeling you got when you'd just given your all and played your best, I would sometimes look around and think, *We're all doing it! We're all playing hard! We're all gonna make our dreams come true!*

Keeping that momentum, holding on to that pumped-up feeling—even when faced with the frustration and heartbreak of waiting to get into Notre Dame—meant everything to me.

At it's best, that's what sports can do.

I kept my grades up—all As and a couple of Bs—and reapplied to Notre Dame again after my third semester. A thin envelope arrived in my mailbox at St. Joe's a few weeks later. Brother John scolded me, once again, for ignoring his guidance and applying too soon. I knew it was wrong. I just couldn't stop myself. I simply had to try. I let it bounce right off of me as I set my sights on my final semester. I kept up the maintenance job. I went for runs around the interior of that beautiful old football stadium, beneath the concrete supports and archways, staying in shape all winter long. I kept working out at the ACC, staying in shape for the day my shot came to join the team.

I happened to be in the ACC one day when I stumbled onto a whole new outlet for all of my frustration: boxing.

The Bengal Bouts are a big, big deal at Notre Dame. The outside world might not know much about it, but on campus, among the students, the annual Bengal Bouts—a series of student-elimination boxing matches that raise funds for the Holy Cross Missions in Bangladesh—drive almost the same sort of passionate devotion and jam-packed stands as the football games. (Coincidentally or not, the Bouts were founded by legendary football coach Knute Rockne.)

I came across a bunch of guys training for the bouts in the ACC that January and asked what they were doing. If you haven't noticed, I don't have a problem talking to people. I talk to everybody! It never fails to make something happen, and at the very least leads to some interesting conversations. I was intrigued by the whole thing and asked if I could train along with 'em. They said sure. No questions. No student ID necessary. I jumped right in, and I loved it. I was a fighter at heart, always had been. Yet no one had ever tried to channel that fighting energy in such a positive way for me before. Working the bag until my heart felt like it would beat right out of my chest, lifting weights with a new purpose, learning to take hits, learning to hit harder—it all felt great, and it was one more thing to keep me out of trouble and away from the party scene or any other distractions that could have derailed my academics.

There were about six weeks of official training for the Bengal Bouts, which happen each spring semester, and I got all the way through the program. I was pumped! Suddenly I was climbing into a ring set up in the center of the basketball court in the ACC. The arena was filled to the rafters with screaming Notre Dame students, and the noise was incredible. *Ding!* Just like that, my first match was underway. I went toe-to-toe with a guy who was quite a bit taller than me. Just about everyone was taller than me, so that wasn't a surprise, but the audience seemed to like the David and Goliath–type matchup. I focused hard, using my height to my advantage and getting in lots of punches to his body. Enough punches to win the decision. First round over. Victorious. Piece of cake. I would move on to the next round.

One problem: the guy in charge of the whole thing came to me in the locker room just before the next match was set to begin and asked pointedly, "Rudy, are you a student at Notre Dame?" I could tell from the tone of his voice that he already knew the answer. I'm not sure if one of the administrators had a conversation with him, or if someone else recognized me from Holy Cross, or what, but I knew the jig was up. I told him the truth. He said he was sorry, but I wouldn't be allowed to fight any more rounds. I had to leave.

I watched the rest of the Bengal Bouts from the stands that year. The most remarkable thing about the whole experience for me was watching how those Notre Dame students always rallied behind the underdog based entirely on his performance in the ring. Everyone would chant the names of their favorite fighters—many of which they hadn't heard of until they discovered them in that room—watching for the great ones to emerge among their fellow students as they stepped foot into that ring, one by one, to do battle for the title and to earn the right to wear a Bengal Bout jacket, which was only awarded to the two finalists in each division. The idea of winning the title didn't interest me: I really wanted one of those jackets! I could picture myself walking around campus wearing that thing. I was excited by the thought of how my fellow students would react once I had that coat on my back.

The immense power of the energy in that room rocked me. Round after round, I pictured myself standing in that ring, seeing just what I would have done to defeat each of those opponents. I sat there with my fists up, bobbing and weaving my head, mimicking the motions from my seat, fighting right along with each match. But the fact that I was outside, not inside, stung like a bee in my gut.

Next year, I told myself. *Next year.*

The Bengal Bouts were one more goal, one more challenge to keep me on course. I *had* to get into Notre Dame. I just had to!

I kept leaning on Freddy for help with my studies, and he came through for me, without fail, every time. Finally, I stopped asking as often because the work seemed to get easier and easier for me with every class I took. I kept leaning on D-Bob, too, for laughs and a sense of family in South Bend, and he came through as well. Neither one of those guys ever showed a shred of doubt that I'd get into Notre Dame. Ever.

That unwavering support meant everything. Especially as the end of the second semester inched closer and I started filling out my final application to Notre Dame, knowing it was my last chance; knowing that everything was on the line; knowing that this was the only application that really mattered; knowing that finally I would get the full recommendation of Brother John Driscoll and that my name recognition among the Notre Dame administration would likely help. I knew all of that but simply did not know with any certainty whatsoever if my combination of grades, determination, and grit was enough to overcome the incredible odds that were stacked against me in every way.

I graduated Holy Cross that May with honors. *Cum laude*, they called it. I walked away with my Associate's Degree and had no idea what an Associate's Degree was good for. I never thought about it. The degree wasn't my goal. I didn't even feel like celebrating. Here I was, the first kid in the Ruettiger family to hold any kind of a degree whatsoever, and it didn't feel like an accomplishment. Not yet, anyway. The accomplishment was still to come. I found myself walking around with a knot in my stomach, wondering when I'd hear from Notre Dame.

I made a stop at the Grotto, lit a few candles, and prayed on my knees in that beautiful spot one last time before moving out of St. Joe's and back to my parents' house. It was strange to be home in Joliet without the absolute assurance that I would be headed back to Notre Dame in the fall. I held on to the powerful feeling that I *would* be headed back, of course, but that confidence and determination is never quite the same as true knowledge. I worried. In fact, I let myself fill up with worry. Let me tell you, that is not a good feeling.

The short walk down our driveway to the mailbox each day was brutal. Opening it up, peering inside, pulling out and sifting through the bills and letters and cards and various bits of junk mail only to come up empty-handed felt like a punch in the stomach every time. Until finally, one afternoon, I think it was late June, I pulled that handle, flipped through the bills, and recognized the Notre Dame insignia in the upper left-hand corner of one envelope. I noticed something different about this one too: it felt a little bit thicker. My heart started racing. Was I imagining the thickness? It wasn't that much thicker, was it? Was I seeing things?

I didn't open it. I hurried back inside and dropped the rest of the mail on the kitchen counter. I ducked into the downstairs bathroom, which was just about the only place to find any privacy in that house. I put the lid down and sat on the toilet seat. I took a few deep breaths, slid my finger through the little open slot at the back of the envelope, and carefully broke the seal. I didn't want to rip it. I didn't want to rush. The knot in my stomach felt like a giant ball of gnarled-up twine as I pulled the folded pieces of paper out and set the envelope on the sink.

I closed my eyes. This was it.

I unfolded the letter, keeping the written side facing the floor. My heart pounded like I'd been working the punching bag at the ACC. I took one more deep breath and turned the letter right side up. My eyes scanned the opening lines with the efficiency I now applied to my studies, using techniques I had learned from my friend Freddy—to scan for the important words, the meaningful words, the words that held the key to my entire future.

"Dear Mr. Ruettiger . . . Your application for transfer to the University of Notre Dame has been . . . *approved* . . ."

I could feel my face tightening. My eyes welled up.

" . . . pleased to inform you . . . accepted for enrollment as a junior in the fall semester . . ."

I couldn't read another word. With my elbows on my knees, I dropped my head forward into the palms of my hands, pressing the letter to my forehead and bawling like a baby. I tried to hold it in. I didn't want anyone to hear me. I was embarrassed to cry! But the knot in my stomach unraveled almost instantly, and the floodgate of everything I'd been striving for, everything I'd dreamed about, everything everyone told me I could never do opened itself up wide, and the emotion flowed out of me like a great lake bursting through a mighty dam.

I'm not sure how long I stayed in that bathroom. I lost all track of time and space. When I regained my ability to breathe without tears, I re-read the letter, from top to bottom, just to make sure it was real. I looked at the envelope, at the Notre Dame insignia, just to make sure it matched up with the letterhead. Just to be sure it was true. I had waited so long and worked so hard, it felt like a dream. Heck, it *was* a dream! An impossible dream that I'd made come true.

I set the letter down and splashed some water on my face, drying it off with one of my mom's neatly folded hand towels before finally finding the strength to open that door and walk upstairs into the kitchen without bawling my eyes out in front of everyone.

My mom was zipping around, getting ready to start dinner. It took me a minute to get her to slow down long enough to realize I had something important to tell her. She finally looked at my face, and I'm pretty sure she could tell I had been crying. Moms tend to notice that kind of stuff. "What is it, Danny?" she said.

"Read this," I said, and I handed her the letter. She read it, slowly, shaking her head as if she couldn't believe what she was reading. Then she looked at me and gave me the biggest smile.

"Did you tell your dad yet?" she asked me.

"No, Mom, not yet," I said.

"Well, he'll be home from work soon. He'll be very proud of you." It's funny how she always used my dad as the reference point, as if he were the most pivotal figure in our family, as if his opinion mattered most. My dad always did the same thing with her. He was her hero, and she was his hero. I remember thinking, even then in my midtwenties, that wasn't a bad thing to be to each other in a relationship.

My dad walked through the door maybe half an hour later with his usual worn-out, end-of-the-day look on his face. The house was buzzing with all the kids as he set his lunch bucket down. "Dad," I said, "I've got some news."

He stopped and looked at me. Like mom, I think he sensed that something big was going on. I handed him the letter and slowly watched the shock and awe come over his face as he read those precious words.

"Danny Boy got in," he said to himself. And then, with a massive smile: "Hey kids, Danny Boy got into Notre Dame!"

My brothers and sisters flipped out, squealing with delight, echoing his words—"Danny Boy got in!"—in their high-pitched voices, patting me on the back and giving me hugs.

"Well come eat, everyone. Come eat!" my mom said, and we all sat down for one of the happiest dinners any of us could recall. My dad seemed totally energized through that whole meal, and I'm pretty sure I know why. My acceptance wasn't just a new point of pride for him; it also lifted a monkey off his back: the crap he got from all of his co-workers at Union Oil.

It felt good to put an end to that misery for him. Of course, I added a whole new monkey for him to carry around about two seconds later, when I told him that getting into Notre Dame wasn't my biggest accomplishment. There was still one more thing I was planning to do. "I'm planning to play football for the Fighting Irish," I told him. My little brothers all thought that was the coolest thing in the world, but I could see in my dad's eyes that he just didn't think it was possible. The only Notre Dame players he had ever seen were the giants on the field. He had never been in the locker room. He had never seen the third- and fourth-string guys who helped make that team complete. He had no idea that anyone who looked like me could even dream about being a part of that tradition. I knew I wouldn't convince him of it either. I'd just have to show him.

The next morning, I called Freddy. He had been such a big influence on me. Without his help, without his academic coaching, I never would have had the grades to get that letter. I wanted him to see it. I wanted him to read it, in person. I asked if he'd meet me at St. Joe's and told him I had something I wanted him to see. He agreed.

I met him there on campus the next day, and of course he was real anxious to know what was going on, but I made him wait just a little bit longer. "Come with me," I said, and I started down the path behind St. Joe's, off to the left, along the perimeter of St. Joseph's Lake. Thick trees immediately behind St. Joe's obscure the view of the lake at ground level, but as we approached the clearing in front of Moreau Seminary, the lake came into full view. There weren't any benches in that spot, but that spot felt right to me. So we sat in the grass there, looking across that water with a crystal-clear view of the Golden Dome and its perfect reflection in the lake's smooth surface. It was in that spot that I finally reached into my pocket and pulled out my acceptance letter.

Freddy read it, and smiled, and nodded. "I knew you could do it," he said.

"I couldn't have done it without you."

"Congrats, man!"

That's about as mushy as we got. But that spot by the lake, and that moment with Freddy, etched themselves into my memory forever. He would be moving on soon; he was headed to Florida to go to law school, following his dream the same way I had followed mine toward Notre Dame. I loved the fact that we were both accomplishing exactly what we had set out to do. It just felt good to be around someone else who understood that feeling, who wanted that feeling, and who was willing to help someone else accomplish their goal rather than tear them down or try to keep them in their place.

I felt as if I were surrounded by those kind of people, now, almost all the time. And man, it sure felt good.

Back in Joliet, of course, the feeling was a little different. There were still a lot of doubters. I tried not to let it bother me. I had proven them wrong once, and I was about to prove them wrong again. I told everyone that I got into Notre Dame. In some ways, I think I lifted a lot of spirits among my old high school friends, and even some of those co-workers from back at the power plant. It's hard not to feel good on some level when you see someone succeed. But there's also a lot of jealousy, self-doubt, and all kinds of other stuff that come into play. I realized that I didn't like being around those sorts of attitudes anymore, so I tried to avoid them whenever I could. Of course, during a lot of these conversations—maybe too many—I immediately brought up the fact that I was planning to go out for the Notre Dame football team. Boy, did that give the old Joliet doubters a whole new set of ammunition! "Keep dreamin', Rudy."

Tell you what; if you interpret that phrase in a way that's not sarcastic, it's a pretty good mantra! *I will keep dreamin'. Thanks!*

Word got around town pretty quickly, and unfortunately that only amplified the chatter at work for my dad. "You think your kid's gonna play for Notre Dame, Ruettiger? Yeah, right."

I shut up about my football dream after that. I realized it was better to just keep it to myself, except around very select individuals. Even so, I took those words and used them to help fire me up: *Yeah, right. Just watch me.*

Walking On

I lived in a closet my first few days at Notre Dame.

I was so determined to get back on campus and to be there for the start of summer football training that I moved back in early July. The campus wasn't open to incoming students yet, and I didn't have a dormitory to go to. Now that I was out of Holy Cross, the special deal they gave me to stay at St. Joe's wasn't available to me anymore. I certainly didn't have the money to pay for full room and board at Notre Dame, and I didn't have the money to rent an apartment in South Bend either. It's funny, though, that once again, when I was taking that leap of faith, moving forward toward my dream, a path just seemed to appear before me.

Who would ever think that being chatty with a janitor would lead to finding a housing solution? Yet that's exactly what happened. I met a janitor named Rudy—another Rudy! I couldn't believe it!—a remarkably friendly older black gentleman, through my work with the summer hockey camp, and he was more than happy to let me crash on a cot in a maintenance closet that July. It was just a place to lay my head at night, and that was all I needed.

Of course, I didn't realize that I couldn't walk onto the football team at the start of the summer season. I showed up at the field one morning and found out pretty quickly that only Notre Dame students who were already a part of the team the previous year, or who had been recruited for the new season, were allowed on the field. I would have to wait until August, when the walk-on tryouts were announced, before I'd have a shot.

I couldn't even watch the practices. They blocked out all the fences so no one from a competing team could spy and see what they were doing, and that meant no one—absolutely no one—who wasn't a part of the team could step foot onto those fields.

Once again, I'd have to be patient. At least it was only for a few weeks.

Oddly enough, I wasn't nervous about starting the school year. I wasn't worried about the academic side of succeeding at Notre Dame whatsoever. Once I got over the hurdle of being accepted, it just felt natural. Like one more step on the path. I had confidence in my ability to take notes and study and pass tests. That allowed all of my focus to go into thinking about football and gearing myself up to go out there and finally get on that field. To be a part of the Fighting Irish. To be a part of the greatest football tradition there was. I knew I wouldn't be a starter. Didn't matter. I was excited just to be a part of that team, whatever part I could play.

Amazingly, while I focused on that dream, the housing situation took care of itself.

For insurance and safety purposes, the ACC always had to have a security guard/maintenance guy in the building. Even at night, when it was all closed up. The school's solution for that was to hire a student to live in the ACC. As luck would have it, the student who held the job that summer had just graduated in May, and when he vacated the position just before the start of that fall semester, they gave the job to me! Joe Sassano, the head of the ACC whom I'd gotten to know the summer before through the hockey camp, set me up with that job, and Rudy, the old janitor, contributed too. One thing leads to another in life. One step at a time. Every time. And building those relationships with people on campus made all the difference in the world.

I moved down the hall from my closet cot to a little dormitory-style room right next to Gate 8, one of the entrances to the very same basketball arena where the Bengal Bouts took place. The room wasn't much bigger than my room at St. Joe's, but I had to share it with a roommate, a wrestler. The windowless room had concrete block walls, but it had a bed, a table, and its own private bathroom and shower. It was everything I needed.

In exchange for the free room, I would walk the halls after hours with a flashlight in my hands, and spend hours going up and down the stairs, sweeping up the messes left behind after games, while gaining free, up-close access to every big event that would unfold within those walls. I didn't miss the dormitory experience. I didn't need that social aspect of college life. I liked the quiet. I liked having the ability to step out of my door and go sit high up in the basketball stadium to do my homework in the after-hours quiet of that magnificent space. And in daylight hours I loved being surrounded by the energy, the athletes, and the coaches who made Notre Dame great.

I also enjoyed the easy access to the weight room and punching bags, where I started training immediately. Though it was months away, I knew more than anything that I wanted to throw myself back into the Bengal Bouts—this time as a full-time Notre Dame student who couldn't be kicked to the sidelines by a technicality. I focused on one of those Bengal Bout jackets and pushed myself as hard as I could, whether hitting the bag or pumping iron. I figured every bit of boxing training I did would only help me out on the football field too, where I knew for sure that I would need to be fit, strong, and ready to take some big hits. I couldn't wait to strap on those pads and pull on that helmet.

Finally, in August, I got my chance.

The walk-ons' tryouts began with a physical first thing in the morning. I passed. Next thing I knew, I was out on the field standing shoulder to shoulder with fifteen other guys vying for a spot on the scout team, a grunt team whose sole purpose was to help the varsity team prep for games. A junior varsity coach, a linebacker coach, and defensive coordinator Joe Yonto looked us up and down, pacing like drill sergeants. "We're gonna put you guys through hell . . . Don't think that just because you come out here you can become one of us! You have to earn it! . . . You're gonna get hit . . . It's up to you if you want to stay here or not, but if you want to go home, go home now, 'cause you're gonna get hit." They made it clear that the only reason they needed walk-on players was so their first-string guys could have some worthy human tackle dummies to knock down on a daily basis. And on this day, they would start testing us to see if we were good enough to serve as those dummies!

The talk was over. It was time to get to work. They immediately started running the fifteen of us through agility drills. Over and over. No pads. No helmets. Just lifting knees through ropes and tires, bobbing side to side, tripping up, falling down, standing up and going again. I was drenched in sweat and ready to collapse by the time they sent us behind the blocked-off fence and up to the bleachers to watch the varsity team practice. I thought it was a little strange that they wanted us to sit there and watch rather than suit up and get in there and show 'em what we could do. But it didn't take long for me to figure out why they did it: they wanted us to see what we were in for.

It was amazing to have that up-close look at how the team worked. I knew they were the best. I knew it took hard work and massive effort to become the best. I just never knew what it looked like, or sounded like, for a football team to work that hard.

Those guys hit each other with so much force, it sounded like a battlefield full of explosions from the stands. Every play was like a herd of cattle coming together—*crash!*—a cloud of dust, a mangled mesh of bodies. Then they'd all get up and walk away, only to do it again moments later.

The plays, the patterns, the workouts, the endurance—all of it was a hundred times harder and faster and more intense than anything I ever experienced in high school football. And there stood Coach Parseghian, whistle in hand, pacing with the stressed-out look of a worried parent, barking orders as he put his team through the paces.

Watching how hard those guys were sweating, the way they'd nearly collapse from exhaustion before getting up and doing it again, and again, brought up all of these little doubts and fears in me. I wondered for a moment whether I had what it took to be on that team after all. That's natural, isn't it? To have doubts?

The thing I had learned by that point was never to let doubts overwhelm me. Doubts are like little spiders: they're only scary if you let 'em be scary. You're a thousand times bigger than those doubts! Just step on 'em! Squash 'em. Put 'em in a cup and dump 'em outside if you want to be all touchy feely about it, but get rid of 'em!

Sitting in those stands, thinking of what the coaches said about not caring if we got hurt, watching those guys kill each other on the field, all I could think was, *I've been through boot camp! They've spit in my face. I've gone to the edge of death getting seasick and still managed to stand watch. Be a man. Suck it up. They think they're gonna scare me off a football team? No way!*

It's all about attitude. Everything is about attitude. Once you change that thought and don't see the negative, you see what you have to do.

As I laid my aching body down in my room in the ACC at the end of day one, I knew that what I'd seen on that field was a guidebook. It showed me that I would have to work a little harder than I first thought. I was fine with that! I had already made the commitment to the team. I had already made the commitment to Coach Parseghian. I was going to be on that team. I couldn't back out. Whether they knew it or not, people were counting on me: D-Bob, Freddy, my little brothers and sisters, the doubters back in Joliet, my mom and my dad. I had to do this for all of them. I had to do this for myself.

The next day only five of us walk-ons showed up. Five out of fifteen! That's how brutal that first day was. I didn't care. I figured that just meant I'd have less competition. I was raring to go!

Once again we hit the agility tests, sweat through the motions, fell down, stood up, and struggled through. By the time we hit the bleachers to watch the team practice, only two of us were left. Me and one other guy! And they *still* weren't sure we were good enough to join the team. This same routine went on for days and days before finally they told us to put on some pads so they could see us in action head-to-head with the varsity guys. Now we were talkin'! I was so pumped up; I could hardly stand still. I was bouncing up and down on the sidelines. I threw those pads on so fast; I was ready before the coaches were ready to call us in. They didn't even tell us where to go; they just lumped us in with the rest of the scout team and yelled, "Offense over here, defense over there!" I was the shortest guy on the field, but I felt ten feet tall and built like a brick wall. I started to turn toward offense, for no particular reason. Coach Kelly took one look at me. He said I was too short for his linebacker crew and threw me over to Yonto. "You take him!" he yelled.

I was happy about that. I liked playing defense!

So down I went, shoulder-to-shoulder, helmet-to-helmet with the greatest team in college football. I wished my dad could have seen me right then and there. I wished my whole family could've seen me. It was unbelievable!

The whistle blew and *crash!* The first of those monstrous players knocked me over like a rag doll. I was stunned. I didn't know what hit me. I wasn't focused. I was too keyed up. Too excited. I picked myself up off the ground and got back in position. Another massive player lined up in front of me, and this time I stared right through his mask, powering my fist into the grass, stomping my legs down into position like a racehorse at the gate in the Kentucky Derby. The whistle blew and I shifted everything I had into pushing that guy back as hard as I could the moment he charged, keeping him up, keeping him from knocking me down, keeping him from getting around me at any cost until that whistle blew again— and I was still standing!

Over and over, hit after hit. I kept going, hard as I could, pushing back with all my might against the strongest offensive linesmen imaginable—the legendary players of Notre Dame! It was awesome. My shirt was covered in blood by the end of the day, and I didn't even know where it came from! I didn't care. Nothing could stop me. I just kept diving in with everything I had.

At the end of the day, they said, "See you tomorrow."

I had done it! I made it through the first practice. I was coming back again the next day. This was it. I was a walk-on player for Notre Dame!

The pain didn't hit me until I hit the locker room. I was moaning and wincing as I sat on the bench and pulled my shirt off. I realized that I had hurried so much to get out there that I had put my pads on backward. No wonder I was hurting!

Finally dressed, I ran across the lawn to the ACC, to the pay phone in the hallway just outside of my room, and called home. My dad picked up. They had just finished dinner.

"Dad, Dad! You're not gonna believe it. I just practiced with the team."

"Slow down, Danny. What team? What are you talking about?"

"Notre Dame!"

He was silent for a second. "Football?"

"Yes, Dad. Football!"

He was speechless.

"You there?" I said.

"You're kidding."

"I'm not kidding! I went to walk-ons and made it through the whole practice. They said 'see you tomorrow,' which means I'll be there tomorrow!"

My dad shared the news with the family: "Hey everyone! Danny just practiced with the Notre Dame football team." I could hear the noise of my brothers and sisters in the background all shouting, "What? Wow! Cool! Congratulations!"

"Will we see you on TV?"

"No, I don't think so, Dad. Walk-ons don't get to suit up. But if I keep at it, who knows."

"Well, I'm proud of you, son. Good work."

That was all I needed to hear. That was an accomplishment. A big one.

My next call was to Freddy, who was so excited for me. Of course, the first thing he asked was when he could come see me play. I had to explain it to him, just as I explained it to my dad. I was just on the scout team.

Then I went over to see D-Bob. "I did it, man," I told him. "I made it through the first practice. I'm on the team!" D-Bob let out a huge yell. "We gotta go celebrate!" he said. That's when I reminded him of his promise—the promise to quit drinking if I ever made the Notre Dame football team.

He said he remembered and absolutely promised he would quit on the day he saw me play. So okay, he wasn't quite ready to quit yet. Celebrating was in order! I noticed that look in his eye, though. For the first time, he was truly thinking about quitting. It was something. It was progress.

He got me thinking: *Would he ever get to see me play? Would anyone?* The fact that none of my friends or family would be able to see me suit up with the team suddenly clawed into my gut. *Man!* I wished I could find a way to sneak them into the stands at one of those closed practices or something. Better yet: maybe if I worked hard enough I could get good and move up the list and dress for a game someday. *Just one game!*

I should have known better than to even think such a thing. There were nearly a hundred full scholarship football players attending Notre Dame University, and some of *them* didn't even get to dress for home games. We were told that from the outset. They made it clear from the moment we showed up for walk-ons that we would never wear that golden helmet, never once have a shot to run out of that tunnel with the big boys. I didn't care. That crazy idea sunk into the back of my brain somewhere and I just couldn't let it go. I had a feeling I could make it happen if I worked hard enough. Why not? *Why not?* I had heard about walk-on players who had gone on to professional football careers. I knew I would never go pro. I simply wasn't that gifted. But I could certainly get to the point where they'd let me put on a uniform and get out on the field, right?

I thought about it all night as I fell asleep in my windowless room, more exhausted and battered and better than I'd ever felt in my life.

Living the Dream

Waking up every morning as a Notre Dame student was a dream come true. Walking into the South Dining Hall, knowing I belonged there, was uplifting and powerful. Strolling along those paths and across those lawns with my book bag, knowing I was now one of those students I admired and marveled at way back in 1966, left me in awe. I appreciated every second of it. I ate up every class. I savored every moment.

There were plenty of other students who didn't feel the way I did. Lots of kids took it for granted, blew classes off, and complained about this or that, and it didn't make any sense to me. I had worked so hard to get here. It had taken so long. Maybe there's something to the whole idea of taking some time off after high school to live a little before going to school. Maybe it makes you appreciate the experience just a little bit more. I've heard professors and administrators talk about the fact that their "older" students are some of their favorites. I can't say whether or not the path I took would be right for anyone but me, of course, but it sure felt good to know that I was in the midst of accomplishing my dream—and that my dream had a ripple effect on other people.

My parents came out to visit toward the start of that fall semester, and the glow on their faces as they walked around said it all. They were so proud. The campus was so beautiful. I could tell it made an impression on them. In fact, my parents finally took a big step on the road to fulfilling their own dreams just as I was fulfilling mine: they bought a little cabin on a beautiful lake up in Wisconsin. It felt as if all of us were breaking free of the expectations and limitations that life had set upon us in Joliet. I loved that feeling! It made me want to keep going. It made me want to do everything I could to make them even more proud than they were already.

Thanks to Freddy and the education I'd gained at Holy Cross, the academic side of Notre Dame was fun and exciting. For a guy who struggled all through school, I know that seems like a stretch. But it isn't. Classes at Notre Dame might have been tougher than classes at Holy Cross, but they were fun because I had a routine and good study habits. Plus, the pressure was off. I didn't *have* to get all As and Bs. I was already in! I picked sociology as my major. I figured, why not? I was fascinated by the way people interact, the way society influences our lives, and the way people influence society. I was fascinated by my time in the navy, my travels through Europe and Boston, witnessing the cultural differences and similarities. The idea that I could earn a degree by studying the very things that fascinated me, fascinated me! The best part was that I managed to complete all of my general-education prerequisites—the math, science, and so on—while at Holy Cross. So my time at Notre Dame was spent knee-deep in my chosen field, working toward my degree. That concentrated approach made sense to me. The clutter was gone. The classes I didn't care about were over. Honestly, it felt kind of easy!

That was a big lesson for me too. At schools like Notre Dame, or at big businesses or private clubs, they build up this wall of elitism. They hold themselves on a certain pedestal, protecting what they have. For people on the outside, it can feel unattainable. There's a false sense that the people who are a part of whatever institution it happens to be are "better than you" or "smarter than you." The thing is, once you get inside that institution, you realize real quick that they're *not* any smarter than you, or better than you, at all! It's all an illusion. It takes a certain amount of strength and determination to break through that illusion, but once you do, you find out we're all human beings. We're all in this same adventure together. We all have strengths to share and weaknesses that need strengthening. Once you're in it, you look back and wonder, *Why did I ever think this would be too hard for me to handle?*

I'm not saying Notre Dame was a breeze. It wasn't. If I didn't pay attention, if I hadn't improved my study habits, I might not have made it. But it wasn't nearly as difficult or unattainable or impossible as I had once allowed myself to believe. Getting through my junior and senior years would be entirely manageable academically. I knew that within the first few weeks of starting classes. So I didn't worry about it any longer.

That freed me up to concentrate on two really big goals: giving my all on the football team in order to earn a chance to dress for a game, and going home with a Bengal Bouts jacket on my back.

There were 130 players on the Notre Dame varsity team. Since only two of us made it through walk-ons, that made me so far down the depth chart that I wasn't even on it! Literally, my name did not appear on the list outside the locker room.

That bothered me.

If there was one thing I learned in the navy, it's that everyone on a team plays a part. No one is above or below anyone else when the chips are down. When it's time for a team to get the job done, as it was during re-fueling, the whole team does it. It's the only way a ship can function, and the only way an athletic team can truly function, as far as I'm concerned.

Unfortunately, just as there was a sense of elitism that permeated Notre Dame, there was a sense of elitism in pockets of the football team. Not every player showed it, but the sense was there: us versus them, the big guys and the little guys, the elite players and the third- and fourth-string guys. Part of it was systemic. Guys like me didn't get our names on our locker like the top players. We never got jerseys with our names on them either. Just numbers. We weren't even supposed to eat with the first- and second-team guys. The rest of it was implied; people just have a way of making you feel lower than them. They pound their chest differently. Even though I was suiting up for practice just like everyone else, I felt like an outsider—at first. Everybody wants to be accepted in life. I just wanted to be accepted as a member of that team, and I couldn't understand why anyone would want to create this feeling of division—as if the walk-ons weren't good enough to be around those guys. Even the walk-on scholarship players treated us non-scholarship walk-ons differently. Granted, we were just human tackle dummies, but tackle dummies are important. The offensive line couldn't improve their game without us. Did we deserve to be made to feel lower than anyone else? We were contributing members of the team!

Part of me wonders why I continued to put up with that attitude. In the early days, no one would have cared if I walked away—except me. But the fact that I faced it put a chip on my shoulder: an "I'll show them" mentality that burned like fuel for me.

To say my days were full at Notre Dame would be a major understatement. Football practices stretched on for hours, every day. We never let up. And when the fall season was over, spring ball arrived in what seemed like no time at all. Rain, shine, mud, snow, whatever the weather could throw at us, we practiced through it. Hard. Balancing practice alone with my classes would have been a lot of work, but I also continued my work with the grounds and maintenance crew at the stadium. It was the only way I could earn money. And I worked at the ACC, patrolling every night, working with the cleaning crew, setting up and breaking down chairs, and staging for various events. That's how I earned my room and board. Yet, somehow, none of it seemed like a burden. Sure, I'd get upset at just how much garbage the spectators could leave behind after a football game. And once in a while I'd get a little ticked that I was picking up garbage at this stadium when I didn't even get to play in it. But most of the time, I just appreciated the amazing opportunity to be a part of it all.

Those work arrangements gave me some awesome access to events at the ACC, which I was able to share with my friends. It was the mid-1970s, and the ACC was a major stop on the concert circuit. I wound up working security for Elton John, the Doobie Brothers, Kiss, Neil Diamond, and

Kenny Rogers. What a thrill to get to hear that great music up close, and for free. Of course, they always needed extra security for those gigs, and who better to hire than some big, strong football players? The fact that I was able to get some of those guys jobs so they could see the concerts for free certainly made them look at me in a slightly different light. I was more than a human tackle dummy at that point, and I wound up truly befriending some of those guys who were intimidating to be around at first.

The biggest concert moment was definitely Elvis Presley. It was one of Elvis's very last tours. The arena was packed, and Elvis was nowhere to be found. It was well past eight thirty, when the concert was slated to begin, and my football buddies on the security team were working hard to keep everyone under control. I was standing right outside my room near Gate 8 when I saw Elvis's Cadillac finally pull up just in front of the double doors. We made sure no one got near it, and we made sure the pathway to the stage was totally clear, just like his team had ordered, but Elvis just kept sitting there in the car. I asked a guy who had stepped out of the car what was going on. "He's afraid to go on stage," the guy said, "'cause of his weight."

Elvis at that point was looking a little pudgy. It apparently took everything he had to gather the courage to perform. Elvis! One of the greatest performers in the history of music. It seemed crazy to me. I guess everybody has their issues to overcome, even the biggest stars on the planet.

After a few minutes, he got one step closer to emerging: he opened the car door, then just sat there with the door open. I'm not sure why I felt compelled to do this, but I ducked inside my room and came out with one of my Notre Dame boxing shirts. I thought maybe Elvis would like a souvenir. Maybe it would break the ice for him. So I went over as close to the car as I could get and tossed it to him. Elvis picked it up and looked to see who threw it. "Hold on, buddy," he said to me. It was so cool to hear that that deep, familiar drawl of his. He leaned back into the car for a moment and then tossed a little stuffed hound dog out to me. A hound dog from Elvis! It was awesome. I wound up giving that dog to my oldest sister, Jean Anne, who was just about the biggest Elvis fan in the world.

She was already inside the arena, waiting and waiting for that concert of a lifetime to begin. It was awesome to be in a position where I could help her get tickets—and even cooler to hand her that toy from Elvis after the show.

Elvis finally did get out of that Cadillac a few minutes after our shirt-to-dog exchange. He beelined it to the stage, where the lights came up and he completely transformed into the astounding performer that he was. I remember thinking that performing must be like boxing, in a way: once you get in that ring or on that stage, your instinct just takes over and you go with it. Takes some courage to get up there and do it, but then all the preparation and a lifetime's worth of experience just kicks in. It certainly kicked in for him. The concert blew the audience away. I read afterward that his South Bend performances were some of the best of the entire tour.

A couple of years later, just before Elvis died, I heard that he had worn that Notre Dame boxing shirt I gave him when he was relaxing at Graceland. I don't know with 100 percent certainty whether it's true or not, but still, it was staggering to think I had shared something with a singer of that stature, of that massive level of fame, through the simple gesture of throwing him a shirt. In a strange way, none of us are too far from greatness. Simply chasing my dreams and pursuing my goals allowed me to get up a little closer to that great musician than most people could even dream. I chalked it up as one more unexpected benefit, one more little bonus that came as a result of my efforts to make my dreams come true.

Still Fighting

I never got hurt on the football field. Bruised, battered, beat-up, swollen, and bloodied, sure. But never injured. I played smart. I stayed low. Other guys got hurt because they didn't play hard all the time. I went hard every practice, every play. I was all-in, all-focused, no room for mistakes. I knew one mistake could get me killed. (Well, maybe not killed, but broken for sure. Those players were huge!)

Walking up to the training table to get iced after a practice, there were times when they didn't have my name on the list of players. "What's your name?" the trainer would say, looking at his checklist. I always managed to keep my composure, but I remember thinking to myself, *I just got the crap kicked out of me for this team. Didn't they see that? Why am I being treated this way?* That lack of recognition, that built-in lack of respect for the scout team never seemed to let up, no matter how many people on campus knew me from the Bengal Bouts or my work at the ACC. Sometimes just the fact that they didn't care if I got injured put a chip on my shoulder. I understood my role; don't get me wrong. Yet I thought about the navy, how they took care of us seamen, all of us, because they recognized that every member of the team was important and needed to feel valued and critical when the chips were down. As I turned the corner into the latter half of my junior year at Notre Dame, I got the sinking feeling that I would have a hard time finding that kind of value and respect anywhere else in life, and that realization made me truly appreciate the times when that value and respect was showed to me in full.

Coach Yonto did that. He treated every one of his defensive players the same. He reminded me of a navy guy, actually. A true leader. He'd show those little moments of caring after I'd take a hard hit. "You alright, Rudy?"

Greg Blache, the junior varsity coach, was great too. Those guys seemed to value all 130 of the players who were out there working together to make Notre Dame great.

Of course, the greatest of the greats was Ara Parseghian. He just had a way about him. He commanded respect because he got results. He pushed every player, big or small, to fight hard and to be their best at every practice, every game. There was no feeling like getting a pat on the back from Parseghian. An acknowledgment from him really meant something, because he didn't give out compliments that weren't deserved. But he also fostered a camaraderie on the team. At the end of each week, he'd bring us all together, offense and defense, training and first-string varsity alike, and challenge some of the guys to come up with skits to lighten the mood. Someone would get up and imitate one of the coaches' mannerisms or tell a few jokes or reenact a botched play to rib the quarterback. It was a simple way to relax everybody at the end of a hard week, and the sense of togetherness and true teamwork that it fostered was important. The walk-on players like me didn't even get to dress in the varsity locker room. We were relegated to the baseball locker room next door, where our laundry sacks full of socks, pants, T-shirts, and shorts that were supposed to get washed every night would sometimes be forgotten. Without Parseghian's efforts to bring us together, in my opinion, that literal wall between us could have hurt the team. It would have hurt morale. It would have left us feeling like second-class citizens. He managed to overcome that, at least to some degree. Fact was, I wanted to do everything I could to get out of that baseball locker room and go dress with the rest of the team. I wanted to wear clean shorts like everyone else! Those little things became huge goals to me, and I promised myself I would work hard to somehow achieve them.

Of course, no one worked harder than Parseghian. I remember leaving my room in the ACC every morning for 6:00 a.m. security rounds and seeing Coach already in, at the desk in his office, almost every day. More nights than not he'd be in there at ten o'clock at night too. That inspired me to work harder. If he saw me, he'd nod hello, and I'd nod back. It was all the acknowledgment I needed. I knew he recognized me, and that was something. Heck, there were plenty of times out on the field during practice when I'd take a hard hit and stay down for a few seconds, and I'd hear Parseghian yell, "Is that kid okay?" If he didn't care, if he didn't see me as a real contributor to the team, I don't think he would have asked that question. And he certainly wouldn't have asked it loud enough for other players to hear. I think it was his way of making sure everyone acknowledged the little guys who were working so hard to help make the big guys great. I liked that. It felt like light-years of accomplishment to me in the three years since I first stepped foot into his office unannounced to share my dream of playing for him. Three years since he uttered those words: "I bet you will."

Of course, in my opinion, the greatest motivator Parseghian gave to any of us to show up to practice and work hard was his promise, at any number of practices, that as long as we kept showing up to practice, he would let all of the graduating seniors—even the walk-ons—dress for the final home game of the season. The fact that he would give all of his players, all the way down to the bottom rung of the ladder, that dignity to fulfill their dreams of running out of that tunnel onto the field was about the most impressive thing I'd ever heard.

I was a junior. I'd have a whole year to wait for my shot. But the thought that I might actually get to dress for a game—that my wild, unrealistic, over-the-top, impossible-to-reach dream was now on its way to becoming true—felt awesome!

I remember telling my parents and my brothers and sisters all about it. What a thrill it would be for my younger siblings to see me wearing that uniform. To see their oldest brother get out there and play for Notre Dame? It felt big. It felt like the sort of thing that would change their whole worldview, you know? I loved that feeling.

For some reason, as December rolled around that excited feeling was replaced by something bittersweet. Maybe it's because the season was almost over. The thought of not playing got me down. Football was the reason I got up in the morning. For many reasons, I didn't want to see 1974 come to an end, even as I dreamed of what the following year would bring. But it couldn't have been more than a week or two into that month when I picked up a copy of *The Observer* and just about fell over, completely sucker-punched by the top story: Coach Ara Parseghian was retiring.

I thought about what it meant for the team. I thought about what it meant for morale. I thought about what it meant for the legacy of Notre Dame football. In his decade in South Bend, which would become known as "the Era of Ara," he amassed ninety-five wins, only seventeen losses, and four ties. That's an .836 average! Unheard of in the modern era! He was kind. He was fair. He was tough. He was everything a coach should be.

I was devastated.

And I couldn't help but think about the one thing that suddenly felt selfish to worry over: *What would this mean for my chances of actually dressing for a game? Would a new coach think of that? What if a new coach didn't like me? I'd have to prove myself all over again to whoever took over next year.*

To say I had a little frustration built up as that football season came to a close would be quite the understatement. Lucky for me, I'd have a place to throw all of that energy: January meant the start of training season for the Bengal Bouts.

Six weeks of training; three days of fights. The Bengal Bouts are like an entire football or baseball or basketball season compressed into a single weekend. The energy on campus is intense. To be one of those fighters and to have a shot at the top, you have to be 100 percent in the game, in the zone, fixated on the task in front of you, which amounts to pummeling the other guy with as many hits as possible to score points, move ahead, and make it to the championship.

I didn't care about *winning* the Bengal Bouts. I just wanted to make it to the final round so I could get one of those championship jackets. I'd only have to survive through three rounds of fights. I was stronger than ever. Still scrappy as ever. That goal seemed entirely attainable to me.

Pulling those gloves on, stepping out into the roar of that capacity crowd in the basketball arena, climbing into the ring under those lights, hearing my name announced over the loudspeaker—"And in this corner . . . Rudyyyyy Rueeetigger!"—it was all a bit surreal. The funny thing about working hard toward any goal, preparing for weeks on end, focusing so intently on something, is that once you're in the actual game, there's almost no room for thought anymore. It all comes down to instinct. It all comes down to preparation. I found the sound of the crowd disappearing as I focused on my opponent. It was just a wash of noise in the background. I didn't think about my hands or my stance or protecting my face or protecting my body. I just did it. "Ding!" I stepped into the center of that ring and just went for it. *Boom! Boom!* Took a couple of hits, then *Wham!* I knocked him hard, following up with a *right, right, right, left!* I just kept going, thinking about that jacket, thinking about making it through, not falling behind. *Keep punching, Rudy! Don't let him in!*

The first fight flew by. The bell rang and I couldn't believe it was over. I closed my eyes, just praying I'd done enough. Judge's decision: "Ruuudyyy Rueeetigger!"

All right. All right. Phew! I caught my breath. I went back to the locker room and wound myself down. *Two more to go. Two more to go.* It's all I thought about.

The next round, I was up against a well-known opponent in the same weight class who was a varsity football player—a halfback. I thought his fame as a Fighting Irish star would put the crowd firmly in his corner. But as we came face-to-face to touch gloves in the ring, something happened in that arena. In the greatest tradition of Notre Dame sports, the students immediately picked me as the underdog . . . and started rooting for me. Loudly.

After taking a few hits in the opening moment, I came back strong and started landing body blows just like I wanted. Suddenly I felt the crowd behind me. It felt like a surge. Like I was carrying their energy. It was all a rush of noise in the background as I focused on that opponent, anticipating his every move from the look in his eyes and counter-striking on pure gut reaction. When the bell rang, I finally heard what that crowd had been chanting: "Ru-dy! Ru-dy! Ru-dy!" They were chanting my name! And they didn't stop. They kept chanting until the judge's decision came in: "Ruuudyyy Rueeeettiger!"

The place went wild. It was awesome. As if the whole student body suddenly knew my name. *Me!* The fact that I defeated a football player was huge.

Stepping into the ring for the championship fight is nothing but a blur to me now. I know I was up against a bigger opponent again, a varsity football player named Mike McGuire, and after what I'd done in the last fight, the crowd was looking for an epic battle. I know the crowd started chanting my name. I also know I didn't give it my all. I lost focus. I had already won! I wanted to make the championship round so I could earn that jacket—and I did. So I let my guard down. I fought, but not to win. And guess what happens when you don't fight to win? You don't win. No surprise there. I lost in a split decision. It didn't matter to me. Walking out of that arena, hearing hundreds of students and coaches and professors say, "Great fight, Rudy!" "Way to go, man!" All those hands patting me on the back of that Bengal Bouts jacket was the greatest win I could have imagined at that point.

The next day, life was different. Notre Dame knew my name. Complete strangers said, "Hey, man! . . . Hi, Rudy! . . . Nice fights, man!" as I walked through the quad. I'd never felt that kind of recognition before. I'd never felt that sort of admiration. What was really strange about it was I didn't feel like I had worked all that hard to get it. It came easier than I would have thought. Just like the academics. I was tapping into something. I was starting to understand something here and there, in little glimpses: focusing on an achievable, accomplishable goal can turn a far-fetched fantasy into an attainable dream. A dream that can become real with a little hard work and perseverance.

There was something more to it than that, as well. I started to realize that accomplishing that goal, achieving that one dream, made a whole bunch of other dreams come true too. I had seen it in my quest to get into Notre Dame and in my quest to land a spot on the football team. When spring football practice came around, I would see it on the team.

Not long after those fights were over, I wore that Bengal Bouts jacket into the locker room on my way to suit up for our very first football practice under new head coach Dan Devine. Devine was a great coach who had been considered by Notre Dame way back in 1964, when Parseghian was first hired. He had spent the previous couple of years with the NFL coaching the Green Bay Packers. Not exactly chump change! I was excited to get to work for the man, even though the depression over Parseghian's departure seemed to permeate the entire football program.

On that very first day of practice, I noticed a whole bunch of my teammates looked at me a little differently. A couple of the first-team players made a point to say, "Nice fights, Rudy." These were guys who had never spoken to me before. My performance in the Bengal Bouts helped change the attitude I faced on the football team. It didn't change everyone's attitude, of course. There are some people who are never willing to let go of that us-versus-them mentality as they cling to their elite status. But it made a difference. It made a difference in the way I felt in that locker room. And the more comfortable I felt, the more included I felt, the harder I wanted to work to become the best football player I could be.

Oddly enough, just as I had predicted in my mind when I heard that Coach Parseghian was leaving, Coach Devine had a very different attitude about team camaraderie. He actually separated the teams, divided the teams, never brought us together at the end of the week for any kind of common exercises, let alone some fun skits. In fact, it was his official policy that the prep teams weren't even allowed to sit and eat with the regular players! That made a lot of us upset, and in fact, there were many times when I flat-out ignored the order. I was friendly with some of those guys, and there was no way I was gonna sit like an outsider and not eat with them. No one could really blame Devine. He came from the NFL. It was a different mentality, and there was definitely a method to his madness. The fact that the prep team was off by itself meant we bonded in our own way, on a smaller scale, like never before. Even so, as the year progressed, Coach Devine would see the differences in the Notre Dame traditions and start to embrace them.

Spring practices were divided up into two shifts so the team members would have plenty of time to study for their final exams. That apparently bugged Devine, but he would learn to deal with it. Academics never took a backseat to football at Notre Dame, yet I understood where Coach was coming from. I was glad I had time to study, but if I could have been out there on the football field both shifts I would have been. I had begun to make a name for myself on that team. I had established a reputation for never giving up, never backing down, always playing my hardest. There were certain players who didn't appreciate that. They thought it made them look bad. I didn't understand how it was my fault if they wanted to rest on their talents and not strive for the best every practice, but that's how they treated it. Even so, there were other players, the guys I became friendly with, who would knock me on the helmet or say, "Great practice, man," as we walked off the field. "Man, you come out here and work your tail off! I appreciate that!" Players like Gerry DiNardo, Willie Fry Jr., Ross Browner, Luther Bradley, and Ken MacAfee lived up to the Notre Dame name in every way. There were times when I'd invite some of those guys to ride back to Joliet with me to have dinner with my family. My mom loved it. Now that a few of her flock had flown the coop, she was thrilled to have a big, full table with lots of big eaters. And those guys liked nothing more than a good home-cooked meal.

D-Bob and I designed custom Notre Dame jackets for those players, with their names on 'em. It turned into a lucrative little side business for the both of us, and the players appreciated having unique keepsakes, so it was a win-win. The camaraderie of all of it grew stronger every week.

As the days grew warmer, the idea of making a name for myself on that team became more and more important to me. I'm not sure why. I guess we all want recognition for the hard work we do in life. But at some point, I also realized that my dream of dressing for a game, of allowing my friends and family to see me play, had a whole other level of depth behind it that I wasn't aware of in the beginning: unless I dressed, and unless I stepped foot on that field during a game, my name wouldn't appear in the history books. My name wouldn't appear alongside the rest of the Notre Dame players in the yearbook. My name wouldn't appear on the bronze plaques filled with player names that lined the walls in the ACC. As far as history was concerned, it would look as if I had never been a part of that team at all. That didn't sit well with me. I don't care who you are or how gracious you are, that's a hard thing to take. Sure, I would know in my heart that I was a part of that team, an important part of that team, forever. That's important. But if a tree falls in the forest and no one's there to hear it . . . I dunno. It just bothered me that no one would know.

During the spring season, Coach Devine never, ever mentioned the notion that seniors would get to dress for a home game. That worried me. I also became aware of a whole new set of NCAA rules that were put into effect that year, rules dictating that no team would be allowed to dress more than sixty players for any single home game. Coach Parseghian had the option to suit up 110 players if he wanted. The NCAA cut it by almost half! At a place as flush with great players as Notre Dame, where there were nearly one hundred scholarship players on the team, that meant there weren't nearly enough dress slots for even the scholarship players to suit up. *How would I ever have a shot now?*

The only solution I could think of was to work hard and try to make an impression. I played as hard as I ever had. I gave my all, over and over again, no matter how tired I was or how much it hurt. I reminded myself, every day, what a privilege it was to be a part of that team. I seemed to make an impression on offensive coordinator Merv Johnson. He would throw out little comments like, "Great effort! . . . Nice job!" I loved that stuff. He seemed to love how hard I made his guys work, which only made me want to work even harder. *Heck*, I thought, *if these new coaches really notice, maybe I'll see my name move up the depth chart and I'll finally get to play!*

I said good-bye to my great friend Freddy at the end of that year. Just as he dreamed, he was heading off to law school in Florida. He was one of the few people in the entire Notre Dame community with whom I had shared my dream of dressing for a game. I was smart enough to know that most people would tell me it was impossible, so I kept my mouth shut, just as I did back in Joliet when I finally made up my mind to quit my job at the power plant and go find a way into Notre Dame. I didn't want to hear all that negative talk. Lucky for me, Freddy—just like D-Bob—never tried to dissuade me. They were both convinced I could do it. And even though he'd be thousands of miles away, Freddy said he'd do everything he could to come back and see me play if I ever got suited up. That meant a lot to me. I was so proud that he was accomplishing his dreams and so happy to have met a guy like him, purely by chance, on my very first day at St. Joseph Hall. I believe certain people come into your life for a reason, and I knew I had better pay attention to make sure I didn't miss another "Freddy" if he or she ever came along.

That summer I moved back home to Joliet and took a construction job as a plasterer. I wasn't qualified to do the detail work, so I took on all the low-level jobs: setting up scaffolding, mixing mud, carrying stuff back and forth to the truck. I liked to do the heavy lifting because it kept me in shape for football, and doing all that grunt work made the other guys happy, simply because they didn't have to do it! All those plasterers chewed tobacco. I had never tried it, and one day I said, "I want to chew some." They said I wasn't man enough, but I fought back, saying I'd been in the navy. Give me a shot. So I tried it, and man, I got so sick! I vomited everywhere, and those guys just laughed and laughed. "Oh yeah, the tough Notre Dame football player!" they said. I never did that again.

The highlight of that summer came in the mailbox. I wasn't expecting it. I wasn't anticipating it. But there in the mail, one afternoon, I spotted a letter with the Notre Dame insignia on it—only this one wasn't from the admissions office. It was from the football team.

Inside was a letter inviting me to come back early to join the varsity team for fall training. I couldn't believe it! It was so out of the blue. I had hoped to make an impression, but this felt as big as my acceptance letter to Notre Dame: it meant I was a full-fledged member of the football team now. Not a walk-on player, but a true member of the team.

Showing that letter to my dad was just as exciting as sharing the news when I first got in. He got really excited too. There were certain guys at work who still ribbed him about his son not showing up anywhere on their TVs and radios during the Notre Dame games. They refused to admit that a Ruettiger was part of the Notre Dame legacy, and they ribbed him about it. My dad wasn't the kind of guy who'd go running into work with that letter in hand to shout over a loudspeaker and let everyone know that his son was a full-fledged member of the football team now, but I knew that he'd carry that confidence with him the next time he stepped foot into that refinery.

That made me proud.

Never Quit

The scout team doesn't travel to away games. The only shot I'd have at dressing for a game in the fall of 1975 was at home, and that shot was most definitely a long one. Despite my dreams, I hadn't moved up the depth chart. Not one bit. I'd walk by the list outside of the locker room every day and not see my name on it. No scout team players were listed. So there was no indication that I was even a part of the team, despite my new "official" status. It frustrated me so much that I started writing my name on the bottom of the depth chart just so I could see it. One day, one of the team managers caught me doing it. Luckily, I knew those guys. The managers were sort of the business managers of the team. They took care of all of the logistical details, and I was always friendly with them, just hanging around and talking to them outside the locker room from time to time. Because I lived in the ACC, I could always make sure they had whatever they needed on short notice. Little stuff like that. They liked me, and I liked them. A couple of weeks later, when the new chart came out, my name was on it. It was still way down the bottom, but at least it was something. I still don't know who was responsible for doing that, or if it was a mistake. Either way, it made me happy. At least it was an acknowledgment that I was part of the team.

I think being friendly with the people who worked with the team, not just "on" the team, paid off in a lot of ways. As I entered that second year, I noticed that my laundry bag was never left behind. I had clean shorts for every day's practice. I wasn't forgotten, and that's a good feeling.

Because they invited me back early for fall practice, I wasn't treated as "just a walk-on" anymore, even though I was still only a member of the scout team. They gave me a locker in the varsity locker room . . . with my name on it. That was huge!

Oddly enough, my name was showing up in lots of other places too. For some reason, the story of my journey through Holy Cross and Notre Dame caught on as a human-interest story around campus. A reporter put together a big article on me that was printed in the basketball brochures they handed out with tickets at the ACC. It talked about my journey through the navy and Holy Cross, to playing on the scout team and coming very close to winning the title in the Bengal Bouts the previous spring. I guess I was such a fixture around the ACC that I seemed like someone worthy of profiling in the press, because *The Observer* did a similar article profiling my Notre Dame experience in its pages later that fall. There was one difference with that *Observer* piece, though: In that piece, they quoted me talking about my ultimate dream—to suit up for a Notre Dame home game, to come running out of that tunnel with my parents watching in the stands, to go down in the history books, and to prove to everyone back in Joliet that I did it. I really did it.

The newspaper played me up as the ultimate underdog, and boy, does Notre Dame love an underdog. They put me as an odds-on favorite to win the Bengal Bouts the following semester, but that was a long way off. All I cared about that fall was football. It would be my last season. I couldn't believe how fast time had flown. I only had three months of football season to have any shot at dressing, and as we got into October, it wasn't looking good.

The first two home games were against Northwestern and Michigan

State, back-to-back Saturdays at the end of September and the first week of October. The dress lists post on Thursdays before each game. I walked down to the bulletin board outside of the locker room on both of those Thursdays, scanned the list, saw my name wasn't on it, and walked away. I didn't say anything about it. I didn't make a fuss about it. After all, other than Coach Parseghian, my family, D-Bob, and Freddy, no one had known I had this crazy dream of dressing for a game and actually playing until that newspaper article came out. Now everyone knew! Still, I didn't want to appear to be making a big deal of it. There were plenty of other guys on that team who would never get a chance to suit up. I'd kick myself sometimes for even dreaming about it. *What makes me so special?* I'd think. *Get over it.*

It's tough, though, when you a have a big dream like that and someone in a position of power, like Parseghian, tells you that it's possible, and then you go and tell other people who mean so much to you; it's tough to think it's not going to come true.

The best way to deal with that frustration was out on the field. I played harder than I ever had in my life that fall season. I went at every play like it was my last, like I was knee deep in the biggest, most important game of my life. In a way, that wasn't inaccurate. This was, once and for all, the last season of football I would ever play.

Coach Devine noticed. There were a couple of times during practice when he gathered everyone around for a pep talk and brought up my name. "I wish you guys had more heart, like Rudy. I wish you'd throw yourselves into these practices 100 percent. Then maybe you'd see the results we all want to see on game day!"

That embarrassed me. I was just doing my job. *Why would anyone want to play for Notre Dame and not work as hard as they could to be the best they could?* The whole thing didn't make sense to me. I was part of the team; I wanted the team to be great. Therefore, *I* had to be great! I had to play my hardest. What else was there to do?

I remember listening to the next couple of away games on the radio—games that would go down in Notre Dame history. The first was against North Carolina on October 11. We were losing 14–0 at the end of the third quarter. My guys just hadn't been able to move the ball. Our quarterback was struggling, plain and simple. It was painful to listen to it! He finally found his footing and caught a break, which brought us to 14–6 with about six minutes to go. That's when Coach Devine replaced him with a freshman hot-shot who no one in the football world had heard of at that point: a guy named Joe Montana. Over the course of the next five minutes, the team came to life. Montana nailed a couple of good passes, scored a touchdown, and made a two-point conversion to tie it up; and then Ted Burgmeier snagged what should have been a simple short pass and turned it into an eighty-yard touchdown to win the game 14–21. The whole campus erupted! You could hear cheers from every window, echoing across the chilly lawns under that October sky. It was awesome. A week later, Joe Montana led the team to another legendary fourth-quarter comeback against Air Force, only this time Notre Dame was down twenty-one points at the end of the third quarter. We managed to rally back to a 30–31 win.

While the fans erupted and the student body erupted and everyone was patting Joe Montana on the back, I knew better than to think that Dan Devine or Joe Yonto or Merv Johnson would consider that kind of a last-minute comeback any sort of a cheer-worthy victory for our team. If we were playing right, if we were playing as a unit, we never would have fallen that far behind.

When the team got back from that Air Force game, I was waiting for them. I knew when they were scheduled to arrive, and I was always there to greet them. But the first thing Coach Devine and Coach Johnson did that day was take the whole traveling team over to the big stadium to run sprints, a punishing workout in return for their near defeat. I could have just gone back to my room at that point, but something in my gut told me I needed to go run with them. We were all in this together. So I grabbed my uniform and suited up.

"Where you going?" Coach Johnson said. "You're not part of the traveling team."

I remember saying something about feeling responsible. The fact that the offensive line wasn't doing its job the way it should was, in some way, my fault. I was their human tackle dummy. I was the guy tasked with working them harder than anyone else so they could prep for those big games! So I went and ran those sprints right along with them.

Even in that chilly October air, the sweat poured off me. I was exhausted. Heck, my legs are half the length of some of those guys', which means I run two strides for their every one! It hurt!

When Coach Johnson blew his whistle and finally called it a day, he came up to me, all pumped up, and yelled loud enough for every other guy to hear: "You're a real man, Rudy. Takes a real man to do what you just did."

I didn't know how to react to that. I knew he meant it as a compliment, but something felt a little off. I wished he had told the rest of the guys who had gone back to the locker room that we *all* had to run sprints. *We're all in it together. We're all one team.* To me, that compliment solidified that feeling of division that permeated the team at that point—one that permeates a lot of great teams. What I did shouldn't have been considered anything special. It should have been what every member of that team wanted to do!

Unfortunately, I think those words from Coach Johnson ticked off a few of the first-team players. They had already heard Dan Devine use me in his "heart" example a couple of times that season, and the whole thing didn't go over so well with some of the full-scholarship players and All-American types who were far more talented and athletically gifted than I was.

That sense of division really came to a head one practice in late October, between the Southern California and Navy games—two of the final three home games of the season. USC kicked our butts, right there on our home field. The final score was 17–24. Morale was low. Tensions were running high. Practices were running long. It was the end of a particularly brutal day, probably the last play or two of the entire practice, and when the whistle blew I shot right through the tired and worn-out offensive line with everything I had and tackled one of our top players. He popped up madder than a hornet, and for days and days he wouldn't let it go. He kept complaining that I was pushing too hard, kept complaining that the practices were too long, kept complaining about everything.

We played Navy that Saturday, and won, which boosted morale as we headed into a week full of practices before our final home game of the season. Yet still, even on that Monday, that one particular player kept complaining about everything. The guy was a fifth-year senior. He was supposed to be a starter but wasn't, so he had a big chip on his shoulder.

Back in the locker room that afternoon, I had heard just about enough. "Quit complaining!" I yelled.

"Aw, you're nothin' but a suck-up, Rudy," he said to me, and he pushed me!

I wasn't about to take that, so I pushed him back, and another player stepped in and stopped us from going any further. Good thing too. With all my Bengal Bouts training I might have knocked his head off! "Knock it off," the other player said, not directed at me, but right at that senior. The message he sent, loud and clear, was, "Why don't you try putting as much energy on the field as you're putting into all your complaining?"

The whole thing was ridiculous. I wasn't looking for a confrontation. All I ever did was work to make the team better and to make those players the best they could be. That was my role. Even though someone else came to my defense, I felt like I was being punished for doing my job to the best of my ability. The whole incident set me over the edge. That us-versus-them mentality was eating me up inside. I was never going to move up the depth chart. I was never gonna get a chance to run onto that field. What the heck was I doing? Why was I working so hard if all it was causing was anguish and agony?

I kept asking myself those questions all week. And when Thursday came around, and my name wasn't on the dress list, I walked out of the locker room thinking I'd never be back. *Why bother?* A couple of players saw how angry I was as I stormed out and asked what was up. "I quit!" I yelled as I kept on walking. They knew why I was upset. They knew I felt like it just wasn't worth it. Like I'd been wasting my time.

There were tears in my eyes when I walked back into my room. I slammed the door and dropped down on my bed—exhausted, spent, and over it.

Couldn't have been thirty seconds later when I heard a knock.

"Come in," I said, wiping my eyes and sitting up.

It was Rudy, the old janitor who lent me the cot in his closet the previous summer. Apparently I walked right past him on my way in. I didn't even notice, but he noticed. He saw my face. He saw my pain. He asked if he could sit. I said, "Sure."

He asked me what was up, and I told him the whole sorry tale. I opened up about the incident with the senior that Monday and the bigger picture of feeling unwanted, unappreciated by the very guys I was working so hard for, and how disappointed I was that I wouldn't get to dress for a game—that no one would even know I had ever played for Notre Dame.

He listened. Really listened. Rudy was one of those guys who always seemed to be smiling. Always content. So I was surprised when he opened up to me about knowing exactly how I felt.

"When I lost my leg, I thought my whole world was over," he said.

"When you what?" I asked. I had no idea he was missing a leg. I don't know what's wrong with me. Was I the most unobservant guy in the world? It was a strange, strange feeling. He lifted up his pant leg a bit and showed me the prosthetic, extending down into his scuffed-up brown leather shoe. I had noticed he had a limp. I never thought anything about it. It never occurred to me that his leg was gone.

"I lost it to diabetes," he said.

I apologized for not noticing.

"Don't apologize, Rudy. You see the good in people. You do. You don't see what's wrong with them first. You don't look for flaws. That's a gift."

He talked to me about landing the job at Notre Dame and how thrilled he was, not only to find work in his condition, but also to land a job at a place he so admired. He was a lifelong Notre Dame fan. He described to me how much he loved the campus, how it felt like a church or a temple to him, how at peace he felt just walking between these beautiful buildings every morning, and how rich he felt to be able to contribute to Notre Dame athletics in his own way.

His name would never be up on a wall. His name wouldn't appear in any history books or yearbooks. Didn't matter. "I'm a part of something great," he said. "And I know it. And that's all that matters."

That started me crying again.

"Don't quit, Rudy," he said. "Don't quit the team. Not now. Not after coming this far. Not after all the hard work you put in. You quit, and I promise you—you'll regret it the rest of your life."

I let out a bit of a moan. "Sorry," I said, wiping my eyes. "I don't mean to cry."

"It's okay to cry. You just think about what I said."

"I will. Thanks."

"No problem," he said, standing up strong and laying his hand on my shoulder. "I'll see you around."

I called home that night. My brother Francis picked up the phone, and I told him what had happened. I told him there was only one home game left, and that it didn't look like I was going to dress for a game after all. I told him I wasn't going to bother going to practice anymore.

"Are you nuts?" he said. "You can't quit the team. It's Notre Dame! What the heck are you thinking?"

Of my six brothers, Frank's the one most like me. The one who got into trouble. The one who finished second or third in his class—from the bottom. The one who suffered from similar undiagnosed learning disorders. He confided with me on the phone that night just how much he'd been influenced by my whole course of action. The fact that I said I was going to get into Notre Dame, and then did it. The fact that I said I was going to play football for Notre Dame, and I did it. It didn't matter if I dressed for a game or not. I accomplished what I set out to do, and that something was much bigger than any of us had ever dreamed possible. He talked to me about his own dreams of becoming a police officer one day, and how he was turning that weight room he'd set up in my parents' garage into a business: Rudy's Gym. It was awesome. He was already starting a business just coming out of high school, and he said I was the one who helped inspire him to do it.

It's humbling to hear something like that from your little brother.

"Don't quit the team, Rudy. Don't let yourself down like that. We all know what you've done. You know what you've done. That's what matters."

Daniel O. Ruettiger,
Rudy's dad, age 22;
Air Force Sergeant, 1945

Betty Ruettiger,
Rudy's mom, age 17, 1943

Betty and Daniel Ruettiger wedding party, May 13, 1945

Rudy's First Communion,
age 10, 1958

Rudy's sister, Mary Eileen, with 6-year-old Rudy, 1954

The Ruettiger Family—Dad, Mom, and 14 children, 1963

The Ruettiger Boys with dad, 1995

The Ruettiger Family, 1984

USS Robert L. Wilson (DD-847), Mediterranean Tour, 1971

Coach Nappy Napolitano, and Rudy; Bengal Bouts Boxing, 1974

Rudy during Notre Dame-Georgia Tech Game

Topps Collectors Card, 2011

Dan Ruettiger, #45,
Defensive End, 1975

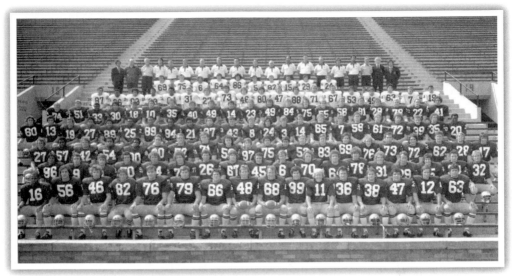

1975 Notre Dame Football Team

Walking out of tunnel,
Notre Dame-
Georgia Tech Game,
November 8th, 1975

The Tackle, Notre Dame-Georgia Tech Game

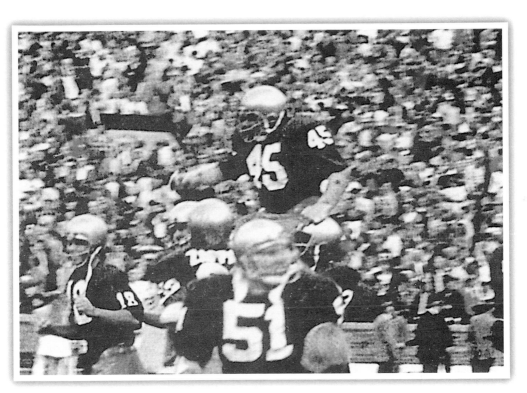

The Carry Off, Notre-Dame-Georgia Tech Game

First job at Pat Ryan & Associates, 1977

Rudy in his condo in South Bend, Indiana, 1992

Rudy movie poster, 1993

Jason Miller, David Anspaugh, and Rudy on the *Rudy* set

Rob Fried, Rudy, Peter Guber, Cary Woods, and Roger Valdiserri

David Anspaugh, Rudy, and Angelo Pizzo

Sean Astin, Rudy, and Jon Favreau on the set

Skip Holtz and Rudy, 1993

Father Joyce, actor Robert Prosky, Rudy, and Father Hesburgh on set at Notre Dame

Meeting Hilary Clinton for the second
time. (This time I wore a tie!)

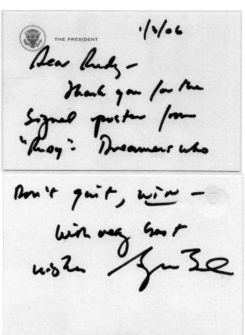

From President George W. Bush, 2006

Rudy with Luke's Wings Wounded Warriors at Walter Reed Hospital, 2012

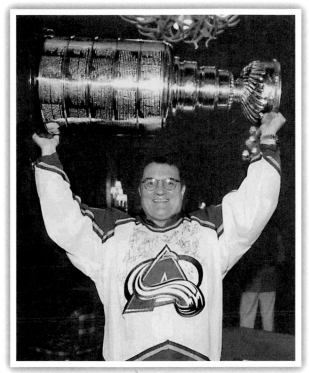

Hoisting the Stanley Cup, after making a surprise appearance during the ring presentation for the champion Colorado Avalanche in 1996.

My first visit to Yankee Stadium in 2011, where the field just happened to be set up for a Notre Dame v. Army game!

Aunt Eileen, Betty, Rudy, and Dan Ruettiger at a special *Rudy* screening, 1994

Betty and Dan Ruettiger at Wisconsin Cabin, 2001

I know I'm a little hardheaded, but I went to bed still thinking I was done with the team. I was confused, of course, and my mind kept spinning, but the anger and frustration seemed to overwhelm the very reasonable arguments for going back.

The next morning, I woke up a little less stressed. There's nothing like sleep to help give you some perspective. Still, it hurt to think that I wasn't appreciated by all of the other players. I had given everything to that team.

That's when a third set of lessons came knocking on my door. First Rudy. Then Frank. Now? Four team members came by to give me a little pep talk before practice. Some of the strongest, most well-respected members of the team: Pat Sarb, Dan Knott, Ivan Brown, and Bobby Zanot. They were all real serious. They just wanted me to know they didn't want me to quit. They all had struggles. They all got frustrated, they said. They were all bummed out about the way the team was playing and disappointed by the big attitudes of some of the star players, and they said it was unforgivable the way I'd been treated by that fifth-year senior. They were also upset about that new NCAA rule that was keeping so many of us seniors from suiting up for our last home game. After all, it was a Notre Dame tradition! But they wanted me to know how much they all appreciated me. They wanted me to know how much they admired me and were blown away by how hard I worked.

"Be sure to come to practice today," they said. "You won't regret it."

It was exactly what I needed to hear, from exactly the people I needed to hear it from. It wouldn't have meant any more to me if Ara Parseghian himself had come along and told me to get off my behind and get back on the field.

By the time practice came around that day, I was embarrassed. I didn't want to dress in the locker room with everyone else. I held off and showed up late. It was the day before the final home game, against Georgia Tech, and I glanced at the dress list outside the locker room on the way to the field, just in case.

My name wasn't on it.

I dressed in the empty locker room. I walked out toward the practice field with my helmet under my arm, listening to the sound of those explosive hits, the crunch of that herd of cattle exploding into each other, the yells and whistles of the game I loved, the team I loved, echoing off the beige-brick walls of the distant campus buildings.

I stepped through the gate, to the field behind the blocked-out fence, reminded of just how privileged I was to be able to pass that barrier, to be on the inside—a part of the team.

"Sorry I'm late, Coach," I said to Coach Devine.

"Glad you're here, Rudy," he said, turning and yelling. "Now let's get back to work!"

I pulled my helmet on and took my position, fist in the grass, determined to give it my all. I could hear my own breath in the helmet—the muffled sound of the quarterback's call. I focused in. Everything on the line. *Time to play.* Instincts fired up. *The snap! Stop him. Smash!*

At the end of the day, Coach Devine told everyone to take a knee and we gathered around him for a pep talk and a rundown of what to expect on Saturday. He talked about how practice had been going well, but it was no time to rest. He talked about Georgia Tech and what we needed to do to win. How we weren't going to let another team come in here and push us around. And he talked about the fact that it would be the last home game in that stadium for all of us seniors. He said he knew what it meant to us all, and that for those players who dressed for the game, he would do everything he could to get them in for at least one play—as long as we were winning.

Everyone cheered.

"And one last thing," he said. "We're going to make one change to the dress list for Saturday. One player is going to give up his uniform . . . and Rudy Ruettiger's gonna dress."

I was floored. Speechless. As the players around me started applauding and hooting and hollering for me, patting me on the back, I just closed my eyes and smiled. I thanked God for giving me that blessing.

Then I opened my eyes, looked at Coach Devine, and said, "Thank you, Coach!"

"Good practice, everyone. See you tomorrow," he said.

As we got up and headed back to the locker room, more and more players came and slapped me on the back. "Alright, Rudy . . . Way to go,

Rudy!" Some of them got real emotional about it. I still couldn't believe it. It was almost as if it wasn't happening. Once again, as if it were a dream. It was a dream. A dream come true.

What I found out years later is that those four guys who came to visit me in my room at the ACC had actually gone to the coaching staff on my behalf and asked if I could dress. "Guys like Rudy deserve a chance," they argued. And Coach Devine agreed without hesitation.

I dressed in a fog, almost dizzy with emotion. *I almost quit!* The thought of it made me laugh! I almost quit when I was so close! What a mistake that would have been. I was overwhelmingly grateful to Coach Devine, to those players who hoisted me up with their pep talk, to Rudy the janitor, and to my brother Frank.

Frank! I had to call Francis right away. I suddenly snapped out of the fog and booked it over to the pay phone in the ACC. Of all the people in that house in Joliet, it was Frank who picked up the phone on the first ring.

"Frank, you're never gonna believe it," I said.

"What?" he asked.

"It's happening. I'm dressing for the game tomorrow!"

"What?" he yelled. "For real?"

"For real, Frank. Coach just announced it in front of everyone at practice!"

He was beside himself. "You've gotta tell dad."

"Is he there?" I asked.

"No."

"Frank, you've gotta tell him. And tell him I've got four tickets to the game. You've gotta be there!"

Frank cupped his hand over the phone and yelled out to the rest of my brothers and sisters, "Hey guys, Danny's gonna dress for the Notre Dame game tomorrow!"

Just as my Notre Dame dream coming true set the whole family off on one of the happiest dinners of our lives, and my making the football team sent the whole clan into cheers over the phone a little more than a year earlier, once again I listened as my whole family erupted with excitement over something I'd done. What a feeling that is, to spread that kind of joy.

I called Freddy, who just about blew a gasket on the phone. He wasn't sure he'd be able to make it up on such short notice, he said, but he'd be there in spirit and he'd be sure to listen to the game on the radio.

I called D-Bob, who flipped out too, and promised he'd be watching the game on the TV at his store.

I ran into Rudy the janitor down the hall and told him the news. He was so thrilled for me. "Come to the game!" I said. "I just might do that, Rudy. I just might do that," he replied with the biggest, broadest version of that smile he always seemed to wear. "I couldn't have done it without you, you know?" I said to him.

"Well, I don't think that's true. But thank you, Rudy. It's quite a story you have to tell."

It was quite a story. I had never really thought of it that way. Even after it showed up in the basketball program and the student paper, it never occurred to me that my story was anything special. It was just my life. But to dress for a game? To actually step into that stadium with a gold helmet? Me? This lousy student from Joliet who wasn't even a "college-bound" type of guy? Yeah. I guess that did make for a pretty good story. People always joke about this sort of thing, but I remember thinking, right then and there, *I'll be telling this story to my grandkids someday.*

That was a pretty cool feeling.

Of course, it wasn't nearly as cool as the feeling that would come my way in the next twenty-four hours.

It's funny, but on my way into the locker room the next day, it still didn't feel real. I remembered what Coach said—and said in front of the whole team—but I still had this nervous knot in my stomach as I walked up to check the dress list. I put my finger on the first name on the top of that piece of paper and dragged it down, down, down the list until finally, there it was. "Ruettiger—#45."

I kept my finger there for a moment, and just stared at it. All that waiting. All that anticipation. All that dreaming, hoping, praying. There it was. It was real.

It was real.

Twenty-Seven Seconds

My parents drove in from Joliet with my brothers Frank and John. I knew I wouldn't see them before the game. I'd be sequestered in the locker room, right where I needed to be. The stadium was packed, fifty-nine thousand strong, as it was for every home game. The noise of that crowd filtering in echoed through the tunnel and down the hallways into my ears every time somebody opened a door. And there I was, standing in front of my locker, looking at my first-ever game jersey—and a gold helmet.

I held up that shirt and just stared at it—45. At first, I fell into that old sense of feeling sorry for myself: everyone else's jersey had their names on it. Not mine. It was just a number. And for a few seconds, that's exactly how I felt.

I picked that helmet up off the bench and held it in my hands for a moment. Just a couple of years earlier I had broken the rules and snuck in here as a Holy Cross student to help touch up the paint on game helmets just like this one. Now here I was, about to put one on.

Nine years had flown by since I first stepped foot in this very locker room as a high school student, an overzealous fan rolling with the flow as the team filtered in from practice. Nine years since Ara Parseghian first laid eyes on me and told me to get out of there. I couldn't help but laugh to myself.

I wished Coach Parseghian could have been there right then.

I remember looking over at the brass plaque on one of the columns— a plaque featuring the famous quote from the film *Knute Rockne: All American*, starring Ronald Reagan as George Gipp: "Rock, sometime when the team's up against it, and the breaks are beating the boys, tell them to go out there with all they've got, and win just one for the Gipper. I don't know where I'll be then, Rock, but I'll know about it; and I'll be happy."

So much history. I just took it in. This one chance, this one shot to run out on that field, to be not just a part of the team but a part of the team's history—it was overwhelming. I was so grateful. I pulled that shirt over my head and caught a glimpse of myself wearing it in one of the mirrors, and suddenly any feeling of disappointment I felt over that silly notion of not having my name on my back went flying right out the window. This was it. I was part of the Notre Dame tradition. Me!

I basked in it for as long as I could.

In some ways, I wished it could have lasted forever—that feeling right before the payoff, right before the goal is reached, right before the dream comes true, when you know for certain there's nothing left to stand in your way, but before it's all over.

Nothing lasts forever, of course, and I was starting to feel the rush. I wanted to play!

Before I knew it, Coach Devine was calling us over to gather round and take a knee. I got down right in front, surrounded by all of my teammates, listening as he thanked us seniors one last time and instructed us to take it all in—reminding us that we would never forget this day for the rest of our lives . . . and that Georgia Tech was the number one offensive team in the nation.

Father James Riehle, the chaplain of the athletic department, led the team in prayer. I closed my eyes, knowing this was the one and only time I would ever have the opportunity to take part in that beautiful pre-game ritual. In my mind, I privately thanked God for the blessing. "Amen," I said, as Coach Devine took command once more. "Now let's go get 'em!" he yelled.

We all jumped to our feet: "Raaaahhh!" The noise was deafening as we made our way out of the locker room, all of those players ritually tapping the signs above the doorway and along the corridor on our way out. I joined right in, slapping my hand against the cold metal, joining the pulsing rap of one hand after another in a steady chain of solidarity.

The sunlight streamed and bounced off of the brick and concrete in the tunnel outside. I looked back over my shoulder, and through the gates at the top of the ramp I caught a perfectly framed view of Touchdown Jesus glistening in the sun. The Notre Dame marching band blew their horns and pounded their drums just outside the tunnel, energizing the crowd for a big Fighting Irish welcome. I could barely see around the rest of the team, they were all so big. I only caught brief glimpses of the field from the back of the group.

"Rudy! Where's Rudy?" someone yelled. All of a sudden some of the guys started pushing me forward. "Rudy, you lead us out!" They pushed me right up front. Suddenly the whole stadium came into view. Fifty-nine thousand people, all looking our way. Man, I thought sitting in the stands was exciting! Standing in that tunnel, feeling the anticipation of all those fans left me shaking. I kept jumping up and down, just trying to throw my energy around. I was so pumped.

I could barely hear the announcer over the roar of that crowd. I couldn't make out all the words. All I could make out was the build-up of excitement in the sound of his voice and the sudden roar of the crowd when, suddenly, *Raaaahhhhwww!*, the whole team exploded forward, bursting out of the tunnel and running onto that field as the band tore into the Notre Dame fight song: "Buuuh, buh buh, bu buuuh, bu buuuh!" My legs sprinted beneath me as my arms rose up in the air, carried by the sound of that crowd and the powerful feeling of running out flanked by the greatest team in college football history. I was flying on pure adrenaline. I could've run sprints from end zone to end zone for hours at that moment and not even felt it.

The photographers, the reporters, the cheerleaders, the guy in the Leprechaun mascot outfit, the site of Georgia Tech's team and coaches all blurred together in the excitement of those glorious, glorious seconds until finally I made my way to the sideline and found my spot on the bench— which is, by far, the best seat in the entire stadium. To sit and watch and feel every breath of every player, the pacing coaches, the physical contact of that team all around you while throwing your energy out to those players and feeling every move along with them, knowing that you're a part of it all and responsible for some of the work that went into creating each play, every move, every instinct that drives them, is greater than any skybox experience at any stadium in the world.

I loved every second of it.

I kept looking up in the stands, spotting familiar faces from all over campus, catching people waving and pointing at me, clearly excited to see me on the bench. Those articles about me had spread even further than I realized. My "story" had caught on. I spotted a few friends from back in my Holy Cross days at St. Joe's too—including Fred Rodgers and Bo Potter, the guy who tackled me in our very first interhall football practice. He was a full-time Notre Dame senior now, just like me, and he stood there with his camera in his hand. I wasn't the only guy who made the leap from Holy Cross to Notre Dame. A bunch of us "misfits" made it. *Look at us now!* I thought.

Funny thing is, I never told Bo or those other guys I was aiming to get on the varsity team. I was in that whole mind-set of not wanting anyone to tell me I couldn't do it. So this had to be a surprise to him. I can't even imagine what he must've thought seeing me sitting there on that bench!

Freddy wasn't there; he couldn't make it. But he was certainly there in spirit. I knew D-Bob was back at his store, watching it all unfold on TV—probably while drinking a few beers between visits from customers.

The game seemed to fly by. The Yellow Jackets of Georgia Tech managed to score one touchdown, but we basically dominated the entire game. In fact, we were so far ahead by the fourth quarter, Coach Devine started playing some of the scholarship seniors who were second- and third-team players, just to give them one final chance to get out there on that field. The fans loved that, and the players loved that. He played so many of 'em, I started to get a little ticked off. I wanted to run out there! I had already achieved everything I asked for, everything I dreamed of: but now I wanted to make sure my name appeared in the history books by stepping out onto that field and getting in the game! Heck, I wanted to get in there and sack the quarterback just like I'd done in practice, over and over for the last two seasons.

I kept looking at the clock. My time was almost up. We had possession of the ball with less than two minutes left to play, and we were up 17–3. There was no way we'd give up the ball at that point. The quarterback's sole mission was to run that clock down and give Notre Dame that victory.

All of a sudden, Coach Devine ran over to me. "Rudy, get out there! Go play!"

"I can't, Coach. I'm not offense!"

"It don't matter. Get out there. Now's your chance. I'll put you in for—"

"No, Coach. It wouldn't be right. It wouldn't be right." I didn't want to take a shot away from some player on that offensive team. As much as I wanted to get out there, it wouldn't be right. It wouldn't.

He looked disappointed. "Alright, Rudy."

Coach walked all the way to the other end of the bench and sent someone else in. He seemed to be distracted for a moment as the team huddled up before the next play.

That's when a minor miracle happened.

For some reason, the quarterback decided not to play it safe. He went against Coach Devine, against offensive coordinator Merv Johnson's orders, and threw a pass. He went for it, and we scored! The crowd went nuts.

Suddenly we were up 24–3 with less than a minute left to play, and our defensive line had to go take the field once more. Coach Yonto spun around and looked right at me: "Get in there, Rudy. Get in there, kid. Get in the kickoff."

I jumped up off the bench and pulled my helmet on, running out behind the rest of the kickoff team when I had to stop and turn back. "Where do I go?!" I yelled. I had never been a part of a kickoff before, even in practice.

Coach Yonto waved me over to the far side of the field, but I couldn't hear him. I just ran as fast as I could and lined up in what seemed to be the only position available. As I ran by the kicker I said, "Kick it to the guy so I can tackle him!" Well, that didn't happen. He kicked it all the way down to the end zone. I looked up at the clock: twenty-seven seconds.

I swear my whole life flashed before my eyes. "Twenty-seven seconds." I was twenty-seven years old. Time had flown but now it seemed stopped. I knew I would remember these next twenty-seven seconds as much as anything that had happened to me in those twenty-seven years. I could feel the weight of it and the excitement of it, all rolled up into one. The coincidence of my age and the clock seemed significant in that moment. So did the fact that the score was 24–3; a total of twenty-seven points had been scored in the game that was about to change my life forever.

I got in the huddle—my first time ever—and they called the play. I was defensive end, over on the far left side of the line. I could see that Georgia Tech's offense was tired. They were over it. They were playing in the final seconds of a horrible loss, and their morale was down. No fire in their eyes. I remember telling myself, *I'm gonna sack the quarterback!*

The snap came off and I broke free, jerking left and then right, arcing around until that quarterback was in my sights. *He's right there!* But he got his pass off too quickly, a high throw over the head of his wide receiver, who just barely managed to knock the ball away to keep our guys from intercepting.

I looked up at the clock again: five seconds. *Five seconds!*

This was it. Last play. Last chance. The Notre Dame fans were going crazy, and some of them were chanting something—this repetitive sound. Then I realized what it was: the student body was chanting my name!

"Ru-dy! Ru-dy! Ru-dy!"

It was unbelievable! The chant grew louder as more of the crowd joined in.

I planted my fist into that grass one last time. I drove my legs in, pounding them like a racehorse chomping at the bit to get out of the gate. I focused hard as ever. *He's mine. He's mine!* I could feel it. I had trained for this. I had worked my whole *life* for this! *If he passes again, I'm gonna get him!*

Adrenaline rushed through me. I could've run through a wall and not felt it. The sounds of the stadium disappeared. The only sound I heard now was my own breath in that helmet and the muffled audibles from the quarterback. All of a sudden he took the snap and I saw him drop back. I jerked left and then right, blowing right through the offensive line to come around right behind him. *There he was!* He still had the ball. I went for it, diving right into his waist, knocking him down with everything I had.

I hit the ground. So did he. The crushing rumble of collapsing to the earth left me rolling and reeling, and two seconds later I realized what happened: I did it. I made the tackle! I sacked the quarterback!

The crowd went nuts. I popped up and jumped in the air as the whole team erupted in victory. My teammates started knocking my helmet and slapping my back. I felt arms around my legs, my body hoisted from the ground. I looked down as two of my fellow players, Howard Meyer and Ronnie Cullins, hoisted me onto their shoulders and a bunch of other players circled around and started carrying me off the field: Tony Zappala, Ross Christensen, Teddy Burgmeier, Pete Johnson, Jay Achterhoff—all these great guys who had always been good to me. And all I could think was, *I almost quit! I almost quit! I was so close to quitting!*

The whole team didn't carry me off. Just that group of guys who felt connected to me. Who felt, much to my surprise, inspired by me. There was still division on that team, and I guess that's just the way life is. But the players who lifted me up did so from their hearts. They were living the dream and appreciating the magic of the moment. And to me, that's all that counted.

The view from that vantage point surpassed every expectation, every dream, every notion I had about what it would feel like to play football for Notre Dame. Blew them right out of the water. Flying over the field on the backs of those players, looking over the heads of my teammates and the defeated players of Georgia Tech to the cameras snapping away, to the crowd on their feet waving banners and shouting and hugging and high-fiving as the marching band played and those drums rattled my rib cage, to my clear view of Touchdown Jesus, who seemed to be looking me right in the eyes was bigger than anything I had ever dreamed. Bigger than anything I had ever imagined. Bigger than anything that anyone—including myself—ever thought could happen to me.

As we reached the end zone by the tunnel, the guys set me down and an AP reporter came running up to me. "I've never seen anything like that. All the years I've been covering Notre Dame, and I've never seen that kind of excitement. You're the first Notre Dame player ever to be carried off the field. It's the kind of thing that only happens in Hollywood!"

I just shook my head and smiled. I didn't know what to say. I didn't know what to do! The adrenaline was still pumping so hard I couldn't think straight.

The kind of thing that only happens in Hollywood. What a thing to say! What a thing for someone to say about something that happened—to *me*!

I still felt like I was floating when I walked out of that locker room. Crowds of friends and parents and fans gathered all around the door right next to the tunnel. In a way, it was like coming out of the Bengal Bouts. People slapping me on the back, congratulating me. I just kept saying thanks over and over. I was so thankful! I could hardly believe it was real.

Then I spotted my parents.

They both had that look in their eye. That look I saw at boot camp graduation. That look they had when I handed them the acceptance letter from Notre Dame.

My dad, though, had something extra written all over his face. Notre Dame football meant so much to him. It was difficult for me to imagine how awesome it must have been for him to watch his son out there on that field, sacking the quarterback no less. He put his hand out to shake my hand, and when I grabbed it, he hugged me. For the first time I can remember. A big, proud squeeze.

We held that hug in slow motion as a bunch of the other players filtered out and that excited crowd milled around us. When we finally let go, I swear I saw a tear in his eye.

To bring that sort of emotion out of him was something. Really something. It felt big, as if our lives had turned a corner. As if everything would be a little different from that day forward. As if what he saw in me had changed something in him. Once again, it just seemed proof positive that the act of pursuing my dreams, of never giving up, had opened more doors and produced more results than I ever could have imagined coming true. Not just for me, but for people all around me.

Across town, D-Bob was sitting in his sporting goods store watching the Notre Dame game on TV, and he told me later how he just about fell off his chair when he saw my number 45 run onto the field. He stood up and yelled at the TV screen: "Go Rudy!!!" When I sacked the quarterback, he said, he threw his beer can against the wall. He stuck his hands into his hair in disbelief, then spun around and grabbed the rest of a six-pack, throwing all of 'em against the wall. That was it. He was quitting drinking. Right then and there.

Thirty-five years later, he's still sober.

My friends. My family. The people I loved. The people who loved me. All of them had been affected by the fact that I followed through and achieved and exceeded this wild dream of mine.

Over time, I'd come to learn that those people I knew were only the tip of the iceberg. The inspiring effects of dreams fulfilled had run deeper than I ever imagined.

—

The semester ended. I went home to Joliet for the break. The holidays came and went, and the glow of the final twenty-seven seconds of that game never faded. Saying good-bye to teammates at the end of the season had been hard, but in a way, I didn't even have time to miss football once I got back to school. I had a whole new challenge in front of me: my final shot at the Bengal Bouts.

This time, riding high from the feeling of topping my wildest dreams on that football team, I decided I wanted the title. Not just a jacket. The title of Bengal Bouts champion.

I hit the gym harder than ever before. Hour upon hour. Six weeks straight. Working the bag, push-ups, sit-ups, weights, and medicine ball twice as hard as I'd ever pushed myself before. I ran every morning, all over campus, no matter what the weather. Everywhere I went I'd get cheers of, "Hey, Rudy! . . . Go get 'em, Rudy!" The whole student body was charging up for the big three-day battle, and with my underdog status solidified with that second-place finish the year before, there was absolutely no question in my mind that I'd have plenty of support in the stands.

My parents and a bunch of my brothers and sisters would be there too. They insisted they wouldn't miss it for the world.

It was difficult for me at times to come to grips with having so much support. I had faced so many obstacles and so many naysayers throughout my life that the idea of my friends, my family, and even perfect strangers lining up behind me now was an unusual feeling. I often asked myself, *How did that happen?* I'd look back at the path I took to reach that point and think, *How did I manage to do that?*

The magic of the entire climb up that hill had been taking it one step at a time. Never giving up. Never losing my faith. Never taking no for an answer, no matter how many doubts and fears I had or how many times I came close to quitting. I thanked God every day for the lessons. I thanked God every day for the gift of laying that path out in front of me every time I took a step. And even in the dead of winter, I stopped by the Grotto to pray for continued guidance and understanding as I made my stride toward yet another ambitious goal.

Six weeks of training. Three days of fights. The routine was exactly the same. The noise in that basketball arena was exactly the same. The matches progressed in almost exactly the same way they did when I climbed into that ring the previous year. First match: landed more punches. Won the match. Second match: against a guy who was bigger than me, got underneath his arms, landed lots of hits to the body. Won the match.

Now it was championship time. I kept my eyes on the prize. Focus.

There was no stopping me. I knew I could do this, no matter whom I faced. Of course, I had no idea that the whole David-and-Goliath factor was about to take on an epic new proportion: In the final match, I wound up facing another football player. A giant. It was amazing to me how different two bodies could shape up in the same weight class. The fans went nuts! The entire student body sat on the edge of their seats, and as soon as that first bell rang they were up on their feet. The place was rocking! Yet all of that noise fell off into the background. The power of focus is incredible, especially when a much bigger guy is throwing fists at your face. One slip, one break in concentration, and I could've gotten my head knocked off.

That wasn't gonna happen.

Round One: I was sizing him up. He was sizing me up. He knew the kind of tenacity he faced. He saw it at practice every day. He just had no idea what kind of punches I could throw. I found myself holding back a little. I didn't want him to know what he had in store. The psychology of the sport is half the fun.

Round Two: He popped me a couple of times, pretty good. I popped him right back. But I was still holding back. Still holding out. *Was he?* We seemed pretty evenly matched so far. I wanted to finish this thing right. That's when the crowd really started to get into it.

Just before the third bell, the start of the third and final round, I heard the sound of a few scattered voices chanting, "Ru-dy! Ru-dy! Ru-dy!" More joined in on the other side of the arena. "Ru-dy! Ru-dy! Ru-dy!"

I had to be careful not to get swept up in it. I had to be careful not to get overconfident. I tried to tune it out. I tried to focus on why I was in that ring. I tried to focus on all of the things in my life that I wanted to punch right out of existence. I thought back to fifth grade and the humiliation in front of my class; to high school and the constant feeling of inadequacy and hurt; to those fights we had down by the river; to the untimely deaths of Big Nick, Ralph, and Siskel; to the surprisingly lonely feeling of never being hugged by my father for all those years; to the jerks at the power plant and the naysayers of Joliet; to my dyslexia; to the elitists who didn't want guys like me to get into Notre Dame, who didn't want me on that football team, who didn't want me to work hard, to be the best, to help push them to victory while reaching my own goals.

Ding!

When that bell went off, I was raging. I put everything on the line. That guy didn't know what hit him! *Right, right, right. Left! Boom, boom, boom.* I never let up. He was tired. It showed. I felt more energized than I did in round one!

When the final bell came down, the sound of that crowd nearly knocked me over. There was no question in anyone's mind that I'd won the fight. They were screaming in victory and cheering me on long before the judge's decision was announced. And when that long, drawn-out, magnificent announcer's voice said "Ruuuuu-dyyy Ruuue-ttiger!" I jumped off the canvas and up in the air, and the crowd went nuts all over again.

This time, when I saw my dad ringside, he didn't hesitate to come straight in for a hug. Things were different between us now. He was different now.

That Bengal Bouts win was everything the sheer glory of victory should be. It was the embodiment of a dream come true. A beginning, middle, and end. An individual dream set into motion, worked at, fought for with nothing left to chance or the decisions of others, everything riding on my own two shoulders and the power of my conviction to win.

The Notre Dame football victory, the sacking of that quarterback, both in my mind and in my heart, were shared with every one of my teammates. This? This victory was mine and mine alone.

It was astounding to me that such big dreams could come to fruition back-to-back. I felt as if I was on a fast-moving train on a track aimed at the fulfillment of every dream I'd ever had—not to mention a few dreams I had never even imagined—since I first allowed myself to envision going to Notre Dame way back on the bridge of that ship, rolling toward Europe in heavy seas in the dark of night.

First came the gift of playing in that Notre Dame game. Second, this pure, individual victory at the Bengal Bouts. Next up? The fulfillment of a third and final dream, the ultimate goal at the end of the path: graduation.

There was only one thing that could derail me, and that was statistics. I thought I was done with math, but a course in statistics was a requirement of the sociology major, and I just couldn't wrap my mind around it. There was nothing about that class that made sense. I worked hard. I asked for help. I used all of Freddy's techniques in my studying. Didn't help. I was failing. With my heart so into the Bengal Bouts, I didn't put in the sort of after-class time that stats class required of me. But I should have.

I mistakenly had reached a point where I didn't care very much about my grades. I figured all that mattered was that I passed, so I could earn my degree. No one in the real world would go back and look at my grades. Once anyone saw that I graduated from the University of Notre Dame, it would be an automatic thumbs-up on my academic abilities!

Unfortunately that attitude, combined with my brain's inability to grasp the intricacies of statistics, added up to trouble. The only way I knew how to counter that trouble was to put in the sort of hard work and dedication that had worked for me elsewhere. To show up to every class. To let that professor know how hard I was struggling. To show him that I wanted to pass. On any given day, only about half of the students showed up in that professor's classroom, so I hoped my constant presence would pay off when he sat down to give our grades. I prayed! Especially as May approached.

They documented my tackle in the Notre Dame yearbook. That 1976 edition of *The Dome* features a photo of me sacking that Georgia Tech quarterback. Seeing a photo of myself in that book, surrounded by photos of all of the great players on that team, was something. There I was, right there with them. A part of the team. A part of that history forever. Just as I had dreamed. Even better than I had envisioned.

Around the same time the yearbooks came in, our class rings came in too. I had my Notre Dame graduation ring, with that *ND* on the side, just like the one that officer wore in the navy. Slipping that heavy golden ring onto my own finger felt like coming full circle. A journey, almost complete.

The journey, of course, had been better than I envisioned. Bigger. More fulfilling. But I still felt remarkably unsettled. Unsure about something. One part of it still felt like a dream.

The graduation ceremony was set to be held in the ACC, the very building where I worked, slept, and lived for the past two years. I helped set up the chairs. I sat in my room as they put together all of the final touches. And when they laid out all of our signed degrees on a great big set of tables, I snuck in to take a peek. Quite honestly, I wasn't 100 percent positive I was going to graduate. It just didn't seem possible! I was sure I had missed something. Some credit. Some class. I was told they would send you a letter if you weren't going to graduate. I hadn't received that letter. Still, I was worried. *What if that stats professor flunked me and never let me know?*

I scanned through the degrees, alphabetically, one after another, skipping quickly through them and over them until finally I found it: Daniel E. Ruettiger. There it was. My degree. My University of Notre Dame degree. I checked to make sure the signature at the bottom was there, just to make sure it was official.

It was. *I had proof!*

I got butterflies in my stomach as I walked back to my room. When my parents showed up, they were dressed to the nines and their faces were flashier than anything they wore. They were beaming. They melded right into that crowd of proud parents—the rich, the elite, the exclusive club that is Notre Dame. They were one of them now. They wore that look of pride that says "My son graduated from Notre Dame." They could wear that look wherever they went now, for the rest of their lives. That was powerful.

We posed for snapshots in my cap and gown, and they went in to take their seats. I joined my classmates in line, and before we knew it we were all filtering into the arena. It was awesome. Such a spectacle. All of those students, some fifteen hundred graduates, and all of those proud parents packing the stands right up to the rafters.

Vernon E. Jordan Jr., executive director of the National Urban League, was our graduation speaker. He was a pretty eloquent guy, from what I remember, and had a few laughs in his speech as well. But all any of us really cared about was getting to the big moment.

With that many students, it would take hours and hours to have everyone come up to get their degree one at a time. So instead, they just had all the MBA students stand up together to acknowledge their commencement, then all the law students, and so forth. And then finally, at the end, came the big group: the undergraduates.

To stand up and cheer with the rest of my graduating class made me feel more a part of Notre Dame than any other moment. I had come to the school through a side door, struggled to find my place before I was ever a student, worked my way through school, lived in a tiny room just outside of this arena, and never quite felt like I was fully a part of it . . . until that moment. That moment when I suddenly felt like no one could deny it. Nobody could take away the fact that I was a Notre Dame graduate. I was a part of the tradition. *This is real*, I thought. *This is great!*

I threw my hat in the air along with everyone else and then rushed right over to pick it up off the floor. I wanted the keepsake! I wanted to keep everything. I wanted to hold on to that proof that I was there, that I did it, that I accomplished what everyone said I couldn't. Every tangible piece I could hold was important to me, and I knew I would hold those items for as long as I lived.

When I met up with my parents after the ceremony, I gave them both a great big hug. And when I looked in their eyes, I decided to let go of one of those tangible bits of my personal Notre Dame history: I gave my Notre Dame ring to my dad. I just felt like he should have it. I knew he would cherish it. He tried to refuse. He said I should keep it. "Dad, I'll buy a replacement, and then we'll both wear one!" He liked that idea. He put it on his finger and looked at it. A Notre Dame ring. On Dan Ruettiger's hand. Just a few years earlier, that would've seemed like the most far-fetched thing in the universe. Yet there it was. He smiled at that. And I smiled right at him.

After all of that glory, all of that triumph, it was a short walk back to my room. Hundreds of parents and professors and coaches and students were still milling about as I stepped in and closed the door. I had already packed up most of my things. The walls were bare concrete blocks again. My bed was stripped. My desk was cleaned off and my duffel was full. I suddenly felt incredibly sad.

I sat down on the edge of the bed and took a big deep breath. I didn't want to leave. *What the heck am I going to do now?* I thought.

For all of my big dreams, big goals, big hopes, I hadn't spent any time thinking about what I was going to do once I graduated. I guess some part of me, right up until that moment when I stood up and cheered and threw my hat in the air, maybe some part of me didn't really fully believe that it was ever going to happen. I prayed for it to happen. I convinced myself that I knew it would happen. I *willed it* to happen. But now that it had, I sat there dumbstruck.

I felt so happy, so fulfilled, so overwhelmed, so proud—and so lost.

What am I gonna do now?

Part III

Up Against the
Red Velvet Ropes

Rocky Too

Graduating from Notre Dame set me on a course not unlike the one I set after high school. For a while, I wound up drifting. Dreamless. Unsure what I really wanted to do with my life. Void of any real goals. I hadn't thought ahead. Maybe I hadn't believed in myself quite enough to make plans for a time after my Notre Dame dream had been achieved. In some ways, all that lack of planning does is leave you vulnerable to saying yes to whatever offer might come along. You'd better hope and pray that the offers you take are good ones, and if they're not, that you at least have the vision to learn something from the experiences that unfold in your directionless state.

That directionless state isn't necessarily a bad thing. Not at all. Sometimes we need that rest in life. A breather. A time to just let loose and see what happens. Those times offer up a great sense of discovery. Outside forces can wind up taking you to places you might not ever have imagined for yourself—the way the Vietnam War era took me into the navy. Without the navy, I wouldn't have gotten to Notre Dame!

Once again, that's easy to see in retrospect. In the middle of it, I wasn't so sure. It's scary to live life feeling trapped or confused or unhappy with your job. It's hard to trust that anything will ever change. But that trust is what you need the most. That faith that you're on the right path, even if it doesn't feel quite right at the moment, is important. The truth in life comes from following your intuition and the gut feelings that God gives you, and then making the right choices when opportunities present themselves. And heck, if opportunities aren't presenting themselves, then it's all about having the guts to make the kinds of choices that *give* you those opportunities.

At the very least, every experience you have, every job you take, and every path you walk will teach you something. Pay attention to the signs along the way, and you never know what new dreams and ambitions will develop.

As I was on my way out of the ACC after the graduation ceremony, I ran into Coach Devine.

"What are you gonna do next year, Rudy?"

I told him I had no idea. I hadn't really thought about it. And right then and there, he told me he really liked the way the younger kids on the team connected with me, and he wondered if I'd be interested in taking a job as his graduate assistant.

"Heck ya!" I said.

I had no idea what that job would entail. I had no idea what would be required of me. All I knew is that an opportunity to stay tied into Notre Dame football just dropped in my lap, so I went for it. After all, what was a football player to do after his football career ended? Coach. Working as a GA would put me on a path toward coaching. It made sense. It's what people expected. It was a normal path for someone like me.

But was it the path I wanted?

I found the answer pretty quickly. Being a GA meant I had to enroll in a couple of graduate level courses at Notre Dame. Sitting in those chairs, listening to lectures, taking notes—man, I was done with school. I didn't want any part of it. I was burned out. I just couldn't do it anymore. And what's the point of taking classes if they're just making you miserable or you wind up skipping all the time?

I remembered back to seeing Parseghian in his office at 6:00 a.m. and 10:00 p.m. at the ACC, and I started watching the routines of Devine and all of the assistant coaches. I realized that coaching for Notre Dame was a 24/7 job, filled with paperwork and politics, pressures from parents, school officials, and the NCAA. It never stopped! I saw coaches playing inferior players over talented players because of political pressures from outside the game. I never realized why they did that stuff until I was on the inside, and now that I was there, I didn't want to be a part of it.

I enjoyed the coaching part of it. They wound up placing me on the junior varsity team, coaching freshmen. Special teams was my assignment, and I loved pushing those guys to be great. I had long ago let go of all those goofy notions that so many coaches hold on to—the stuff about yelling and screaming and putting kids down. I got out there and worked them hard, praised them for their work, made sure they stayed focused, jumped in and showed 'em how it should be done by example rather than words, and did everything I could to encourage their camaraderie while inspiring them to be the best. During regular practice, Devine put me in charge of the scout team, so I was coaching kids who were just like me— the outsiders, the human tackle dummies, the walk-ons. It was awesome. They all knew my story. They all knew about Rudy. They wanted to *be* like Rudy! That was a strange feeling. They all wanted a shot at running out of that tunnel and seemed to understand the hard work and sacrifice it would take to get there. So they listened to me, and I helped make sure they all felt like they were part of the team, valued resources on the gridiron. I loved that.

Still, the coaching aspect seemed to be the thing that consumed the smallest amount of my time each week. Instead, it came down to the assistant work. Grunt stuff. I had done a lot of that sort of work in life already, and my heart just wasn't in it anymore. Then there was the paperwork. The organizational tasks. Sitting for what seemed like endless hours in meetings in which no decisions were ever really made, and the only thing anyone agreed upon was the date and time of the next meeting. Not exactly the kind of stuff that makes you jump out of bed in the morning.

Another graduate assistant and I were tasked with splicing game film together for the coaches; it was a tedious task and not an easy thing to do when you've got dyslexia. I kind of liked working with the film. I liked the idea of editing things together to make everything make sense so the coaches could use that raw film in teaching. Of course, when I was distracted (as I was pretty easily, and often) a couple of times I would grab the wrong bits of film and splice 'em backward. I'd wind up putting the offense with the defense so the sequence made no sense at all. That wasn't a help to anyone.

As the end of that first semester as a post-grad approached, I realized the whole thing made no sense. It just wasn't me. It wasn't the way I wanted to be spending my time. It's funny, but unless you have a real direction in college—unless you know that you're inspired to be a doctor, for instance—you're left at the end of those four years with a tremendous feeling of uncertainty. Everyone thinks college should be all about education, but if you don't have dreams that you're applying those lessons to, what good is all that education? If you don't know where or how you're going to apply that education, is it really going to stick in your brain?

By December 1976, I was desperately in need of some inspiration. I didn't realize it at the time. I wasn't consciously seeking it out. I didn't prepare for it. I wasn't looking for it when it came. It was a typical Saturday night, and all I was doing was going to the movies. But as I sat down in that South Bend theater and the lights dimmed, a whole new path was set in motion right in front of me. A whole new path that God laid down, that would take me places I had never even dreamed.

The film I was there to see was *Rocky*, and it was unlike any other movie I had ever seen. I always enjoyed going to the movies. I often thought fondly of my teenage days at the old Rialto Theater in downtown Joliet. I loved the escape of disappearing into another world for a couple of hours at a time. But this? This movie was about people who seemed to come from *my* world. As if the cameras knew who I was. The setting in the grittier, downtrodden, working-class neighborhoods of Philadelphia reminded me of the power plant and the bars and the criss-crossing train tracks of Joliet. And this character, this "Rocky Balboa," reminded me, just a little bit, of me! He wasn't the best-looking guy. He certainly wasn't born with a silver spoon in his mouth. He talked a little funny. He was stocky. Gruff. In a lot of ways, people would look at him like any other working-class bum. But there was something about him. A little fire in his belly. A passion. A dream. And when he saw a shot to go after that dream, he set his sights on the goal and just went for it. The harder he dreamed, the better things got. People came into his life who would help him. His coach, Mickey, was a gift—almost the way Freddy was a gift to me at Notre Dame. He found love and support from a new girlfriend, Adrian, and his buddy named Paulie, who reminded me a little bit of D-Bob when it came to his sense of humor. He wasn't a naturally talented boxer. He wasn't a naturally talented athlete. But he had heart. He had passion. And his dream wasn't to be the world champion. His dream was just to get into that ring and go toe-to-toe with the best. To last all fifteen rounds— something no one else had done against the mighty champ named Apollo Creed. I could relate to that dream! It was awesome!

Having been in the boxing ring myself, I swear that I could feel every punch, every swing, every broken nose and bruised rib those guys took during the fight at the end of that movie. The music had me up on the edge of my seat. The power of that whole story grabbed me and set my heart racing like I was right in that ring myself. And when Rocky did it, when he made it, when that final bell rang and he knew he had made it through all fifteen rounds—that he had accomplished the impossible, the thing no one said could be done—I cheered out loud! I had never done that in a movie theater. I had tears in my eyes. I could hardly believe the way my emotions poured out of me. Over a movie!

I walked out into the frigid air of a wintery South Bend night, my breath gathering in clouds all around my face as I strolled back to my little off-campus apartment, thinking, *Man, I want to make a movie like that! I want to make a movie like that about* my *story! How cool would that be?*

It wasn't much more than a thought at that moment. A ridiculous fantasy. I knew nothing about Hollywood or movie-making whatsoever. All I knew was that film had created a feeling in me like something I had never felt before. All I knew was that whenever I told my story of my twenty-seven seconds of glory on that Notre Dame football field, people reacted. They were blown away. All I knew, way deep down inside, is that seeing *Rocky* had somehow changed my life. Maybe I wouldn't make a movie. I wasn't delusional. But there was something about the message of that movie, the inspiration it planted in my heart that would serve me going forward. I knew it. I just knew it.

The spring semester began and I sat in the stands watching other people, younger people, take to the ring at the Bengal Bouts; spring football got underway, and I found myself out on those same fields, coaching a bunch of kids and participating in the recruiting process as it went into full swing for the following year. But I simply felt lost. I felt like I was sitting in the stands at high school football games, reliving old glories, Friday nights under the lights. It felt exactly the same as it did back in those post–high school years. I didn't want to be there anymore, but I also had no idea what I wanted to do, where I wanted to go, or how the heck I was going to get there.

With all of that confusion, I felt like I needed a coach for my life that was as good as the coaches I'd had in football. *I need my very own Mickey! Like Rocky!* I thought.

Well, guess what? My wish was about to come true. And the Mickey would be someone I had known and admired for years.

Ara Parseghian had stayed right there in South Bend after he left the job as head coach, and he always seemed to be around campus. He was moving on with his life in many ways, transitioning from coaching to becoming a commentator for ABC Sports. He'd always say "hi" when he saw me, and we'd wind up talking about whatever was going on with the team. He seemed interested in what I was up to, and I was very interested to hear what he was up to. I was fascinated that a guy could move from one unbelievably successful career into another the way he was later in life. It developed into a friendship of sorts, which my old self couldn't really have imagined. He seemed like such a god from afar. Then almost like a father-figure type once he was my coach. Now? He was just a good guy who I was always happy to run into. I guess people are people, no matter how great or talented they are. The fact that I find myself talking to everyone, no matter what their position is in life, has proven that to me over and over again. There's no reason to hesitate to talk to anyone in life. At heart, we're all just people. You know?

Toward the end of that post-graduate year, I got into a real serious talk with Parseghian about my future. "I don't want to coach," I told him. "I don't know what I want to do."

"You should go sell insurance," he said to me. "You'd be great at it."

"I don't know anything about insurance. Where would I go sell insurance?" I asked.

"Go see Pat Ryan. Pat Ryan & Associates up in Chicago. I coached him at Northwestern."

Given my lack of direction, I figured the best thing I could possibly do with my life at that moment was to follow Coach's advice. So I did. Turns out Pat Ryan was one of the richest guys in the world, and his insurance agency was a huge, successful organization. One call from Parseghian got me in the door, and I wound up getting interviewed at 9:00 a.m. a few days later.

The long and short of that meeting was pretty simple: "You're not qualified," the interviewer told me.

"Well, what do I need to do to get qualified?" I asked.

"You need to be around the business more."

"Is that all? Okay, then. I got it," I said. If he wanted me to be around the business, I figured I'd stay right there and be around the business as much as I could. Starting that very moment.

I left his office and took a seat in the lounge. Stayed right there. All day. Never moved.

Around six o'clock, that interviewer came out of his office headed for home. He spotted me sitting there. "Hey," he said, "didn't I interview you this morning?"

"Yes, sir," I replied.

"Ruettiger, right? What are you still doing here?"

"You said stick around until you get the experience, so that's what I'm doing."

He kind of chuckled to himself. "Alright, Mr. Ruettiger. You come and see me tomorrow. You're hired."

Hey, the way I saw it, when Ara Parseghian tells you to go get a job, you go do it! I wasn't about to fail. If he didn't hire me that day, I would have kept coming back until he did. Call that hardheaded, but it's basically the same way I've accomplished all of my big accomplishments. Why change what's working, right? Perseverance is everything.

The insurance business wasn't easy. It required a lot of math and a pretty decent understanding of statistics, which of course I was no good at. It took me three or four tries to pass the test just to get my license. But I was great at sales meetings. The primary thing we were doing was selling insurance add-ons to car dealerships—extra insurance policies that the dealerships could sell to their car-buying clients to protect for all sorts of damages and circumstances not covered by regular car insurance. It was great for the dealers and great for us; it amounted to basically nothing but profit in the long run because so few of these policies ever resulted in real claims. Talking a good game came easy to me. My Notre Dame connections and my little tale of sacking the quarterback in the final home game my senior year was a hook for just about anyone I met who was into sports. People loved my story! And when they loved my story, they almost always wound up buying whatever it was I was selling. It was pretty cool.

It wasn't the most exciting or inspiring business to be in, of course. It was easy to get down. Easy to feel like I was just going through the motions. That's pretty true for anyone working at a big company, I suppose. But Pat Ryan & Associates was great about doing little things to keep employee morale up, including sending each of us to training seminars. They were basically coaching sessions aimed at firing us up. Like pep rallies. And man-oh-man, did they work! I remember this one speaker who got up in front of this room full of insurance salesmen in shirts and ties and just about tore the roof off. He just had this way of talking, almost like a great preacher or a coach, that got us thinking big, dreaming big, imagining how much money we could be making if we really applied ourselves, really got to work, really thought outside the box and went after every sale like it was the most important sale on earth. He made us feel good about our career choices. He made us feel like we should be grateful and happy to be helping people and helping ourselves while working for a big powerful company and contributing to a team that included the best of the best in the business, which meant that each and every one of us were among the best of the best! By the end of that guy's motivational speech, we were all on our feet cheering. We walked out of that boring beige hotel conference room like we were running out of the locker room into the Super Bowl. All just to sell insurance!

How the heck did that guy do that? I wondered. *Man, I would love to be able to give talks like that someday!*

I was so fired up, I started seeking out bigger, better assignments. I was single and willing to travel, so the company started sending me all over the country to tackle the biggest jobs out there. All the while, my bank account kept growing. I cleared over $40,000 in a single year! This was the late 1970s. It was almost unimaginable.

All my life I dreamed of having that kind of money. All my life I dreamed of not wearing hand-me-down clothes, or driving on bald tires, or skimping on the food I bought. It was wonderful. Having money at my fingertips certainly made things easier.

I was off working in Baltimore, at a dealership with all kinds of problems, when my job started to lose its fire. I don't know why. Maybe I needed another pep talk. Maybe I needed another seminar. Or maybe, just maybe, the fact that I was good at something and making good money at it wasn't enough for me.

Maybe, I started to think, *this isn't my calling.*

By the time *Rocky II* hit in June 1979, I was ready to move beyond my insurance career. I was ready to move on, period. The inspiration of *Rocky*, the idea that it's possible to conquer your dreams, to drive your own fate, was amplified in that sequel, and I felt like it was time to find a sequel to all of that success I had unlocked at Notre Dame.

That's when I turned the fantasy of making a movie based on my life into a dream. A dream I could work toward. I started writing down ideas for scenes. I had no idea how to write a screenplay, no idea how to get a

screenplay made, who to call, or who to give it to. Didn't matter. I started
jotting these ideas down in a notebook. Started sketching out the way my
story followed the arc of a movie. I thought back to that AP reporter, who
said to me right after my teammates carried me off the field, "This only
happens in Hollywood!" That guy had planted the seed in me right then
and there! It felt like fate. It felt like destiny. It didn't feel like a fantasy—
something that would never actually happen; it felt like a dream in the same
way playing Notre Dame football had been a dream, a distantly attainable
dream.

But I also had a more immediate dream: to quit the insurance business
and go to work for myself. It almost didn't matter what business I went
into. I just wanted to be my own boss. I was tired of answering to someone else all the time. I was tired of not knowing when and if I might get
transferred to some other part of the country. I was fed up with the same
old routines and fed up with being a salesman. It seemed like I spent 90
percent of my day getting turned down. "No! . . . No thanks . . . Let me
think about it and call you tomorrow . . . Sorry, no." Any great salesman
will tell you it takes a ton of no's to get to one yes, but that process is tiring.
Exhausting. I was ready for a change.

I remember watching the crew that came into the car dealership in
Baltimore to buff the floors each night. I found out what kind of money
those guys were getting paid, and it was pretty good. I had plenty of
experience picking up soda pop and all kinds of sticky stuff at the Notre
Dame stadium and helping around the ACC. It seemed like the kind of
work I could get into without any training, and there were certainly lots
of offices and businesses that needed cleaning crews. Selling businesses on
hiring me would be a heck of a lot easier than selling insurance. And the
work would be good. Manual labor. A start and a finish. Not these endless
days of just getting to the next sale.

So I jumped in with both feet. I started picking up side jobs while
continuing the insurance gig. I convinced a guy to let me live at his ware-
house while I got my act together and bought the equipment I needed.
I was scraping it all together and making things work however I could,
just like I did back at Notre Dame. As weeks went by, more work started

to come my way. I needed help and added a couple of guys to my crew. I actually enjoyed buffing floors, at least for a while. There was something meditative and pensive about it. Holding that machine, listening to that whir, my mind would wander—and it almost always wandered to my movie idea. I just couldn't let it go. I kept picturing my life from the outside, through a camera. I thought of splicing the pieces of my life together like splicing the practice films back at Notre Dame, putting the pieces in order so they all made sense. The people in my life started to come alive to me in a whole new way, like characters on a screen.

I made sure to do top-notch work everywhere I went, hoping that my good work would shine bright enough to attract the attention of other clients and garner strong word-of-mouth recommendations from the clients I had. It was tiring, juggling the two gigs. But it worked. A few months into it, I picked up a chance to take on a major client—a client that would require me to hire a real crew; buy bigger, better equipment; and really turn this thing into a full-fledged cleaning business with me at the helm. The income it would produce would allow me to quit the insurance business for good. There was just one problem: in order to get started, I'd need a chunk of cash up front.

I wasn't real good with saving my money. I had never had money before, and I enjoyed spending what I had. I didn't have enough history or any kind of a business plan that would allow me to go to a bank for a small business loan. So I really only had one choice: I had to find myself an investor. Someone willing to loan me the money and let me pay them back, with interest, of course, when I could.

There was only one person I could think of who might be willing to do that. So I hopped a plane back to South Bend and went to see my Mickey: Ara Parseghian.

Parseghian heard me out. He listened to my plan. He loved the fact that I had already landed this big contract even though I didn't have the money to get the job done. It was forward thinking. It was risky. But he also knew how hard of a worker I was, and that I wouldn't let him down. Parseghian was involved in an insurance business of his own at the time, with a business partner. He didn't even take time to think about it. He heard me out and right then and there he turned to his partner and said, "Write him a check. Rudy's gonna make it." When his partner asked how he could be so sure and wondered whether or not they should take a day to think on it, Parseghian said, "No. I coached him. I've seen how hard he works. He's gonna do this."

The deal I made with Parseghian was a handshake deal. There wasn't any contract. There weren't any lawyers involved. It was simple. He was a man of his word. I was a man of my word. That's all that mattered. We shook on it, and the deal was done.

I was pumped! With twenty grand in my pocket, I high-tailed it back to Baltimore and bought everything I needed. I put my crew together and lined everything up. I got behind one of those buffers, always a part of the team, showing my workers how dedicated to the job each and every one of us had to be in order to make this company shine, and we buffed, and polished, and swept, and mopped, and repeated that process day in and day out, working nights when the workplaces were empty and the rest of the world was out grabbing a beer and watching the game on TV.

Then suddenly, eight months later, I woke up one morning with a start. *What the heck am I doing?!* I wondered. I thought about the back-breaking night before and looked ahead to the backbreaking day in front of me and realized that I no longer enjoyed running this little company at all. Here I had created a wildly successful, already profitable business, almost overnight, and I couldn't stand being in charge of it. It was too much pressure. I couldn't think of anything else. I had started to let my movie dreams slide in favor of budgeting and schedules. I needed to change that. But I couldn't just drop it and not pay the loan back to Parseghian.

I've gotta sell this sucker!

I had met a guy with a fire in his belly who kept peppering me with questions about how quickly I'd grown my business. He owned a fire clean-up business, the kind of operation where they come in after a fire or other disaster and remove all the smoke and damage. That was a great business, but it was unpredictable. No steady client stream. What he needed to augment his business was a steady routine, like the one I had developed. I went to him and offered to sell him all of my contracts for twenty-five grand. "Yeah!" he said, and we signed the deal in a matter of hours. I gave Ara his principal back, but with no interest. I needed to keep that extra money to live on, and he respected that. As part of the deal, I stayed on for a couple of years running the cleaning side of things for the new owner. Knowing that I wasn't the real boss anymore felt like someone had released a pressure valve on the top of my head. Funny how after years of wanting to be my own boss, the demands of that particular career turned out to be a little more than I bargained for. Once all that steam went out, I suddenly had space to think about my real dream again: the dream of making my movie.

It's a strange thing when you talk about your dreams, especially big, far-out dreams like mine. Some people laugh. Some people think it's really cool, but then the conversation moves on to something in their own lives and that's the end of it. Then every once in a while someone gets so fired up about your dream that it unlocks a dream of their own. Those people are fun to be around.

During my time in Baltimore I met a high school coach. Great guy. Enthusiastic, fun to be around, great coach who believed in inspiring his kids to be their best. When I told him my story, he went nuts for it! He loved inspirational movies, and he was a total movie junky. We would ride around in the car, go to lunch, meet up for a beer somewhere, and spend the whole time talking about Hollywood and the great movies we'd seen, trying to pick apart what it was that made certain movies so great, so powerful, so emotional. He asked me if he could help write a script for my story, and he was so pumped up about it, how could I say no? I suddenly had a partner in this, a partner who took it as seriously as I did.

That coach did a whole bunch of studying and reading up about the art of writing screenplays, and then the two of us would get together and write. Mostly I would talk, he would type, and we'd just put stuff down on paper. He'd show it to me, we'd edit it; we'd rework it 'til it felt good, reading the parts out loud to each other as if we were actors. We didn't really know what we were doing. It didn't matter. It was fun. And by the time my contract with the cleaning company was up, by the time

I decided it was time for me to get the heck out of Baltimore and try to pursue this movie with everything I had, the coach and I had completed a screenplay that was nearly two hundred pages long. It didn't even feel hard! Working on it a little bit at a time the way we did, it just happened. It didn't feel like work.

It wasn't a very good screenplay, and we never wound up doing anything with it. As time went on, I would learn that a screenplay translates to about one minute of screen time per page, on average. Which means the movie he and I developed would have been over three hours long! Something in the range of 90 to 110 pages would have been more appropriate. *But how the heck could you fit a whole story into ninety pages?* I wondered. It seemed like a complete mystery.

What wasn't a mystery was my desire to go to the place where I thought I would find lots of support for this movie. No, not Hollywood. Not New York. I'm talking about a place steeped in the traditions that flooded my story. A place full of history and pride and a reverence for the ideals and the positive message I wanted my movie to promote.

Of course, I wouldn't be moving anywhere without a job and some income. So the first thing I did was go crawling back to the insurance company to ask for my old job back. Luckily for me, they remembered who I was, and I didn't burn any bridges when I left. After seeing the initiative I had taken in starting my own successful business, they even did me one better: they promoted me to district manager. So leaving that job, taking that risk, taking that leap, following my gut on the way in, and on the way out, yielded positive results all around. I learned from it, wound up better off because of it. No harm, no foul. It was nerve-racking and a little worrisome at times to have my life in that kind of flux. But I was very glad I did it.

There was one more very important benefit to come from that whole endeavor: now that I was a manager, the insurance company agreed to let me manage the Michigan/Indiana territory. And that assignment allowed me to move back and set up my home base in exactly the place I wanted to be for the sake of getting my movie made: South Bend, Indiana.

14

Chalk Talk and Hollywood Dreams

It was 1986 when I bought my first condo about a mile from the Notre Dame campus. Ten years had come and gone in what felt like ten minutes. It had been ten years since I threw my graduation cap into the air and walked out wondering, *What now?*

A decade of my life had flown by, and I still didn't feel like I had the answer to that question. I had a dream. I had my movie. And that was enough to keep me going. But putting that dream first was hard. It's hard to do that. It's hard to keep a dream alive when life and all of its worries are in the way. How was I supposed to find time to work on a movie idea when my job kept me on the road, traveling, selling, filing paperwork, making phone calls, taking phone calls, and attending meetings, seminars, and more? Let alone finding some personal time to spend with friends, or even think about dating or settling down. It's a wonder anyone ever finds a way to turn a dream into reality. When years go by, and nothing happens, it's easy to just forget about it.

But that's the one thing I never, ever did. I never, ever let myself forget about my dream. One way I did that was to tell everyone I knew all about it. I basically went around blabbing to anyone who would listen that I was going to make a movie about my life. If they knew my story already, they would either believe it and support my dream, or they wouldn't. No skin off my back. If they didn't know my story, I would tell it to them; and in all those years of telling my story, the tale of where I came from, of how I pursued my dream, of making it onto the football team and then getting on that field and sacking that quarterback in the final moments of our final home game, to get carried off the field for the first time in Notre Dame history . . . the story never failed. I never met one person who didn't get excited by it, who didn't say, "Man! That really is a movie!" Not one.

That's what kept me going. That's what kept my dream alive, even in the face of real-life rejection.

One of the first things I did in South Bend was to bring my movie idea to a series of administration officials at Notre Dame. A lot of them liked the story. They loved my enthusiasm. I had it in my head that my movie would be really good PR for Notre Dame—after all, it would be a heartwarming movie with a positive message, I told them. I even went to the PR department with this idea in my head that they might be willing to fund part of the movie, because it would send such a strong message to potential students.

That whole idea turned out to be a fantasy. Notre Dame was doing just fine in the PR department. The school had more applicants than they could ever desire. They liked their elite position in the world, and it became very clear that the idea of doing a film about some kid who didn't really accomplish that much, who came into the university through a junior college in his junior year, just wouldn't cut the mustard. Plus, they hadn't let a film crew step foot on campus for almost fifty years—not since the filming of *Knute Rockne: All American*—and the legacy of that film was strong enough to carry Notre Dame throughout history, as far as the administration was concerned. They weren't going to let Hollywood play around with their image. So no matter how many times I went back, they simply wouldn't read the script, and they rejected the notion that they would ever allow another film to be shot on campus. The final decision seemed to rest with the University Relations department, and their polite but firm message to me basically amounted to, "Get lost!"

I suppose a lot of people would have given up the dream at that point. I mean, if the school where your dream movie is set doesn't want you and says it's never going to happen, then what good is the dream, right?

Don't forget, though: everything about Notre Dame had been a closed door to me from the very beginning. When it came to that school, I had learned through experience that "no" simply didn't mean "no." What I had to do was find a side door, maybe even find the secret keys in order to step inside that castle. My film wasn't ready yet, anyway. I had time. And that's always a good thing.

So as ridiculous and unrealistic and impossible as it seemed that Rudy Ruettiger could get a movie made about his life story, that dream never died. Not even for a moment. Not even while it sat dormant, covered in frost, while I worked hard just to pay my bills and to learn to stand on my own two feet in South Bend.

Coincidently or not, another film came along the very same year I returned to Indiana, a film that would fire me up and inspire me all over again to keep going: *Hoosiers*. An underdog story, on lots of different levels. A small-town Indiana high school basketball team. A coach with a questionable past. A town drunk. A victory as powerful as *Rocky*'s, with a positive message that brought audiences to their feet. It was just what I wanted my own movie to be. I knew the elements were there. I just wished with all my heart I could find the right people to help me bring it to life.

What I should have done is taken notes. I should have sat there in the theater and watched the credits and written down the names of every person who helped make that film. I should have sought those geniuses out one by one. I wasn't smart enough to do that. Not yet. Maybe the process would have been shorter if I had. It's strange, but in some ways, I didn't think of movies being made by individuals. The whole thing seemed so big. "Hollywood" seemed more like an untouchable entity than just a bunch of individuals doing good work and forming teams to get that work to the big screen. I didn't understand any of it yet.

Things happen in their own time anyway. God has a plan. I have no doubt about that. The thing I needed from *Hoosiers* at that moment, in the fall of 1986, was the inspiration—and maybe a sign—to tell me that I was headed in the right direction and let me know that the powerful, positive message I could send with my personal story would be valued. After all, *Hoosiers* wound up being a big hit, nominated for multiple Academy Awards. This was the '80s, when every other film in theaters seemed to be about a big adventure, special effects, teenage drug use, or sex. And yet this little film with a positive message about a basketball team won the hearts of audiences all across America. If I could make a film with that much heart and that much inspiration—a film that was anything like *Hoosiers* or *Rocky*—I knew for sure I'd have a winner on my hands.

Even with all those thoughts rattling around my brain, I never could have imagined just how much of an influence *Hoosiers* would have on my life. A few years later, that film would be the key to everything. Everything.

Life in South Bend for me was a lot like life at Notre Dame: I was happy to be there, appreciative of the whole situation, and able to share my enthusiasm just about everywhere I went. I talked to people. Everybody. The shop clerks, the waiters and waitresses, the Notre Dame faculty, the townspeople, the garbage men, the legendary local barber, Armando, who cut all the football coaches' hair in his old-fashioned meeting-place style barber shop. I introduced myself to new Notre Dame football coach Lou Holtz, and I got to know some of the legendary players from my youth, including 1966 champion Bob Gladieux, who became my roommate at the condo that year. A lot of people I met around town knew my story. They knew the legend of Rudy. They wanted to help me. There was a priest from outside of Notre Dame who offered to help me turn my story into a book. Players wanted to introduce me to people they knew who were involved in the movie-making business. It was great!

In fact, it was another legendary Notre Dame player who suggested I bring my story to Jason Miller.

"Who is he?" I asked.

"Did you ever see *The Exorcist*?"

"Yeah," I said.

"Jason's the guy who played the priest."

It struck me as a little strange. I remembered the movie really well. I remembered what the priest in the movie looked like, with his dark hair and big soulful eyes. But why would some actor be the right guy to write my movie?

Turns out that Jason Miller won a Pulitzer Prize for writing *That Championship Season*, the 1972 play that had recently been turned into a film starring Robert Mitchum—the story of four guys who get together with the old coach of their championship basketball team to relive their glory days back in the '50s. A sports movie that wasn't really about sports at all, but about life and drama and who we are as people. It was really deep stuff. Jason Miller was a personal friend of this new acquaintance of mine, and he was a Notre Dame nut!

I was floored. The idea that I might be able to get my story into the hands of a Pulitzer Prize–winning writer never even occurred to me. Maybe I hadn't been dreaming big enough!

A little time went by and we set up a meeting. I drove to Scranton, which is this scrappy, blue-collar place full of brick buildings and big old stone churches, and when Jason Miller came around the corner I thought I was in *The Exorcist*! It really took me back. He looked just like the priest in the movie. I don't know what I expected, but it really knocked me over for a second. "Hey, Rudy," he said, and he was a real nice guy. No twisting heads or projectile vomiting. "Let's go to my favorite bar," he said, and we went off to this real working-class place full of coal miners. Rather than tell him my story in a private corner where no one could hear us, I started telling my story within earshot of all these hard-working guys with beers in their hands—and they were riveted. I built the whole thing, just telling my story from start to finish, and when I got into the stadium with those last five seconds to play, and the crowd chanting my name, and I dove in to sack the quarterback, those coal miners cheered!

It was awesome.

"You got a story, Rudy," Jason said to me, grabbing my hand in a big, firm handshake. "We're gonna write it."

I wasn't sure who the "we" was at first, until he introduced me to his ghostwriter. Jason's talents were in storytelling and acting, so the way he liked to work in those days was to dictate to a ghostwriter who would then go off and write and polish the raw ideas. They were right in the middle of working on another movie project at the time, but they promised not to put mine on the back burner. They loved the story, and Jason insisted he could handle it.

I went home feeling like I'd just sacked the quarterback all over again. Truly, I couldn't have imagined a better outcome, a better meeting, a better plan, a better alignment. It's like everything fell into place. Jason really was a Notre Dame nut. He knew Ara Parseghian backward and forward and could stand up and imitate his mannerisms, his voice, everything! It was uncanny. I remember thinking he should play Parseghian in the film. But mostly, I thought he was the perfect guy to get inside my story and bring out the heart of it. He was passionate. Creative. Perfect for this. I felt it in my bones.

Six months went by, and I never heard another word. I kept calling Jason to see what was up, and he kept saying he needed just a little more time. I was so impatient! This was my life story. I felt like I'd already been waiting ten years for this thing to get off the ground. I didn't want to wait anymore!

Finally, Jason came to visit me in South Bend. He brought his son, Jason Patric, along and the whole gang had tickets to a Notre Dame football game. It turned into quite a party, actually. Jason Patric, of course, is a talented actor in his own right, the maternal grandson of Jackie Gleason, and one heck of a good-looking guy. He was dating a young actress named Julia Roberts at the time—yes, *that* Julia Roberts!—and he brought her along to a little post-game gathering at my condo. I really didn't know who she was at the time so it didn't affect me. I didn't talk to her all that much, but she seemed real nice. And who could ever forget that smile, or that laugh of hers. When I found out later who she was, I almost fell out of my chair! Seeing her on screen, I remember thinking her smile was as big off screen as it was on. Their agent was with them, who was a really powerful person in the film business at the time. It's like all of Hollywood came to my doorstep! Some people might get nervous in that kind of a situation, but not me. I think it goes back to the fact that I just like talking to everybody. It doesn't matter what people do for a job or how successful they are. At the heart of it, we're all people, and we've all got our struggles and passions. They were all passionate people, which is always fun to be around, and they were so fired up about my story. It felt like progress. I felt like this whole movie thing was really on the verge of taking off.

The very next day, Hollywood left town and the excitement seemed to leave with it. As the weeks flew by, it simply felt like Jason might never get around to writing, and a call from his ghostwriter basically confirmed my hunch. He just had too many other things going on. So I wound up hiring that ghostwriter myself. He moved into my condo in South Bend, and I agreed to pay him one-thousand dollars a month to work on the script. I was still selling insurance, traveling around to twenty-six different car dealerships spread over three states. It was exhausting. But knowing that ghostwriter was back at my place working diligently on my real dream kept me going.

There was just one problem: after a few months, it became clear to me that the "work" that ghostwriter was doing wasn't so "diligent." His girlfriend had moved in with him. The progress on the script was way too slow. Then one day I came off the road to find him and his girlfriend fighting in my kitchen . . . and my kitchen was on fire. Literally on fire! They were yelling and screaming at each other while the stove burst with flames behind them. I grabbed the extinguisher and put it out, and right there in the middle of that hazy cloud of white and smoke, I told him he needed to leave. "Forget the screenplay," I said. "Just get out of here."

The two of them packed up and left the next day. I was floored. I felt like a fool.

It seemed every attempt I made to partner up with someone to get this movie made turned out to be a mistake. And yet, there were always moments that kept me going. Even with that ghostwriter, the journey wasn't over. We reconnected, and he apologized, and he wound up bringing a major producer on board: Frank Capra Jr., the son of the great director of *It's a Wonderful Life*, among other classics. After feeling so low, that lifted my spirits right up!

Capra wanted to meet with the powers that be at Notre Dame to make sure we'd have all the clearances we would need to shoot this film on campus. After all, Notre Dame was as big a character in the movie as I was. We would need to capture the look and feel of that campus, and there was no way to reproduce that anywhere else—especially in what would be viewed as a fairly low-budget movie. This wasn't *Star Wars*. We weren't going to be building a fake Notre Dame set on a studio lot somewhere. Without the real Notre Dame as the setting, the whole film just wouldn't work. Everyone agreed on that.

I put in a call to University Relations, told them Capra was on board, and asked if they'd take a meeting to discuss the project. Lo and behold, they agreed!

Capra took the red-eye in from L.A. just for the meeting. A bunch of us sat in this little conference room at Notre Dame, pumped up about the possibilities and psyched to get this thing off the ground, when suddenly a Notre Dame official came in and said the meeting was over. They were sticking by their original decision not to let any more movies be shot on campus.

My emotional whiplash continued.

We all sat there in stunned silence. I think I was the first to finally speak up and apologize to everyone. I had no idea that meeting would go the way it did. I felt like a fool. Like I'd wasted everyone's time, not to mention their money.

After a bit of discussion, Capra looked at me and said, "Rudy, they're not going to listen to us. The only person who can get this movie done is you." He told me I shouldn't rely on ghostwriters or anyone else to get the deal done from this point forward. I was the one with the connection to the school and to the football team. I was the one who had the perseverance to make my story a reality, and I was the only one who would have the perseverance to see to it that my movie would ever get made.

I knew he was right. I had been leaning on the knowledge and experience of others. I had been leaving my fate in the hands of other people, just because I was too naive and too busy with the rest of my life to take the time to really do my due diligence and figure out how to make my dream a reality on my own. I needed to take charge.

I never heard from Capra again after that. I simply retreated into my life and started thinking about what would come next.

The first thing I had to do was find a way to stabilize my day-to-day existence. I was on the road too much. The insurance business was eating me up—the same way it had been eating me up back in Baltimore. I loved going to sales meetings. I loved standing in front of a bunch of guys who were eager to make some money, and getting them fired up about the job. I would talk to 'em like a coach at halftime, digging deep, pulling out all sorts of energy and feeding off of their energy in return. But when it came to the rest of it, the organization and paperwork, the constant traveling, it wasn't my calling. I needed to find a way out.

Funny how when you really need something, when you're asking for it and praying for it, certain opportunities will fall right into your lap. It might not be the exact thing you were imagining. But as long as you're paying attention, that thing could be the opportunity that rescues you and sends you in the direction of your dreams.

No sooner did I start thinking about getting out of the insurance business again than the owner of a car dealership right there in South Bend offered me a job. He saw what kind of a salesman I was. He knew my reputation. He knew my story. He had heard about the way I fired up my sales team—and he wanted me to pour that energy into his business. He asked me if I'd like to become the new car sales manager at his dealership. A dealership that was two miles from the Notre Dame campus. The one dealership in town where all the coaches and Notre Dame staff seemed to go for all of their new-car needs.

"Heck ya, I would!" I said, and the deal was done. No more traveling. No more wasting hours and hours driving all over creation. No more insurance.

For a while, my film dream went back under the frost. I knew spring would come again. I never let the dream die. In fact, I kept a copy of the latest script that ghostwriter and I had put together tucked in my top desk drawer at the car dealership. I wasn't sure when it would happen, but I knew that at some point, my movie dream would sprout up from the ground once again. In the meantime, I dedicated all of my energy to being the best new car sales manager that dealership had ever seen. Part of me knew that it still wasn't my calling. It wasn't what I was meant to be doing in life. But it was good work. Solid work. It provided me with a really good living. In fact, I earned enough that I bought myself a much better condo, a townhouse with a deck just perfect for barbecuing. I made friends all over town and stayed in touch with the Notre Dame crowd by hooking them up with the best deals I could.

One day, toward the very tail end of the 1980s, one of my salesmen came to me all worried and upset, looking for help. "I can't close this guy," he said. He had a customer on the floor who really liked a particular car, but he didn't like the price and was ready to walk out the door. This salesman really needed this sale. So I told him to bring the customer in to see me.

The guy looked at the name on my door as he walked in, and he stuck out his hand. "Rudy," he said, "I graduated when you graduated. You fought in the Bengal Bouts and played in that football game. Boy, you were a real inspiration around campus."

Spring had sprung.

The fact that a fellow graduate remembered me and thought of me as an inspiration reminded me what I needed to do. And from that moment forward, I once again began my quest to turn my movie dream into a reality.

I contacted all sorts of old friends and various Notre Dame alumni, and found that almost anyone I spoke to was willing to try to help if they could. I wound up making trips to California on the weekends, to take meetings and lunches and coffees with all sorts of Hollywood characters—friends of friends of various alumni, none of which seemed all that interested in helping me, and instead wanted to know if I could help them. It struck me that my career as an insurance salesman had prepared me for all of that rejection. I heard "no" a hundred times a day, for years, so I didn't let any of the negativity get me down. I just chalked it up to experience and learned firsthand what that town was all about: Hollywood was full of dreamers and not a lot of doers, it seemed.

In the meantime I started holding regular gatherings at my new condo. I had sort of an open-door policy on Thursday nights, and whoever wanted to stop by was welcome. We'd throw on some barbecue, watch a football game on TV, watch movies, and just sit around talking—whoever showed up. My old pal D-Bob was always there. So was his buddy Paul Bergan, a great educator and renowned high school football coach in Michigan (who would be inducted into the Michigan High School Football Coaches' Hall of Fame in 1991), whom I had met when I was a student and became great friends with as an adult. Young, old, alumni, a bunch of the current players from the Notre Dame team who wanted to get away from it all and blow off some steam, and even out-of-towners and well-known individuals would hear about Thursdays at Rudy's and want to stop by the condo: guys like Jerome Bettis, Roger Clemens, and President Ford's son, Jack Ford. It was amazing who'd come walking through that door, and the connections that were made. My buddy LeShane Saddler, a student and football player at Notre Dame at the time (who became a high school teacher and who now works in the Notre Dame admissions office), met a girl named Kellie who lived upstairs from me, and the two of them wound up getting married. So the connections ran deep! I felt like some sort of matchmaker, like I'd helped shape this guy's future just by giving him a place to hang out. My condo was simply a good place to relax, have fun, and talk. And almost every week we'd wind up talking about my story, envisioning the movie, imagining what actors could play which roles. All of a sudden there were a whole bunch of people dreaming about the movie version of my life. It was wild.

Some of those friends and acquaintances would open up about their own dreams too, from playing in the NFL, to buying a house in one of the more exclusive parts of town—whatever it was, everyone knew that Rudy's condo was a judgment-free zone, and a place where dreams could be spoken out loud. There was magic in that. Looking ahead, making plans for things that weren't quite real yet all of us were aiming for. It was almost like a lowbrow version of the "salons" I'd read about in school— like back in the 1800s, where a bunch of intellectuals or authors would gather around and share ideas and stories, and inspire each other to do great work. Only we didn't think of it in those kinds of terms. We called it "Chalk Talk." We'd be sitting there with a big white board, sketching ideas for my film, or whatever the topic of the day was. It was kind of like sitting in the locker room in front of a blackboard, planning plays for upcoming games. The games weren't real yet. You never knew how things would unfold in real time, under real circumstances, but that didn't stop you from planning. You'd grab a piece of chalk and go ahead and set things into motion as if they were real, right there in that moment, and whoever held the chalk held the floor. That's exactly what "Chalk Talks" at my condo were all about—except we weren't talking about a game. We were talking about our real lives, our real goals, and our real ambitions, no matter how far-out those ambitions seemed to be.

I also started talking up my movie idea around town again—to anyone who would listen, from the mailman to a local hotel manager. They all loved hearing about it. People get caught up in dreaming. We all love to see enthusiasm in someone else, and so many people I talked to got caught up in this positive, forward-thinking attitude I let flood back into my life. I felt like I had people rooting for me everywhere I went. Even at work: I'd wind up talking about my movie to the sales team, to certain customers, with clients on the phone.

One guy who wound up being a customer of mine was an assistant coach at Notre Dame. A guy by the name of Barry Alvarez. He had heard of me before he came into the dealership, and he asked me, "Why are you selling cars?"

"'Cause I'm gonna make a movie someday," I said. That was my answer! I knew this car thing was just paying the bills. I knew it.

"What kind of a movie?" he asked. And I told him: not just a movie about my personal story, my life's journey, but of the inspiration behind that story, and the message I hoped to share with other kids who are look-ing for a way to move forward in life.

"Wow," he said. "You're really gonna do that. I can feel it."

I loved getting that kind of support.

"Well, what are you gonna do, Coach? I bet you're not going to be an assistant coach your whole life," I said.

"Nope, I'm gonna be a head coach. I'm a dreamer, like you, Rudy. Just watch me."

Those were the kind of conversations I'd have. The movie dream just followed me wherever I went, all the time. And it felt great—despite all those fruitless trips to Hollywood and the lack of what most people would consider any real progress toward making that dream come true.

I'm not sure what was driving me. It was just a feeling in my gut. One of those gut feelings that I've spoken about before. Those gut feelings that I firmly believe are the voice of God, and need to be heeded. I felt as if I was doing the right thing. I felt like I was making progress. I trusted that feeling.

Well, lo and behold, that feeling was right.

One day, one of those random people I had shared my story with, a local hotel manager, called me up on the phone. "Rudy, my brother's coming to town and you need to meet him."

"Why?" I asked.

"Well, to be honest, he was roommates with Angelo Pizzo and David Anspaugh back at Indiana University. Do you know who they are?" he asked.

I had no idea.

"They're the guys who wrote and directed the movie *Hoosiers*," he told me. "I got talking to him about you, and he thinks you have a valid story to tell."

I just about dropped the phone. I could hardly believe it. Here I'd been messing around going back and forth from Scranton to Hollywood getting involved with the wrong people for years, and this guy right here in South Bend had a connection to the team behind *Hoosiers*? Are you kidding me? It blew my mind!

"I'd love to meet him!" I said.

The meeting happened, and before I knew it, I was back on a plane to California, trekking out to Santa Monica to meet Angelo Pizzo— the *Hoosiers'* screenwriter—at a little Italian restaurant. I sat at Louise's Trattoria on the corner of 10th and Montana and waited. And waited. And *waited*. I sat there for three hours! I had been stood up.

I couldn't believe it. *Was this one more dead end?* I walked outside to get some air. That's when I saw this older mailman walking by with the biggest, friendliest smile on his face. L.A.'s not necessarily full of the most genuinely friendly people in the world. I don't think that's any secret. So seeing this big, friendly smile surprised me. And to tell you the truth, he reminded me a lot of Rudy, the old janitor at the ACC. "Look at that smile!" I said to him as he passed by. He kind of laughed and looked at me, and I guess he could tell right away that I wasn't the usual L.A. type either. "Where you from?" he said. I told him, and he told me he was from Michigan. Two midwesterners, crossing paths in La-La Land. "What are you here for?" he asked, and I told him the whole story—of how excited I was about this big meeting with Angelo Pizzo, the writer of *Hoosiers*, and how he told me to meet him at this place right here in his neighborhood and how he hadn't shown up. Well, you'll never guess what happened next. Even though he could have gotten in a lot of trouble, that mailman saw how genuine I was, and how passionate I was, and he walked me down around the corner and led me right to Pizzo's front door.

Angelo was surprised to see me. "How did you find me?" he asked.

"Never mind that," I said. "You're late for lunch."

He had forgotten. He had been up all night writing. "Look," he said. "No offense. I know that you probably got excited about coming out here to talk to me, but I'm not going to write another sports movie. Ever. And on top of that, I hate Notre Dame!"

I was taken aback. But I also hadn't come all this way to be turned away so quickly. If you haven't noticed, I don't take no very easily.

"Well," I said, "you could come to lunch at least."

He paused for a moment, looked in my eyes, and said, "Yeah, I'll go to lunch."

Back at the restaurant, I avoided talking about the movie. We just shot the breeze and talked about our backgrounds. I learned a lot about Angelo that day—his family background, how his parents wanted him to become a doctor but he was sort of the rebellious one, swimming against the stream and trying to find his own way in the world against a whole slew of obstacles. The fact that he had come to Hollywood and found his own way to success was inspiring to me. I could see that there was a fire in him. A confidence. He hadn't let anyone tell him no. That aspect of his personality reminded me of me! I kept thinking to myself, *He's the perfect guy to write this story!*

I shared just enough about my journey and he already knew enough about my journey to know it was a good story. But he didn't give me any kind of affirmative answer before I left town. He basically left me with the same impression that he gave me right off the bat: that he didn't want to write another sports movie, ever; and that he really, really despised Notre Dame.

I flew back to South Bend with a broken heart. My hopes were so high on the way out there. It seemed like fate, having that introduction out of the blue. *How could he not want to write this movie? He could have another* Hoosiers *on his hands. Who wouldn't want to strike lightning twice like that?* I wondered.

It was early December, and leaving sunny Santa Monica behind for the gray-skied chill of South Bend certainly didn't warm me up any. It felt like my chances had gone cold. My whole attitude fell cold. When you come so close and then take a blow like that, it's hard to recover. It's certainly hard to keep up that positive attitude everyone around me had gotten used to. I remember talking to myself on the way into the car dealership that Monday, reminding myself that the dream wasn't dead, that so many people believed in my movie, that I had to do everything I could to get my positivity back—and most of all that I needed to set those bad feelings aside and really give everything I had to selling cars. I was good at that, I thought: focusing on what had to be done in the moment. I felt focused as I hung up my coat and sat down behind my desk, ready to tackle the day.

No sooner did I plant my behind in that chair than my phone rang. It was the owner. He wanted to see me in his office. He had never really called me into his office that way before. My stomach dropped. It felt like I was being called into the principal's office at school for some reason— and I honestly had no idea what that reason might be.

"Rudy," he said, "I'm sorry, but I'm gonna have to let you go."

"What?!"

"Your focus is not on my business. Your focus is on making this movie. You're talking about it, thinking of it. I don't need half of you here. I need all of you."

I knew he was right. I wasn't passionate about being in car sales, just like I wasn't passionate about selling insurance. I just couldn't believe his timing.

"It's December. It's almost Christmas," I said.

Right here's where he taught me a lesson. "Life is tough, isn't it, Rudy?" he said.

"But I don't have any money saved. I've been spending my money! What am I supposed to do?"

"Rudy, life is hard," he said. "But I have a feeling you're gonna get that movie made. I think I'd just be hurting you by keeping you here. You need to give it your all, be 100 percent committed. So you go do that. You go get that movie made."

I was really ticked off. In a way, I was more ticked off at myself for knowing he was right! After the whole experience with Frank Capra Jr., what was the lesson? *I was the one who had to get this movie made.* So why wasn't I 100 percent committed to that pursuit? Why was I trying to juggle it around a career in the car business? Well, the same reason everyone does what they do, I suppose. We all have needs. We need to make money. We need to live day-to-day. I dunno. I felt so lost and confused at that moment, I had no idea what to think. Had I made all the wrong choices? Was I a fool? Was that feeling in my gut just plain wrong? I questioned everything. My past. My present. My whole mind-set. I questioned my faith. Everything.

My first concern was how in the heck I was gonna make my mortgage payment the next month, so I went to the condominium association and asked if I could take over maintenance at our development. I told them all about my experience at Notre Dame, and thankfully they went for it. So that became my job: shoveling snow, being the fix-it guy, and when the spring of the brand-new decade—the 1990s—came around, I was the guy out mowing the grass to earn my keep. It's like I was right back in my freshman year at St. Joe Hall at Holy Cross—only my dream of making a movie about my life felt even further away than my dreams of playing Notre Dame football ever did.

Lou Holtz's son lived in the same condo development. I gave him a copy of the script one day to share with his dad. He said he would, and then I never really heard anything more about it. Except for occasional conversations with D-Bob and Paul, I pretty much stopped talking about the movie. Once again, that dream fell dormant. It wasn't dead. Something inside me would never let it die. It just sat there. Frozen. Again. While I spent my days mowing lawns.

One Hurdle at a Time

"Rudy, do you have a lawyer?"

Nearly an entire year had passed since I'd seen Angelo Pizzo in Santa Monica. I had called him and bugged him about my story a few times, but he just never seemed all that interested. Now here he was on the phone, calling me, and those were the first words out of his mouth. *Great*, I thought. *What, is he gonna sue me?*

"Why?" I asked.

"Because we just sold your movie to Columbia. We've gotta write a script. Fast. We need to get going."

"What?" I said. "What do you mean?"

He explained the whole thing to me. A producer by the name of Rob Fried (pronounced "freed"), who worked at Orion pictures back when *Hoosiers* was made, had a new job at Columbia TriStar. One day over lunch, he asked Angelo and David Anspaugh if they had any sports movie ideas. Turns out Columbia Pictures had set aside a small budget, maybe $20 million or so, for a little sports film, and he had come to Angelo and David to see if he might be able to strike lightning twice.

At first Angelo said no. But after lunch, David said, "You should tell him about that kid from Notre Dame!" And they called Fried back, together.

Apparently Fried's ears perked up. "What kid from Notre Dame?"

They told him my whole story, and Rob Fried loved it. For some reason, the way they told it, Rob got real emotional and said he'd have a deal in place the very next day. And he did. But then there were some shakeups at Columbia and the film got shelved—one more hurdle.

All of this stuff happened without me knowing anything about it! While I kept mowing lawns and shoveling walkways and making ends meet in South Bend. Life is strange that way sometimes, isn't it? How all this stuff that could affect your life is happening and you don't even see it. It's wild to think about.

Anyway, some time went by, and Rob Fried took the *Rudy* idea over to Columbia's sister company, TriStar, which was run by a guy named Marc Platt—and they fell in love with the project and wanted to jump on it right away. Another producer named Cary Woods got involved, and he was just a super guy too. But Rob was the guy who really made it happen. He believed in the story so much, he just kept pushing forward with the project. He wouldn't let it go, despite some of the obstacles that popped up. I guess, in some ways, that makes him a real Rudy in his own right, right?

When Angelo called me, he needed all the rights and clearances from me to get started, which is why I needed a lawyer.

Given everything I had been through with this movie idea, I still had doubts about whether this whole thing was real. It seemed too good to be true. I needed to do some digging, and I quickly found a way to get some digging done for me.

One thing led to another and I eventually got in touch with a Hollywood entertainment attorney who had connections with Columbia Pictures. When I first called him looking for representation, he said he couldn't take me on unless I paid him a retainer. "Look," I said, "I don't have any money to pay you, but I've been told that there's a deal in place at TriStar. Check it out. If the deal is there, if it's real, I'll cut you in for a percentage. If the deal isn't there, if it's not real, then I don't need you anyway."

He decided to dig. A few hours later, he called me back. "Rudy, there's a deal. This is for real. Here's what we've got to do . . ."

We were off and running.

As we rolled into 1991, Angelo Pizzo flew out to see me. He met D-Bob and all of the various characters in my life. We spent hours and hours just walking around the Notre Dame campus. He listened to me tell my story. He didn't roll tape, or take notes. He just listened intently to everything I had to say, knowing the big moments and the reality of it all would settle into place in his mind and be there when he needed to write. It was cool just to watch him think. You could see him putting scenes together in his mind. I had spent so much time thinking about this movie, I could speak it in scenes! What I still didn't understand was how on earth you could tell my whole tale, and get to the essence and power and meaning of everything that had happened in my life, in less than two hours of screen time.

Angelo said I just needed to trust him. And after spending all that time with him, I did. I trusted him implicitly. I felt like he got me. He got what I was all about. He got what the message of my story was all about. He related to my story, personally, and I got the sense that he would infuse some of himself into the screenplay—as all great writers do.

Then he went away. It was six months later when he sent me a copy of the script. I sat down and read it instantly, without stopping.

I cried.

It was beautiful. It captured the essence of who I was. It captured the flavor of everything I had done, but reduced it to these beautiful moments that made it all so clear. I had questions, of course—like, why didn't he include my entering the Bengal Bouts? "Too many victories," he explained. In a film, if there were too many victories, it would water down the story and take away some of the impact. That made sense too, and I suddenly understood that I had needed each of those victories in my real life to propel me forward. But the film version of my life had to be more to the point. More of an allegory. More picturesque in some ways. Like a poem with just the right words, just the right scenes to get the point and the meaning and the feeling across, and nothing more.

He had made my dad a little less supportive than he was in real life, but that was just to make the tension clear, and to make it relatable to so many people who struggle to break free of the confines of their parents' worldviews. That was exactly the struggle I had been through; he just filtered it through the eyes of a screenwriter.

I was worried that he made Dan Devine out to be more of an obstacle to my success than the real champion of Rudy that he was, and Angelo explained that it simply had to be done to drive the point home, succinctly, about just how uphill and impossible my climb toward dressing for the final game had been. It all made sense! (He also promised to talk to Dan Devine about it before filming began, and he did. Dan wasn't real happy about it, but he understood it was a movie and there had to be some dramatic license taken. He was such a supporter of me that he didn't put up a stink.)

There were several instances where he combined multiple characters into one, all to save time on screen and to drive home the messages and lessons I had learned from various folks along the way, from Siskel and the priests at Holy Cross and Notre Dame, from Freddy, from D-Bob, from Rudy the janitor. He made it all make beautiful sense and drove home the essence of everything I had been through, and everything my life had come to represent in the eyes of those who knew and were inspired by my story.

Angelo was a genius.

He was the right guy for the job. My initial instincts on that first flight out to Santa Monica were right. The funny thing is, he just didn't know it himself. He needed convincing. He needed time. Both my dream and his ability to capture that dream needed time in order to emerge from their dormant states in the frost. It all made sense to me now. I could see the path that God laid out for all of us on this project. It was there all along. Life happens in God's time—not ours, no matter how hard we push.

The studio was just as impressed with the script as I was. They green-lit the project (that's Hollywood speak for actually funding it and putting it on the schedule) immediately. They started talking about casting and peppering me with questions; they wanted me intimately involved from the get-go, to make sure everything was accurate and to utilize all the pre-planning and dreaming I had already done to help get the film up and running as quickly as possible.

By June 1992, they were ready to rock and roll. I got a conference call from Angelo, David, and Rob Fried. "Alright, Rudy. We're ready to go. We want to shoot in the fall, September if we can do it. October at the latest, before there's snow on the ground. We do need to have the approvals in writing to shoot on campus, though. Who is it you've spoken to about that?"

Uh-oh. In all this time, no one—including Angelo—had ever asked me about getting Notre Dame's permission to shoot the film. And I never thought to bring it up. They all assumed, like almost anyone would, that the school would be thrilled to have this kind of attention . . . until I explained it to them.

"You don't have permission?" they said.

I gave them the whole story, about the University Relationship department and how they hadn't let anyone film since the Knute Rockne days fifty years ago, and how they had rejected me. They were really upset, as you can imagine. They went back to the studio, and the studio head was absolutely irate.

"Rudy, they've given us forty-eight hours. If we don't get approval," they said, "they're going to drop the project."

That call came on a Thursday. I told them to come to Notre Dame that weekend. I'd get us a meeting. I was making it up. I had no idea how to get us a meeting. I had already been rejected. I was flying by the seat of my pants. At that point, I had everything to gain and nothing to lose. Suddenly, with my dream on the line, there were five seconds on the clock and I felt like the only player on the field.

I walked out of my condo not knowing what to do. I happened to see Lou Holtz's son across the parking lot. "Hey, did you ever give your dad that movie script?" I asked.

"Yeah!" he said. "He loved it!"

Lou Holtz loved the script. And that was an early version of my story—nothing like the powerful, passionate, inspirational script that Angelo had turned out. If Lou Holtz loved my story, why shouldn't Notre Dame get behind it?

That inspired me.

I decided I couldn't go back to University Relations. The rejection there had been too final, too complete. I needed to talk to Rev. William Beauchamp, the university's executive vice president, who oversaw Notre Dame's entire athletic program—not just the administration, but also the philosophy of it all. He had joined the university in 1987, had come to the priesthood later in life, and just seemed to me, from afar, like the type of man who might look at this whole thing with fresh eyes.

I xeroxed three copies of Angelo's script. I put on a suit and tie. I walked over and climbed the steps under the Golden Dome and headed straight into his office. I could see him at his desk. He wasn't on the phone. There was no one with him. It seemed as if my timing was perfect.

I had a little bit of inside information up my sleeve for this meeting. I had heard there was a book called *The Tarnished Dome* in the works; it was a real negative book about the downfall of the Notre Dame football team. The fact that that book was on its way had to be worrisome to the university. It was the worst kind of PR nightmare. Perhaps my film could counter that with a positive message and a beautiful look at what an inspirational place Notre Dame really is.

"Can I help you?" Beauchamp's secretary asked. I asked if I could see him. "Father's very busy right now," she said.

"No disrespect to you, but I can see him right there," I said, and I just walked past her and barged into his office. I had nothing to lose and no time to waste.

"Father, hi, I'm Rudy Ruettiger."

"I know who you are," he said.

I hoped that was a good thing!

"Come in. Have a seat."

We chitchatted a bit and then I told him I was hoping for his guidance.

"I've had this project that I've been trying to get done for I don't know how many years now," I said, and he told me he knew all about it. "Well, what have you heard?" I asked.

The story he had heard came from folks in University Relations. It involved a lot of negativity, and this vague idea that I wanted the university to fund my movie. "Can I tell you my side? The movie's been approved by TriStar Pictures. We don't need any money from you. The money is there. The power is there. It's the team behind the movie *Hoosiers*. Have you ever seen that film?"

He hadn't.

"They've set aside about twenty-five million dollars for this movie, Father," I told him.

That impressed him. "You're kidding," he said. "Well, tell me about the story. How will it reflect on the university?"

I told him it was a message everyone needed to hear. I explained how Angelo Pizzo had taken my personal story and distilled it into a message of hope, perseverance, and never giving up on your dreams. I explained how Notre Dame was like a character in the film, a powerful presence that inspired me to keep going, one that never gave up on me. It was a place that welcomed the underdog and helped someone like me find a place of glory and confidence in the world.

"Rudy," he said, "I feel it. Let me look at the script and let's have the meeting on Monday—10:00 a.m. I can't promise I'll get to read the whole thing this weekend, and I certainly can't promise we'll let you shoot here, but I'll consider it and we'll see."

"Thank you, Father. Thank you. Just give us a chance. If you say no, I won't ever talk about it again. But they will not shoot this movie unless it's shot here at the University of Notre Dame. They're set on that."

We shook hands, and I left that building with hope.

That weekend I picked up Angelo and David at the airport, and we went out to grab some dinner. I recognized a long-time Notre Dame professor at another table at the restaurant and we decided to chat him up. I introduced the guys, and the professor was real excited to meet them. He loved *Hoosiers*.

"So what do you think the chances are that Notre Dame will allow us to shoot our movie on campus?" I asked.

"Ha! About a million to one," he laughed. "They'll never let it happen."

It wasn't exactly the pep talk we were looking for. On the drive back to my condo, we tried to reassure each other that it was just one guy in a bar. No need to worry. We had magic in this script and this story. Still, David was real nervous.

"Rudy," he said to me, "I gave up another project to take this on. I don't know what I'll do if it falls through."

He was just as nervous as he sat in the front seat of my car on the way into campus the next morning. Angelo sat in the back, much more confident. David wore his heart on his sleeve; Angelo didn't. Maybe there was something about that balance that made them such a good team.

As we walked toward Father Beauchamp's office, it struck me just how great a team they were. They were the pros here. It was my story, sure, but so far my past attempts to woo Notre Dame had failed. I suddenly had a strong gut feeling that I needed to bow out of the meeting. "You guys go in without me," I said, as painful as I knew it would be to wait outside and not hear what was going on. "I think it'll be better that way. He's already heard what I have to say. Let him hear you guys without any distraction from me."

David and Angelo agreed and stepped in; I waited outside for what seemed like forever. When they stepped out, I couldn't really tell what the outcome was. Their heads were down. They didn't say anything. Then Father Beauchamp emerged with a Notre Dame picture book in his hand. "Wouldn't this look great on the silver screen?" he said to them, holding up a picture of the Golden Dome. They both agreed that the dome would look amazing.

"Alright, let's go over to University Relations," Beauchamp said.

"I can't," I said. "I've been rejected too many times."

Father Beauchamp looked at me and said, "Don't worry, Rudy. I'm their boss." He gave me a great big smile.

As we walked over, I whispered to David, "Do we have it?"

"Yeah," he said, "but don't get too excited. Play it cool."

Wow! I thought. Just wow. What the heck had they said to him to sway it our way? This was fifty years of restrictions against movie making on campus about to come to an end—for my movie!

I still almost didn't believe it, until we got to the office and the man in charge came right over and shook my hand. "Rudy," he said, "congratulations."

"For what?" I asked. I really wasn't sure about this whole thing yet.

"We're a part of your team now."

What a turnaround! I could hardly believe it was true. This was it. With Notre Dame in my corner, this was a done deal. There was nothing to stop us! I found out what really sold Beauchamp too: after I saw him in his office before the weekend, he went home, had some dinner, and then sat down to watch *Hoosiers*. He was so moved and inspired by that film that when he met David and Angelo, he really only had one question for them: "Can you give us that type of movie in a Notre Dame story?" They promised they would. He had already spoken to University Relations about it before the meeting, and since there were plenty of *Hoosiers* fans in that office too, that pretty much sealed the deal. They knew how powerful a little film could be, and how much it could do for the reputation of Notre Dame. They saw that the message wouldn't be all about me. I think that was the thing they feared most—that all I was doing was trying to promote myself. Why would Notre Dame want to promote some messed-up kid who came into their great university through a side door? What they needed to understand, and what they finally understood, was that my story was about a message, a feeling. We wanted to show other kids that they could make it too, if they followed their hearts and followed their dreams. Once they understood that, and once they had the confidence of the team behind *Hoosiers*, there was simply no stopping us.

Or so I thought.

━

Nothing in life is easy. That sounds like a sweeping statement, and maybe a flat-out cliché. But it's true. The more I've come to accept that truth, the easier it has been to deal with the roadblocks and difficulties that get in the way of my dreams. Once you recognize the fact that nothing—*nothing*—is easy, you just come to accept that the hardships are part of the job. Whatever that job is. I didn't know that when I first got started. Every time a roadblock popped up, I got mad. Sometimes that was okay, because I used my anger to propel me forward. But there's something to letting that anger go. There's something to dealing with the roadblocks, taking them one step at a time, thinking of them as little tests to make sure you're really ready for the reward at the end of the path God lays out for you. There's some peace in that, but it's a peace I certainly didn't have as we got ready to make this movie.

The fact is, my own naïveté, my running around like some chicken with his head cut off desperately trying to get my film made, had set up a whole bunch of roadblocks and problems—going all the way back to the very beginning. The biggest problem of all is that I got involved with people from time to time who didn't have my back. They were out for their own selfish interests. I assumed they were good people with good intentions, whether by association or my own easygoing nature. But once a big Hollywood studio was involved and this movie was really getting made, all of those faulty associations came back to haunt me.

Right in the middle of the preparations, Angelo called me, just beside himself. "Rudy," he said, "they're not going to give me screen credit. I'm not going to get credit for this movie."

I didn't understand. He wrote the script! What did he mean they wouldn't give him credit?

"You wrote an earlier script with a ghostwriter, right? Well, he registered it with the Writers' Guild, Rudy. Whoever wrote the first script gets the credit. That's how it works. It's the Guild's call."

"What?!" I was flabbergasted. "He had no right to do anything with that script. I'll fix this, Angelo. Let me call my lawyer. I'll get in front of the Guild, or SAG, or whatever I have to do."

I couldn't believe that old stuff was still haunting me. As if the fire in my kitchen weren't bad enough, I soon learned that not only had the ghostwriter taken our script and registered it with the Writer's Guild, but he had taken my name off of it entirely! As if it were purely his own

original screenplay. He then went and optioned that screenplay to two or three different production companies through the years, making a little money for himself all along the way—money that should have been shared with me. It was my story. He was still stealing from me!

I was livid. I went out to Hollywood and spoke to the Guild; my lawyer stepped in, and we took care of it. I couldn't believe how much that one guy had taken advantage of me. Clearly I needed to do a little more due diligence in checking out the people I partnered up with. This one guy had now caused me problems for years! Not to mention nearly destroying the screen credit of a genius writer who had come through for me. I felt awful. And it was just the start.

TriStar kept calling me with all kinds of problems and clearance issues. I had to pay back an earlier producer who was involved with the Frank Capra Jr. deal a total of $20,000 before the production could move forward, and he was still included and credited in the movie. Even after all he'd done, that ghostwriter stood up and claimed I owed him money for the work he had done in story development. There were a couple of other producer types who had attached themselves during the Frank Capra Jr. period who claimed some ownership as well, and my attorney basically told me I had no choice but to write everyone a check. "You could fight it, and you'd win," he told me, "but while you're fighting, they'll cancel the film. The movie will never get made."

The most important thing to me was to see this film come to completion. I wound up spending nearly every penny TriStar had agreed to pay me for the rights to my life story before the film even started. Nearly every penny went to pay off this series of guys who claimed they had rights to my story. So all those riches people assumed I was making, the piles of cash everyone expects to gain from a big Hollywood break like this, wasn't anywhere near the millions, or even high six figures people assume you get. And no one ever could have imagined the payouts I'd have to make just to keep the film alive. I basically made no money from the film. My only income at this point, still, was from mowing lawns and fixing stuff up around the condo development! It didn't matter. The excitement of it all fed me more than any money ever could.

Throughout the summer there were panic calls from TriStar because they hadn't received official word from Notre Dame about the right to shoot *Rudy* on campus. I started making phone calls and pestering everyone until, finally, University Relations sent me an official letter on September 3, noting that they had agreed to allow filming but asking to have a meeting with me to discuss it before it all became public. They were still worried about it right up 'til the eleventh hour!

On October 14, 1992, *Variety*—the official trade magazine that documents all the business happenings in Hollywood—printed an article titled "TriStar Pix kicks off 'Rudy' film," highlighting the fact that the film had overcome all kinds of rights hurdles at the last minute. Little did anyone know that most of those hurdles were put there by me and my business dealings with all of these hangers on!

Scheduled for a fifty-day shoot, TriStar set a start date of October 26.

A start date. For the movie I'd been dreaming about since the late 1970s.

I could feel it, deep in my gut: my life was about to change. Everything I had been preparing for and aiming for, the summation of everything I had been learning in all of my flailing around, for all those years, was about to come true. It was that same sort of feeling I had in the locker room before the final game. That feeling of knowing it's real. It's all about to start. My whole life was about to change.

It felt big. It felt scary.

It was awesome!

Making *Rudy*

Λ law student. Λ janitor. Λ hotel managcr. Λ mailman. It's astounding when you stop and think about the people who show up in your life when you need them. As October rolled on and the first day of shooting was upon us, it was those people I wanted to focus on. I tried to let go of all the negativity and the problems and the hangers on who had basically taken every penny out of my pocket.

But God had one more little test for me.

On the first day of shooting, first thing in the morning, I received an angry call from the head of TriStar and producer Rob Fried. "We've got a problem, Rudy," they said. "There's a priest threatening to shut the film down. Says he's filing a lawsuit and will get an injunction to shut us down today. Did you write a book about your life with some priest?"

I couldn't believe it. The priest from outside of Notre Dame whom I shared my story with, who talked about writing a book with me but never lifted a finger to actually do anything, had suddenly come back to haunt me like all of those other hangers on. A priest! Never in a million years would I have expected that kind of behavior from a priest. But by this point, nothing totally shocked me anymore. I asked them to give me his number and to give me a little time. I promised he wouldn't sue them. I promised he wouldn't shut the film down. I told them to just move ahead and I'd handle this guy. I knew him. No problem.

In reality, I had no idea if I could stop him. I couldn't even imagine what this guy was up to. I got him on the phone right away.

"Father, what is going on?!" I said.

After some hemming and hawing, he basically told me that he was in some financial trouble. He really needed the money. "You've got to get me some money from this. Please, Rudy."

I said, "Look, you know this movie was not your idea. You know none of this was your effort."

"Well, we talked about it. We shared ideas, Rudy. I deserve something for this."

He didn't "deserve" anything, but I needed to save the movie. It was all that mattered.

"What do you need?" I asked. "Just tell me how much you need."

"I need ten-thousand dollars."

I sighed, closed my eyes, and said, "Fine."

"And I also want a part in the movie," he said.

"What?!"

I didn't know if I could deliver that. I wasn't in charge of casting. He insisted he would fight me if he didn't get a part.

With no choice, I hung up the phone and called David Anspaugh. Fortunately, there was a bit part that hadn't been cast yet. We were using lots of locals and townspeople for little parts in the film. It was cheap, made sense, and gave the whole production a good feeling. David agreed, and I called that priest back, and we put the whole thing to rest.

That priest was the last of the hangers on who nearly messed up the movie. The last obstacle. Yet another lesson for me to never blindly trust anyone who tried to become a part of my life and a part of my dreams. It wasn't a lesson that sat well with me. I didn't want to be a hesitant, distrustful person. But perhaps I needed to be a lot less naive about the ways of the world.

It just goes to show, even the people who show up in your life in a negative way are really positive: they teach you a lesson, every one of them, as long as you're open to learning. The lesson I needed to heed, and a lesson I would continue to struggle with for many years to come, was not to blindly trust in everyone I met, but to verify. To do my due diligence. To be careful that the people around me were really who they said they were, that their actions matched their deeds, and that their intentions were honest and forthright. It's up to each and every one of us to be careful with whom we align ourselves.

Once that priest was paid off and out of the way, I felt as if my alignments were finally, finally in place. My life's story was now in the hands of an incredible ensemble. They were a group of people who would wake long before dawn, raring to go, day after day, ready to throw their hearts and souls into making the most out of my life story for the next two months.

While I had been busy sorting out the various payoffs to get the film off the ground, the movie-making machine had forged ahead. The power of Angelo's script attracted the best of the best at every level. The crew was phenomenal. All of them. Truly. I've never seen such a well-oiled, professional bunch of people so dedicated to their work in my life. It was like a navy crew, but every one of them wanted to be there and truly loved what they did. They all seemed happy to just be a part of the movie-making process, and every one of them played a vital role. What an awesome way to live! Watching the sensitivity and brilliance of David Anspaugh at the helm, I saw the way he worked as both an artist and a leader at the same time. I don't think I had ever seen that combination in a human being before. From the moment that first camera rolled, it was simply a thrill.

Of course the cast, which I had some input into selecting, was nothing short of sensational. First off, Sean Astin—a talented young actor who had just appeared in *Encino Man* and *Memphis Belle*, and who made a big impression even as a youngster in *The Goonies*, was awesome. I was thrilled to have him play the on-screen version of me. The guy really gave it his all too. He had two stunt doubles at the beginning of the shoot, and the football sequences were so hard, both of those stunt doubles got injured. One of them broke his hip! So Sean had to jump in and do all of that stuff himself. Now get this: Sean Astin had never played football in his life. He didn't know how to get in a stance before he started rehearsing for this film. You would certainly never know it by looking at the finished product, and that's a testament to what a strong actor he is and what a dedicated, focused guy he is. He learned more about football in two days than some kids learn in their entire high school and college careers! It was awesome to watch.

There were also two super-talented newcomers to the feature-film world: Vince Vaughn and Jon Favreau, two great guys the studio discovered through Second City, the comedy troupe based in Chicago. This was the first big Hollywood feature film for both of them. They had basically only done some extra work and TV work before this, so for both of them, it was like playing the Super Bowl fresh out of high school! It was a big leap, and they loved every minute of it. Vince's part was smaller; he played the All-American football player who cut me down on the field and nearly made me quit the team (based on the fifth-year senior who pushed me in the locker room). Favreau played D-Bob, which was a composite character in the film, a combination of both D-Bob and Freddy. There were lots of composites in the film, and that was part of the genius of Angelo's script. When they say "based on a true story," that's exactly what it means. All the elements of my story were true, but they were adjusted to their finest moments and reduced to the finer elements to drive home the meaning of the scenes and situations. It would take too much screen time to set up two friends, so why not combine the best of both—the comedic relief of D-Bob and the tutoring ability of Freddy? It worked.

Despite his relatively small role, Favreau was on that set every day, quietly observing the whole process. He peppered people with questions now and then, and he kept his eyes close on David Anspaugh. It was clear he had ambitions that extended far beyond acting. Of course, he and Vince would go on to make *Swingers* just a couple of years later, an inside story about young people trying to make it in Hollywood, which would become a huge cult hit and launch both of their careers to new heights. Vince would become one of the biggest actors of the '90s and early 2000s, and Favreau would go on to become one of the most bankable directors in all of Hollywood, anchoring the *Iron Man* franchise. It's amazing to think they got their starts in my little movie.

On the other end of the spectrum, everywhere I looked there was an actor I recognized. Robert Prosky was Father Cavanaugh (a composite of Cavanaugh; Father Burtchaell, the University Provost; and a couple other influential members of the order of Holy Cross). John Beasley was one of the assistant coaches. Charles S. Dutton perfectly embodied all the heart of the old janitor, Rudy, ACC director Joe Sassano, and some of the other staff who helped me out with jobs and living arrangements and advice around campus all combined into that wise, almost mystical character Fortune that Angelo crafted so brilliantly.

Then, of course, there was Ned Beatty, who I swear could have passed as my dad's real-life brother. My parents and siblings were on set often, and seeing my dad and Ned Beatty side by side was a treat. Ned picked up on the timbre of my dad's voice and some of his mannerisms. It was wild! Everyone loved my parents, and it brought back that whole glowing feeling of pride they had when they first came to visit me on the Notre Dame campus. Their presence made the whole film feel like a family affair as well. It was as if it was something we were all a part of, a dream come true. It was an accomplishment we could all share in. There was a scene that mentioned my birthday, August 22; Sean Astin got to talking to my mom, and he wanted to be sure the script was accurate, so he asked her when my birthday was. She answered August 23! Once again making the same mistake that she'd made since I was a baby. Sean listened to her instead of following the script and changed the date, so my birthday is stated incorrectly on screen now for all eternity.

My parents were interviewed for TV. There were news crews that came around and reported on the filming—not only local news crews, but national crews. There was something magical about this story and this film that was catching attention everywhere, even during the filming process.

That's pretty unusual. Most films don't get much hype or publicity (or at least they didn't back then) a whole year before they hit theaters. But we couldn't keep the press away. These crews wanted to talk to me, go back to Joliet with me to see the old neighborhood, and shoot all over Notre Dame's campus. It was awesome, and I really got into it all. It was fun for me to tell the tale again and again. I think it was fun for the whole cast to see that kind of attention being paid so early in the process. It helped contribute to the feeling that we were all involved in something important.

I could go on and on about the cast. They were all so good. From Lili Taylor as the girlfriend (who mirrored the girlfriend I had back when I first laid eyes on Holy Cross), to Scott Benjaminson, who played Frank—a completely fictionalized version of a brother, created by Angelo, since none of my brothers were adversarial. He was a character whose purpose was to symbolize all the tension I felt with the naysaying crowd back in Joliet. And then there was Jason Miller. I was real excited that we were able to bring Jason on to play Ara Parseghian. Despite the fact that he never wound up writing my script, I had great affection for the man. He was such a Notre Dame fan and such a passionate, artistic guy. He still knew all of Ara Pareseghian's mannerisms. He had the guy down pat! I don't know how he did that just from watching him on TV. He was such a gifted actor. Now here we were all these years later and he was pacing the sidelines with his whistle in hand; we couldn't have had a better guy for the part.

Jason almost got us into trouble one morning right at the beginning of the shoot, though. The call came at 4:00 a.m. The football players were all called to set that early so they would be there at first light. The cinematographer wanted all of the football practices to be shot in that early morning glow. The "magic light," they call it, just before the sun actually peeks over the horizon. Well, on this particular morning, we walked out onto one of the practice fields and the whole place was filled up with this beautiful morning mist like a radiant fog. It was spread all over the campus, and the cinematographer went nuts for it. He knew how rare and beautiful it was, and he wanted to capture every second of it. He and his crew started shooting all kinds of visuals right away while they rushed everyone into costume and hurried the football players onto the field faster than anyone anticipated. There was just one problem: some of the cast and crew had been out drinking the night before, and Jason Miller was among them. He was nowhere to be found, and filming the team without Ara Parseghian on the sidelines just didn't make any sense.

There were frantic phone calls and knocks on doors. Finally, they found him in his hotel room fast asleep with the phone unplugged.

When they got him up and into costume, he showed up on that set. I swear, it was like he had slept for eight hours and prepared himself to win an Oscar. He was perfect! He knew his part so cold, he just became Ara as soon as the cameras started to roll, and the cinematographer got his shots, which in some ways set the tone for the whole film. The beauty, the majesty of the campus, highlighted in all of that mist and beautiful early morning light, set the tone for everything.

We couldn't use the real Notre Dame football team for any shots because of NCAA rules. I don't think Notre Dame would've risked their real guys getting hurt in our practices anyway. But there was no way David Anspaugh was going to cast a bunch of extras with no football experience to put on those uniforms and play the parts. It wouldn't look real. Even paying a bunch of stunt people to do the football scenes would have failed, for one big reason: TriStar had hired NFL Films to shoot all of the big football sequences. NFL Films has special cameras and patented techniques for shooting real football games. They have super-slow-motion capacity, where you see the ball flying through the air, and the guys' faces through their face masks, and the sweat pouring off of them. Their shots all have that grainy, feature-film look that takes you right down on the field and makes it seem like you're right there in the game. Other football movies might get by with extras filmed from afar, or by using trampolines or other tricks to get guys jumping and flying through the air when they take a hit, but the NFL Films crew didn't know how to work with any fakery. It could have been a problem, finding enough real football players to fill the film's teams. But the beauty of all those chalk talks at my condo and the fact that I had spent so much time dreaming about this film and planning for this film—even before we had a script that worked and

Hollywood finally stepped in—is that my friends and I were prepared for every question that could possibly arise.

The studio had brought Al Cowlings in to coordinate all the football sequences, and he was a super-talented advisor when it came to working under traditional Hollywood setups. But when we decided that the football needed to be real, and I mean "really" real, I introduced David Anspaugh to my friend Paul Bergan. He and his son, Bill, put the word out, and they wound up pulling in forty-four ex-college and semi-pro football players from all over the region. These were massive guys—like six foot six, 310 pounds—who had all played football in recent years and were now working, teaching, or coaching all over the region. The magic of it was that all of those guys had had dreams of playing for Notre Dame, and now, in a small way, they were going to get the chance to do it. You can imagine how pumped they all were.

David and Paul agreed that if we wanted it to look real, we'd have to practice with the guys, come up with real plays, get them playing like a real team. David had taken a similar approach with the basketball teams on *Hoosiers*, so he knew what needed to be done: five days of practice, treating all of these guys as if they were full-on Notre Dame legends.

They passed out uniforms, and most of them were too small, which left the costume department scrambling. They weren't expecting such giants! The biggest pair of shoes they had was a fourteen, and one of our guys was a size seventeen. We blew out a dozen or more pair of those gold pants before shooting even started in earnest. We were using period helmets from the early 1970s, and these guys were hitting each other so hard, we cracked half the helmets on the first day! We had no choice but to switch to stronger, modern-day helmets, and anyone with a sharp eye will notice that period mistake in the film.

The fact that all of these players had jobs meant they couldn't hang around for five or six weeks to film on a Hollywood schedule. So Paul arranged for them to come in for a series of four-day weekends. David rearranged the whole shooting schedule around that, so all of the football scenes could be shot on the weekends. Weekdays were dedicated to other scenes. It worked out perfectly for everyone; the guys loved it. This was a union film, with full catering and craft services. At dinner, they'd serve a choice of steak, prime rib, or shrimp, and the guys would order all three! A few of them gained twenty pounds or so over the course of the shoot.

Paul was right in there on the sidelines, doing the real coaching for all the football scenes—and there were a lot. The script only called for about five minutes of football, but we got this team looking so good, we shot something like sixteen hours of football; we wound up filling almost seventeen minutes' worth of screen time in the final edit, which is huge in the course of a less-than-two-hour film. The fact that Paul was called upon so often led David Anspaugh to finally just ask him to play an "assistant coach" in the film, so we wouldn't have to waste time clearing him from the sidelines when the cameras rolled. Poor Paul had to shave off his beard and moustache. The crew insisted there were no coaches at Notre Dame in the 1970s with facial hair, and they were constantly looking for period accuracy in the piece. He went home that night and his wife barely recognized him.

Paul's family got into the filming too. His wife played a nun on screen; two of his sons, Shawn and Nick, showed up as an assistant coach and a defensive back, respectively; and his other son Bill helped pull the team together, was the one-on-one coach for Sean Astin, and played quarterback in the football sequences.

There was so much good energy on this film that I was constantly taken aback when we hit obstacles. Notre Dame had opened up the campus to us, which was remarkably generous; but there were so many departments involved, and various factors made it difficult to get answers and clearances at times. Mid-shoot, they would tell us we couldn't use certain fields or couldn't set up our cameras in certain areas. Since I was the local consultant on the film, I'd always be the one left to fix things. I'd scramble and call old buddies around town to get us a space to shoot elsewhere, including a field off campus that wasn't even a football field. We just mowed the grass ourselves—I was good at that!—and made it look like a football field. In fact, there's a memorable scene in the film where the guys are playing in the rain and mud, and that whole thing was filmed on that random field, just off the side of the main road into South

Bend. They were forced to use a rain machine to pull that off, since we were blessed with so much good weather for the whole shoot.

Of course, the big shoot, the penultimate scene, the moment when I dressed for a game and finally stepped foot inside that stadium to get my twenty-seven seconds of glory on the field—that could only be shot in one place: Notre Dame Stadium. That was one of the greatest challenges of the entire shoot. If we didn't get that scene right, the whole movie would have failed. That's a lot of pressure under normal circumstances. Seeing me run out of that tunnel to a stadium full of people, seeing me head into the game for the final kickoff, seeing and hearing that crowd chanting my name, watching me sack that quarterback and get carried off the field was the equivalent of Rocky winning the fight in *Rocky II*. I can guarantee you they spent days and days filming those fight scenes, getting everything right. Just the final knockdown alone, I bet they shot it from lots of different angles over the course of a series of hours, if not days. You don't mess around with the climactic scene of a movie.

Well, Notre Dame couldn't give us days on end with a stadium full of people, and we couldn't afford to pay sixty thousand extras to fill the stands anyway. So we shot a lot of close-ups on other fields, shots that would be combined in the editing room to make the whole thing come together. We shot a few scenes with approximately four hundred people in the crowd on weekdays, when the stadium wasn't in use. And then finally we got the Notre Dame marching band to agree to give up part of their halftime show at a couple of games, to allow us to film at the stadium during real Notre Dame home games.

Halftime is only seventeen minutes long to begin with. Do you know how long we had to get the shots we needed? Six minutes. No joke. Six minutes, to film all of it.

Talk about pressure!

Notre Dame was up against Boston College that Saturday. When halftime came around that day, we were just killing the gang from Beantown. It was something like 28–6. So the crowd was all pumped up when the real team hit the locker room and our movie team huddled in that famous tunnel, raring to go.

It's hard to even imagine the logistics that went into shooting this thing. We had to clear everyone off of the sidelines. Had to hand out 1970s-era Notre Dame banners to people in the front rows, as well as some Georgia Tech banners and shirts, since we had played against Georgia Tech in that final home game back in 1975. NFL Films set up something like nine cameras in the stadium to capture the action from every angle possible. Paul had worked the movie team forever, knowing they'd have to basically nail the plays the first time out—Sean Astin included. Everyone knew there were four things that absolutely needed to be accomplished: capturing the team running out of that tunnel with Sean at the front, basking in the magnificence of that sixty thousand–strong crowd; the kickoff; the two plays I was involved in, including my sacking the quarterback; and the moment when I got carried off the field on the shoulders of my teammates. David Anspaugh made sure it was rehearsed meticulously, so it would all go off like a dance. Like a ballet.

I was up in the press booth looking down at this whole thing. Everyone was wired up with headset radios so we could coordinate everything perfectly.

Paul Bergan was down in the tunnel with the whole gang of players, and he gave them a pep talk to keep everyone focused: "When you go into that stadium, remember who you are. You're not the schoolteacher or accountant anymore. You're a Notre Dame football player. It's the only chance you'll ever have to be one, so don't embarrass yourself. Stay in character. Stay in the game. You're only gonna get one chance to come through this tunnel. So make it great!"

He told me all of this afterward. I was so psyched that he did that. He drove it home for those guys. After all, if just one of them had stopped or gotten off track, or waved to someone in the stands, it could have messed up the whole shoot.

Little did he know there was a whole other reason that they would need to stay focused: at the last minute, our whole communication system went dead. All of a sudden we couldn't talk to anyone. David Anspaugh was silenced. I couldn't hear anyone in the booth. No one could give the signal to Paul to let him know when cameras were rolling so he could send the guys from the tunnel out onto that field. It was awful! To this day we don't know exactly what happened.

Paul stood down there just waiting and waiting for someone to give him the signal. The Notre Dame band kept playing, waiting for us to get started. The scoreboard had been reset. The sidelines were cleared of real coaches and players and filled up with our movie guys. But then no one knew what to do.

It's kind of hilarious if you stop to think about it: if you were in those stands and went to the bathroom at the start of halftime, when you returned to your seat, you would have seen the scoreboard reset (to 24–3) and a different opposing team on the field. I'm sure there was more than one person in the crowd who felt like they'd entered the Twilight Zone!

Finally, some Notre Dame official said to Paul, "Forget it. You've missed your window. Shoot's over."

But then something magical happened. Someone else—to this day, no one recalls who it was—said, "Go, go, go!" and Sean Astin led that whole 1975 Notre Dame team out of the tunnel and onto the field. Everyone did just what Paul told them to do, stayed focused, and pretended they were really in the game. The guys from NFL Films were in tune to the whole thing, so used to capturing the action without a script (because, after all, there is nothing predictable about a real-life NFL football game), that they all just rolled cameras as soon as they saw there was some action, and they kept shooting to the best of their own abilities despite the lack of coordination between them.

Nobody—absolutely nobody—would know whether we got the shots we needed until they developed the film and took a look in the editing room.

We had auditioned eight or ten different guys to do the kickoff. The ball was supposed to be kicked all the way to the Georgia Tech end zone, and that's not an easy thing to do. Luckily, we found a guy, and he had nailed it in every single practice. He was one heck of a long-range kicker. There was just one problem: he wore glasses. As he ran out to do the kickoff on this one-and-only shot we had, one of the production assistants on the movie grabbed the glasses right off of his face. "Those aren't period!" that PA told him. His glasses were simply too modern for 1975.

This poor guy didn't know what to do, so he just ran out there and tried to kick the ball—a ball that was nothing but a blur to him! Well, he totally miffed it. The ball only flew about twenty feet. Luckily, it didn't matter. With all of those NFL Films cameras going, they followed the rest of the team, and those guys ran the play as if the ball flew all the way to the end zone. So despite not seeing the ball fly through the air, the whole thing would look fine on film. *Phew!*

Next thing we knew, our fake Notre Dame and Georgia Tech teams were lined up and running the two plays they had practiced. The guys running the clock nailed it. The crowd nailed it. And with seconds to go, Sean Astin nailed it—soaring through the air and sacking that Georgia Tech quarterback with all the gusto I did back in 1975. It was awesome! It was like leaving my own body and watching myself through the lens of history. It's hard to even describe that feeling.

That's when his teammates gathered around him and hoisted him right up onto their shoulders. Sean raised his hands with all the glory of a real winner, basking in the roar of that massive crowd, in that magical stadium, as he gazed over the North Wall to the magnificence of Touchdown Jesus—and the cameras captured it all.

The dance was complete.

Six minutes. Six minutes to capture the entire climax of this movie.

And we did it. First time out.

Good thing too: the following weekend, when Notre Dame played Penn State, South Bend got hit with a blizzard. There was a foot of snow on the ground. If we had waited to shoot, or if we had flubbed it up the first time, none of the shots would have matched the snow-free close-ups and plays we had shot in different locations around town in the weeks prior. In other words: the film never could have come together. The whole thing might have died right there, or at best been cobbled together in a way that would have sent it straight to video instead of straight into the multiplexes.

I could hardly believe our good fortune. It was hard to count the number of little miracles that happened in order for that film, even that one final scene, to come together.

The whole thing felt blessed.

Before the shoot was over, Jon Favreau made a big point of coming over and thanking me. "Thank you, Rudy," he said, shaking my hand, serious and sincere. I thought that was very cool of him. I thanked him too. I was glad he could be a part of the movie. Both he and Vince Vaughn were great to work with and great on screen. Perfect, actually. I couldn't imagine anyone else in those parts.

Saying good-bye to everyone at the end of that shoot was tough. We all bonded so much that it felt like we were roommates, classmates, and teammates in every way. It was emotional, especially with David and Angelo. I couldn't thank those guys enough for what they had done. And they thanked me too. Just like Jon. I gave major props to producer Cary Woods, a USC guy who fought the good fight for us, and of course, Rob Fried as well. The movie never would have been made if it wasn't for Fried's perseverance. He is a great businessman, a Cornell graduate, and I knew exactly where I stood with Rob, always. He is very sincere with a great big heart, and he knew there were big lessons that could be learned from sports, big messages that could be delivered through a film like *Rudy*. I truly would never be able to thank him enough for getting my movie off the ground and seeing it through.

Once everyone left town, the emotional release of sleeping in, of not making those 4:00 a.m. set calls, of not worrying about what obstacle we'd have to overcome in any given hour, was a lot for me to take. Plus, I had spent the last decade talking to people about this dream of making a movie, and that dream came true! Like anyone, you find yourself riding on adrenaline through intense high points in life. When they're done, it takes a while to settle down.

The thing is, I didn't want to settle down. I wanted to hold on to that feeling. I wanted to hold on to that inspiration and passion for the rest of my life.

━

So that was that. My film was a wrap. I would follow it closely through the editing process, watching the film come to life scene by scene whenever

I could, especially as the music was added. That orchestral score by Jerry Goldsmith was so powerful. I still hear that music played at sporting events and all kinds of emotional ceremonies all the time. It gives people chills!

I watched as the TriStar team put together promotional items and started getting ready to do press, and they asked me to make myself available for TV interviews to help promote this thing. But basically, the film was made; it was set for release in October 1993, and it was done. I had accomplished yet another seemingly unattainable, incredible, awesome dream in my life. I knew that once that film hit theaters—the equivalent of a final game or graduation day—I very well could have gone back to repeating the same old pattern in my life: asking myself, "What now?"

That was a pattern I didn't want to repeat, and this time, I was ready. This time, with the help of a friend or two and a little forethought, I was prepared.

What now?

The answer was, "What *not* now?"

I knew how powerful this film was going to be. We all knew it while we were shooting it. You could feel it. The energy was radiant. Plus, I knew how much press I was doing. The media world was very interested in this little movie with a big heart, and in learning the real-life story behind the tale. So even though the up-front money I should have made from that film went walking out the door before the shoot even started, I knew that a whole slew of entirely new doors were about to open for me, and that I had to be ready to walk through each and every one of them.

For the first time in my life, I prepared myself for what would happen after the dream came true. I prepared myself for the future. And that would make all the difference.

Part IV

Dream Bigger

Red Carpets and White Gloves

A lot of films are lucky to have one or two red-carpet world premieres.

Rudy had four of 'em.

First, it was selected as the closing film of the Toronto Film Festival. I put on a suit and tie and walked down the red carpet that September in Canada, answering all kinds of questions from entertainment reporters from all over the world. I stood there alongside Angelo and David, Rob Fried, and Sean Astin, and we basked in all of that applause. In some ways, the whole thing is just a blur to me. I'd never experienced anything quite like it. It's a strange feeling to walk into a giant, ornate theater like Toronto's El Capitan, knowing a couple thousand film buffs were about to sit and watch a film based on your life for the very first time. *What if they hate it?* In my heart I knew they wouldn't. I had seen it already. I knew what we had. The film moved me to tears. It was everything I ever dreamed it could be. *More* than I dreamed it could be. But you can't help but have those doubts. It didn't help any that once we took our reserved seats, right down in the middle of the front section, we noticed that Gene Siskel and Roger Ebert were sitting in the row right in front of us. Movie critics don't seem to have quite as much sway today as they did back then, but in 1993, the "two thumbs up" or "two thumbs down" from Siskel & Ebert on their weekly TV show could make or break your movie! It was big. I couldn't help but be a little nervous.

On a side note, Dennis Hopper was in the audience, sitting right in front of me, for that Toronto premier. He just happened to be in town and came to check out our movie. He turned around to me after it ended and said, "Boy, you've got a hit!"

Of course, that whole audience loved *Rudy*. It was a huge hit. There were tears all around. The applause at the end seemed to go on forever. I had goose bumps.

The same sort of reaction happened at the next three premieres as well. Los Angeles was the biggie, of course, where all the big US press outlets are based. Then we had two full-blown premieres for the film's hometown crowds: one for Notre Dame, at the very same movie theater in South Bend where I had seen *Rocky* back in 1976; and another in downtown Joliet, at the grand old Rialto theater where I had gone to movies as an escape while I was growing up in that rough-and-tumble town.

The Joliet premiere was held the last week of September, and when I got up on stage at the old Rialto to speak to the audience before the start of the film, I said, "There are really only two heroes to this story. That's my mom and my dad."

They stood up on that stage with me, and the audience gave 'em a big round of applause. That's a magical feeling. I wish everyone could get a chance to do that sort of thing for their parents. In my case, it truly was my parents who stood by me, who put up with me, who raised me in a way that would give me the strength to pursue everything I pursued in life. I wanted them to have all the glory that night. After all, this was their hometown. I had moved on. But this was where they lived and worked and had grown up and raised their fourteen kids. To get that applause from that audience had deep, deep meaning to them.

Of course, the glory wouldn't stay focused on them. No matter how hard I tried to deflect it, there was a whole bunch of attention paid to me, which was certainly a turnaround considering how a lot of people in Joliet treated me when I was growing up. The mayor even declared it "Rudy Ruettiger Week," and they read a whole proclamation after the film was over, pointing out that the movie would serve as "an inspiration to the youth of America." That was a pretty cool thing to hear, and I sure hoped it would be true.

I then got up and spoke a little bit more.

"It is an honor to bring a motion picture to Joliet, because when I was growing up, going to the Rialto, sneaking in to watch *The Ten Commandments*"—that line got a good laugh—"I never thought I would see the day that Angelo Pizzo would write my story. He hated Notre Dame and didn't want to do another sports story about Indiana because he had already done *Hoosiers*, which was a great success. You guys remember *Hoosiers*?" The audience applauded at that too. Angelo and David were both present, and they each took a bow. We all made the rounds to these various premieres as a team. The whole thing was such a team effort. It was fun to reconnect with those guys and to spend time together again, really enjoying the fruits of our labor.

I tried to introduce the real D-Bob that night. He had gathered back at the house with my whole family and ridden over in one of the limos we rented for the big occasion. But by the time I introduced him, he had already left the theater. Typical! He and I would be good buddies forever, and by then, we both certainly knew that. The thing was, he had dreams of being a comedian, and seeing my Hollywood dreams come true had sent him on a brand-new path in his own life. He had gone on the road doing stand-up, and found a niche as the guy who opens up on national tours for famous comedic hypnotists, those guys who get audience members to do silly, embarrassing things in front of their friends. I was real proud of him for that. Of course, I always say he's funnier just being himself than he is telling jokes. I wish he'd go off the cuff rather than write stuff down! But we always give each other guff about everything, and neither one of us will ever really change. I love the guy. I really wished he had stuck around to come up and take a bow.

Then I got the chance to introduce Sean Astin, and Sean got up and spoke, wearing a bright red sport jacket: "It seems to me that the more I'm involved in this movie, big institutions and families and schools and universities keep welcoming me into their homes and into their hearts. I appreciate you for letting me come and be in this wonderful, wonderful theater. We're obviously very proud of the movie, and we appreciate your support coming out here today. Hopefully we can get everybody else to go out there and, you know, fight for the Irish."

That got big applause. He was so humble in his whole presentation; the audience just ate it up. What Sean was talking about there, what he was busy finding out, what we were all finding out, is just how much this film was being embraced. It was more than just entertainment. There was something to this whole thing. There was something to the message. That feeling we all had about the power of the story, the inspiration behind it, was real. And it would only become more real as the film continued to roll out, with a preview audience screening in New York City, the opening slot in the Chicago Film Festival on October 8, and the wide opening, in theaters all across America, on October 13, 1993.

The press was astounding. I remember Connie Chung introducing a segment on CBS that included interviews with me and Ara Parseghian, and basically teed up the whole story by calling me a great underdog, like Rocky, except for the fact that Rudy was real. It was six or seven minutes long, which is really long for a TV news segment. That was awesome! And it was just one of many. I wound up going to New York City to sit for an interview with Charles Gibson on ABC's *Good Morning America* more than a week after the opening. I did Montel Williams's show. Regis Philbin, a fellow Notre Dame alumnus, went on and on about the movie. We all know how fast the world moves. The film continuing to get prime press attention weeks after it opened showed what a phenomenon it was becoming.

It was great to see other Notre Dame heroes talking about the movie too. Dan Devine was on one show where he was quoted saying, "Teams can't exist without people like Rudy." Joe Montana, who was a freshman when I was a senior, and who of course became one of the most famous quarterbacks in the world through the 1980s, showed up in an interview on another show describing the moment when I sacked the quarterback in 1975, saying, "All the guys just went crazy on the sidelines. It was like we had won the national championship almost. That's how excited everybody was for him."

I barely knew Montana, so it was great to hear him share that kind of enthusiastic memory of my moment. The whole thing just grew and grew, and the phenomenon never stopped. *Rudy* only grew more popular as it went to video and started showing up on cable in regular rotation.

The fact is, I knew we were on to something big in those first few days. Really big. And the biggest realization of all came to me just two days after *Rudy*'s nationwide release.

There I was: October 15, 1993. My hands were stuffed in my pockets against a cool fall breeze as the sun dropped down and gold leaves shimmied across the sidewalks of our nation's capital. I could see the tip of the Washington Monument over the treetops as I hurried along the perimeter of the black wrought-iron fence.

For some reason, it never occurred to me just how big a deal this was.

I was about to screen my film for the president of the United States. Okay, it's a big deal to meet the president. I understood that. But I hadn't gotten here from nowhere. I got here one step at a time, the same way I managed to get to every accomplishment in my life. It had been a long road! I had already been through all of those big red-carpet premieres. I had welcomed Julia Roberts in my condo back in the day. I had worked with the best writer-director team in Hollywood. This is what my life was now. So as I left the hotel that late afternoon, this thing that I was about to do didn't feel far-fetched or unreal to me. It just felt sort of natural. Like one more step along the path.

The reason the screening came about was pretty straightforward: California senator Barbara Boxer's daughter, Nicole, had worked as an assistant on the *Rudy* set when we shot the film in the fall of 1992. She was there firsthand to see my story unfold, and she felt that the inspirational message of the movie might be something her mom would enjoy. She was right. So her mom, the senator, like any proud mom with those kind of connections might, made the arrangements to screen the film for the president and first lady—and lo and behold, they invited me to come along.

The White House held a dinner first, but I couldn't make it. I had a prior commitment that day, and I was running so late I didn't even have time to put on a tie. I just threw on a white shirt and a blazer and left the hotel with a few minutes to spare, thinking it would be fine. It only occurred to me that this might be a bigger deal than I anticipated when a Secret Service agent at the East Gate handed me a laminated pass to clip on my lapel.

"What's the *A* stand for?" I asked him.

"All-access," he said.

I gave him a funny look.

"You're allowed to go anywhere on the grounds or inside that you choose. Just make sure that pass is visible at all times."

An all-access pass? To the White House?

A United States marine in full dress, white gloves and all, opened the door for me as I approached the building. Inside, an assistant greeted me right away with a big handshake and "welcome." They ushered me down a magnificent hallway toward the Blue Room, where they said everyone was gathering before the film.

Everyone? I thought. *Who's everyone?* I knew Angelo Pizzo and David Anspaugh were both invited. Our producer, Robert Fried, would be there too. Yet when I walked through that door there were fifty-nine people in the room. Congressmen and senators, including Senator John Glenn—a man who had walked on the moon! I saw faces I recognized from TV. Men and women dressed to the nines. *Is that Larry King?* The reception was so large, it spilled over to the adjoining Green Room as well. I started to feel just a bit overwhelmed. Then all of a sudden, First Lady Hillary Clinton slid through the crowd with a big hello. She shook my hand, and before I knew it she was introducing me to the president of the United States.

It all happened so fast, I hardly remember a word that was said.

Bill Clinton's handshake was strong, and I do remember understanding very quickly why everyone said he was charismatic. In an instant, he made me feel welcome, as if I were a friend, as if I belonged in a room full of leaders at the White House. If there had been any sense of elitism, any "us versus them," any hint of the discomfort that a guy like me might feel in a room like that, President Clinton made it all slip away in an instant. Angelo, David, Rob, and I presented him with a tie—we had heard he loved ties—and we gave him a *Rudy* baseball cap. He seemed genuinely appreciative and spent time congratulating each one of us on our hard work and perseverance in getting the film made.

It's a funny thing: when you've accomplished a big dream in your life, there's a mutual respect that comes with it. There can be other things too: jealousy, envy, and the like. But none of those were present on this night. I truly felt like I belonged there. It just felt sort of natural. And that's how President Clinton treated our introduction too.

Before I knew it, they began ushering everyone down the hall into the screening room, including Chelsea Clinton and one of her friends. The whole family was there. Watching people filter out, I was simply stunned by the logistics: *How many people did it take to arrange all of these schedules and all of the security for all of these people in powerful positions to get them in a room at the very same time?* That blew me away.

Yet before I stepped out into the hallway I saw something that truly stopped me in my tracks. There were portraits of former presidents hanging all over that room, and right by the door I spotted a portrait that made my heart pound.

Suddenly, I was ten years old, standing in front of the whole class as my fifth-grade teacher blasted me, over and over again, with the same stupid question that I just couldn't answer: "Mr. Ruettiger, who was our fifth president?" she said. "Mr. Ruettiger, answer the question!" I didn't know. *How could she expect me to sit and study the names of the presidents last night when the Yankees game was on?*

She humiliated me in front of the whole class. She made me feel worthless. She and other educators at that school had already told me, flat out, on numerous occasions, that I was a lousy student and that with "my bad attitude" I would never amount to anything. On that day, she hammered that message home in front of my peers.

I believed her. For a very long time, I believed her. I believed all of them. It had been a long time since I had even thought about that memory.

"Who was the fifth president, Mr. Ruettiger?"

As I stood there looking at that portrait, I knew, once and for all, just how wrong she was to do that. How wrong they all were to do that to any kid. In my mind, I shouted it to her across three decades of frustration and anger. "*The fifth president was James Monroe!* You want to know how I know? I know because *I'm standing in the White House, looking at his portrait!* You want to know how I got here? Not because I was the best student. Not because I followed some prescribed notion of what I 'needed to know' to get ahead in life. And certainly not because I memorized the names of the presidents as a ten-year-old. I'm here at the White House because I followed my dream. I followed my passion. I did my best wherever I could. And I didn't let you stop me!"

Maybe I didn't say all of those things in my head as I stood there, but the feeling was pretty dramatic. What I realized fully as an adult is that the humiliation and inadequacy I felt in that fifth-grade classroom derailed me for the rest of my school-age years. That's not what school's supposed to do. Teachers shouldn't *stop* kids. They should *inspire* kids. Kids need inspiration. Heck, we all need inspiration. It doesn't matter if you can't pass some test or memorize some list, or if you suffer from learning disabilities the way I did. What matters is that you're fired up and inspired to go out and learn about what matters to *you*; that you're so passionate about whatever it is you want to accomplish that you don't let obstacles stand in your way. I wish every kid in America could find the sort of inspiration and passion I found after those miserable school years were over.

The sudden memory made me really upset. Despite the fact that I had accomplished so many of my dreams and gone out and made a movie about my life story, it took me until that very moment—standing in front of James Monroe—to realize just how big that message of *Rudy* really was and how important it was that I take that message of pushing on, of dreaming, of never losing hope, just as far and wide as I could. I felt that new mission burning inside of me as I left that portrait behind and followed the ornate hallway down to the White House movie theater.

As I stepped inside, I couldn't help but shake my head and smile: they saved me a seat next to Larry King, and as the lights dimmed I fully realized what a "big deal" moment this was.

What would that fifth-grade class think of me now? I wondered.

President William Jefferson Clinton sat there and watched the entire movie. Every frame. He never left to take a phone call or to pick up a memo. No advisor ever whispered in his ear. The leader of the free world, arguably the most powerful man on the planet, sat there watching the story of my life for 114 minutes. Larry King kept whispering to the lady next to him. It was kinda bugging me until he told me afterward what he was telling his friend: that the story reminded him of his own life.

In the scene where Rudy finally receives his acceptance letter after three semesters of trying (and failing) to get into Notre Dame, and he opens the envelope as he sits on a bench by the pond looking out at the school's famous Golden Dome—the very same spot where I took my pal and mentor, Freddy, to show him my Notre Dame acceptance letter in real life—I saw congressmen and senators and even the first lady wiping tears from their eyes.

They got it.

When it was all over, as the lights came up, First Lady Hillary Clinton stood and said, "Way to go, Rudy!" in such a commanding voice that every person in that room paid attention. And then she said something else: "Every kid in America should see this film."

I sat there awestruck. I could hardly believe it. Why would the first lady feel so moved that she would stand up and say something like that? In front of all of those influential people, including her husband?

There could only be one reason. It was the very same thing I had just experienced during my little personal moment with President Monroe in the Blue Room: she was moved by the message. She was moved by the message of inspiration and hope that came from my story.

God sure works in mysterious ways, doesn't He?

It all just hit me so hard in that moment. After all, who am I? I'm not that special. I'm certainly not that talented. I didn't accomplish anything at Notre Dame that most people would ever consider a "great feat." I'm just some kid from Joliet. A kid who made a few good choices (and even a few bad ones) here and there, who worked hard, never stopped dreaming, and never gave up. And now here I was, in the White House.

When the crowd left, the president brought a few of us into the Oval Office. He showed us some of the tchotchkes and bits of memorabilia he kept around—personal reminders that helped keep him grounded. The whole thing was so surreal that I truly can't remember what we talked about, but I do recall that neither he nor First Lady Clinton could stop talking about the inspirational message of the film and how important a message that was for our educational system. In the coming days, the president wore the *Rudy* baseball cap we gave him out in public. That's how into the message he was! In fact, from what I understand, the only reason he stopped wearing it was because his staff made him remove it. It was an election year, and primary season was right around the corner. Apparently some people were confused and thought his hat was an endorsement of an entirely different Rudy: New York mayor Rudy Giuliani, who was a serious contender at that point to become his potential Republican opponent!

My point is that *Rudy* had quite an impact on both the general public and on some very influential and powerful people. What became clear to me that October 15 in Washington, clearer than ever before, is that *Rudy*, in a sense, wasn't about me. It wasn't even really about what I had done. It was the *message* that came through my story, the *message* that came about, because of my perseverance, that was not only meaningful but powerful enough to move a first lady to tears; to ring true to a legendary media personality like Larry King; to seem familiar and uplifting to a senator who had once walked on the moon; and to entice a president to invite me into the Oval Office for a little chitchat.

The *message* is what mattered. And that message needed to be heard.

The funny thing is, as I sit here today looking back at my life, I can't imagine anyone ever predicting that young Daniel Ruettiger would become any kind of a messenger. (Least of all, me!) But that's exactly what I had become now. That's exactly where God's path had led me. And I was just getting started.

Sharing the Message

Starting a new career in mid-life is a challenge many people face, even when they don't want to. It's never easy, either way. But I dare you to ask most people who started a whole new career path in their late thirties, early forties, maybe even their fifties if they're happy about what they've accomplished. I bet you nine out of ten of them will say, "Yes! Absolutely. I'm so glad I did it. I wish I had done it sooner!"

Change is good. Life is all about change. The question to ponder is whether you embrace the changes and learn to grow both from and with the changes, or whether you let those changes scare you into retreat.

After the filming of *Rudy* ended toward the end of 1992, I knew I'd have less than a year to get my act together. Less than a year to prepare myself to take advantage of the opportunities that the film's release would present to me. A movie is a once-in-a-lifetime thing for someone like me. If I didn't take advantage of it in some way, I may never get another shot. I knew that.

So I started asking myself some really serious questions. Mainly, what did I want to do with my life? I knew I didn't want to keep shoveling snow and mowing grass, that's for sure. I had been down the coaching route early on, and I still had no interest in that. I knew I didn't want to go back and sell insurance, and I didn't want to get back into the car business either.

What did I really want to do? What got me fired up? What got me out of bed every morning? What was that feeling I had when we were making the film? What were the best, most productive times of my life? What could I focus on that would keep me happy (and hopefully well paid) for the rest of my life?

The thing I kept thinking back to was early in my insurance days, when I went to a seminar aimed at firing us up, and I saw that guy give a speech that brought all of us insurance salesmen to our feet. I kept thinking back to that feeling I had as I walked out of that room—that feeling of, "Man, I want to be able to do that for people some day!"

I thought long and hard about what that guy did. I thought long and hard about what the movie *Rudy* was going to do for people. And I knew, once and for all, what I wanted to do: I wanted to inspire people. I wanted to take the message of *Rudy*, the message of my life's journey, and infuse that message wherever I could—to companies big and small, to the military (building on my navy background), to colleges, to high schools, to middle schools, maybe even to elementary schools.

I wanted to get up in front of audiences, big and small, and inspire them to change their lives; to do great things; to follow their hearts; to work hard; to dream big; and to chase after their dreams with everything they've got, because this is the only life we've got to do it in!

The long and short of it was that I wanted to make a career as a public speaker.

Some of the skills I would need, I already had. I always gave great pep talks at sales meetings when I was on the road with the insurance company. I knew how to fire up my sales team at the car dealership too. I had fired up my players during my short stint as an assistant coach at Notre Dame, during my graduate assistant year. I had learned how to talk to Hollywood types, famous people, even the president! And to do it with relative ease.

But how would I formulate a speech? How would I come up with enough to say? I didn't want to just wing it. I wanted to be ready. I wanted to practice, and for that, I turned to my buddy Paul Bergan. He wasn't just a great football coach and coordinator; he worked for many years as a regional director for career/technical education in Michigan, and he was great at his job. He was a real educator who knew how to inspire his own teams in his school district, and I hoped he could inspire me and teach me how to organize a great speech.

We worked tirelessly in the basement of my condo, in the very same place where the chalk talks took place. We worked with the white board, and we started hanging up poster boards all along the wall, mapping out the perfect Rudy speech that would work in front of the widest audience we could imagine. It involved some retelling of my story, and some big inspirational words; we developed a flow from beginning to end, with peaks and valleys in between, and built toward a climactic ending, just like a movie!

The problem was, I was lousy at memorization. So while all that work got me thinking in the right direction, I just wasn't able to grasp it all. And I certainly couldn't take all the posters along with me to pin to the wall whenever I gave a speech.

Still, all that preparation did me good, and I'll forever be grateful to Paul for taking the time to do that with me. He believed in me. He believed I could be not only a good public speaker, but a great one. And it helps to have someone believe in you no matter what endeavor you're taking on.

Just after the movie came out, and the media went wild for it, my prediction that doors would start opening for me came true: I got a call to do my first speaking engagement in front of a group of fourth and fifth graders right in South Bend.

I was told that the teachers had shown *Rudy* to all of these kids. That was a good thing. At least they'd know who I was. I didn't realize that the teachers didn't explain to the kids that the guy who was coming to see them was the "real" Rudy, and not Sean Astin! So when they introduced me, the kids were massively disappointed. That is no way to start a speech. One little boy even spoke up: "You're not Rudy. You're a fake."

"No, no," I said. "I'm the real Rudy. I lived the life that the movie was based on."

It didn't matter. I had lost them right from the start. They weren't interested in anything I had to say because the setup was all wrong. They weren't primed to listen. They were primed to reject me from the get-go.

My speech was a flop. I lost track of what I was talking about. I lost the flow. It was just a disaster. I left that school defeated and questioning whether I was cut out for public speaking at all. But that feeling was short-lived. I knew I just had to practice. As with anything else in life, I had to find my groove. I had to stand up, dust myself off, and get back in the ring to keep fighting. If I couldn't do that now, then what good were my speeches anyway?

So I got back out there and did it again. And again. The phone didn't stop ringing. The power of the film led to lots of requests from all over the country. Corporations, schools, teams—all sorts of people wanted me to come give them a pep talk or a motivational speech of some sort. The movie's power was simply undeniable. Slowly but surely, the more I did it, the more I realized I didn't have to give a perfect speech. I didn't have to be Zig Ziglar, you know? What I had to be, what the audience wanted me to be (when they were expecting to meet me and not Sean Astin, that is), was Rudy! The fact that I was a regular guy was the whole basis of what made my story powerful, and it was the same thing that would make my speaking engagements powerful.

I learned to get up there and just have a conversation with the audience. I learned to not be overwhelmed by the audience, not to look at the whole audience—whether it was ten people, five hundred, or five thousand—but to look at individuals in that audience to get a read on whether or not my words seemed to be resonating. Getting them to smile was a big deal, of course. You make people smile, and you've got 'em. I saw that right away at our film premieres, like when I made that little joke about sneaking into the Rialto to watch *The Ten Commandments*. It didn't take much to make people laugh, I found. And most people who are attending a speech are really rooting for you. They want you to

succeed. They don't want to be bored. They want to be entertained, and down deep, they really, really want to be inspired.

One of the clearest examples of that lesson, for me, came around because of an old connection.

Not long after the movie came out, I got a call from Barry Alvarez. Way back in the late 1980s, when he was an assistant coach at Notre Dame, we developed a relationship through the car dealership. His dream of becoming a head coach had come true, just like he said it would—he was now head coach at Wisconsin—and he was well on his way to becoming a Hall of Famer.

"Remember that conversation we had?" he asked me.

Who could forget it? We were both locked in, dreaming of a bigger, better future. That conversation was one of those little steps in life that helps you reach your dream.

"Yeah! Of course I remember," I said.

"Well good, because I want you to come talk to my boys. I want them to hear your story, from you. We're playing Ohio State, Rudy, and if we win, we're going to the Rose Bowl. Can you do that for me?"

"Oh, man!" I said. "I'll be there!"

I went to Wisconsin the day before the big game, and I tagged along on the bus as the whole team went to a local movie theater together to see Rudy. Barry didn't tell anyone who I was. He saved it. I was just the mystery man along for the ride.

Sitting there watching that film with a bunch of top-notch football players was powerful. Like most young guys, they were a little talkative and goofing around with each other in the theater at first. But then we hooked them. The whole theater fell silent. They started to identify with the message.

After it ended, we all went back to the Holiday Inn and huddled up in a conference room. Coach Alvarez talked to them about a few housekeeping things, and then he said, "Look, you saw the movie Rudy tonight. Now, I'd like to introduce you to the real Rudy. Rudy Ruettiger."

They all went silent. As I stood up I saw tears coming down some of the guys' faces. It was all I could do not to cry right back at them! It's a powerful thing to move people, and that's exactly what that film did: it moved people.

Barry's setup meant the world.

Before I even said a word, one of the seniors stood up and said, "I'm gonna give the best I can. My life is gonna go on that line tomorrow for every one of you guys!" Another senior stood up and said, "Me too!" Then another. Boom, boom, boom! The energy in the room just exploded as those guys pumped each other up. It was a real inspirational moment for all of them, and all I did was stand there. It was a big lesson for me that amplified the idea of properly setting up my appearances. When the power of the film was present, and when the introduction was heartfelt, just my presence would have an impact on the audience. For that football team, the day before such a big game, it's as if knowing that I was real, simply knowing that I existed, drove home the whole *Rudy* message to a point that far exceeded anything they felt when they left the theater.

The next day, those players gave it all they had. But Ohio State was a mighty foe. With about twenty seconds left in the game, it was all tied up. Wisconsin had the ball. They had managed to push within twenty-five yards of the end zone, and they had a great kicker lined up and ready to go. All they needed was that field goal to win and they'd clinch their spot in the Rose Bowl. The dream game!

But it all went wrong. Just as he went to kick the ball, Ohio State's defensive end came around, and Wisconsin's offense missed him. He leapt up and blocked the field goal. The clock ran out. The tie game would stand. Getting into the Rose Bowl would now, in part, be out of their hands.

Everybody's heads went down and they headed into the locker room in a funk. But here's where Barry Alvarez stands out as one of the great ones. "Get your heads up," he told his players. "You won that football game. They didn't beat you. And you know what? They're gonna get their behinds kicked next week at Michigan State, and we're gonna beat Indiana, and we're going to the Rose Bowl!"

Who knew if any of that was really going to happen, but the point was that Barry Alvarez wasn't about to let his guys get down after holding their own against one of the strongest teams going. He's a dreamer. He's a doer. And he's a great coach.

His prediction unfolded exactly as he said it would. Wisconsin wound up playing in the Rose Bowl—and they won.

Watching that game on TV, knowing that my movie, and my story, had a little something to do with giving those guys the extra push they needed to get the job done was an amazing feeling. Knowing a guy like Barry Alvarez who never gave up on his dream, even though he got derailed for a while and was working as a police officer before going back to the game he loved and becoming the head coach he always wanted to be—that kept a fire in my belly. I wanted to stay in touch with people like him for the rest of my life.

Thankfully word of that first failed school speech didn't spread anywhere. In fact, a division of *Reader's Digest* called QSB, which does fund-raising in schools all over the country, wound up hiring me to tour and speak to schools all over America for a full two years after *Rudy* came out. Two years! And that was on top of the various calls that came in through speakers' bureaus around the country, from big corporations and sports teams looking to fly me in for an afternoon. I never had to seek out a speech. Ever. Never had to market myself. Because of the power of the film, and the message of the film, the calls came in to me.

When the *Reader's Digest* tour ended, I was contacted by Amway to give speeches all over the country as well. Another steady contract. A deal that would keep me on the road for years. I was blown away.

The reward for my preparation, the reward for being ready to tackle a new career after my dream of a movie came true, the reward for not giving up after my first failed attempts, was a career far bigger than anything I ever imagined. Suddenly, I was making more money than I ever had in my life. Thousands of dollars per speech. Thousands. In time, I found that I could make more money from a single corporate speech than my father made in a month at the oil refinery. I could make more money in a single week, if I hustled, than I used to be proud to make in an entire year! I had no idea that speakers were paid so well when I got started. And I was blown away by the fact that I could get paid the same amount of money for a speech no matter how long the speech was. If they wanted me for forty-five minutes, or for fifteen minutes, what they were basically paying me for was the impact of my presence and the inconvenience of getting me to whatever location I needed to get to on their schedule.

Perhaps the most amazing thing about the whole endeavor was that the money wasn't my motivation! My motivation was to inspire people, plain and simple. This wasn't chasing the almighty dollar through some job I didn't love so that I could make ends meet and then hopefully find a way to go after my dream. This *was* the dream. The money came along almost as a side effect.

Why? I wondered. *Why did that happen?*

It's a question I would ponder long and hard for years to come. A question that would eventually be answered, but like many things in life, would only come to me after I made a few mistakes.

Receiving the Message

Inspiration is a powerful thing. The power that one person can have to influence dozens, hundreds, thousands, even millions of lives is amazing. We recognize it in the great inspirational figures throughout history, from Abraham Lincoln to Martin Luther King Jr.; from Mother Teresa all the way back to Moses.

And yet, in many ways, one of the great sources of inspiration I see in life comes from a much humbler place. It comes from the everyday pursuit of dreams. It comes from the remarkable ripple effect that one person's dreams can have on the people around them. What I realized after *Rudy* hit theaters, and after I started traveling the country speaking to people from all walks of life, ages, and backgrounds, is that the inspiration of the *Rudy* story had spread far and wide long before the movie was even made.

It's a strange thing, because I didn't set out to try to inspire anyone! I was *seeking* inspiration. I *needed* inspiration. I craved it every step of the way. It took tremendous amounts of inspiration for me to find the strength to get out of the power plant, to get out of Joliet, and to pursue my dreams to begin with. I hope no one mistakes my message as anything but one intended in the most humble way. I'm in awe of what happened. I'm constantly amazed by it. Because what happened, with every step I took toward my own dreams, is that other people were inspired to chase their dreams too; to break free of the confines of their own goofy thoughts (as I like to call them); and to seek out the paths that God might open up to them once they took a leap of faith—even if that "leap" was just one small first step toward the life they wanted to lead.

There were even people who used my dreams and the story of the pursuit of my dreams as a direct way to inspire others. They used me and my story as a life lesson, as part of their own personal "motivational speeches." That was an astounding thing for me to discover.

Remember Pat Sullivan? He was the school counselor back in Joliet who helped me put my transcripts together to get into Holy Cross after I got out of the navy, just after Siskel died. He believed in me and gave me hope and helped me uncover the benefits of the GI Bill that would pay for my education. He came into my life and played such a powerful role. Well, come to find out, he had been using me as an inspirational example to dozens and dozens of students for a full twenty years before *Rudy* hit theaters! He would tell my story to students who were struggling, students who weren't the "college-bound" type, and use my example as a way to encourage them to go to community college. For twenty years, he had used my story of walking into Holy Cross unannounced, and then jumping from Holy Cross to Notre Dame, as a way to inspire supposedly unteachable, untrainable kids (like me) to chase higher-education dreams of their own. How awesome is that? Do you know how good it feels to learn that something you accomplished has been having that kind of influence on dozens of other kids over the course of decades? It blew me away. Of course, he continued using my story for those same purposes to even greater effect once the movie came out. The added cache of the movie helped him make his point even stronger. But the simple fact that I did it was enough to inspire dozens of kids under his care to accomplish educational dreams they had previously been told were impossible to achieve.

The ripple effect of my dreams hit closer to home as well: after I got into Notre Dame, all of my thirteen siblings—every one of them— wound up going on to some form of higher education. For most, it meant stepping foot into community college, but some of them went on to four-year schools as well, and all of them—without exception—became successful adults with successful careers and families. I attribute most of that success to my parents. I truly do. There was something perfect about the way they raised us, as tough as the circumstances were. They did the best they could. And they loved us with all of their hearts. That made all the difference in the world. My role wasn't a big one, yet it was significant. What I did was open the door. I allowed my siblings to peek into a world they didn't really know existed for them. I allowed them to see beyond the preordained life of factory work and hard labor that had been laid in front of them from the beginning. By chasing my dream, I opened up new dreams for all of them.

I want to focus specifically on my brother Francis for a moment. He's the one who was always most like me, who struggled through school with some learning disabilities and an attitude that sometimes got him into trouble. He's also the one who told me directly how much I inspired him by going to Notre Dame and landing a spot on that football team. I inspired him to chase his dream of turning the little home gym he set up in our garage into a business, Rudy's Gym, which opened and became a big, big success. It's still going strong today! The thing is, Francis also faced challenges in his adult life and wound up taking on a mid-life career change that would serve as an inspiration to lots of other people too.

Francis was built like me—short and stocky. I took that body and applied it to football, and later boxing, but he applied it to weight lifting. An older friend of his saw him working out way back in the early 1970s and said, "You're pretty strong for a little guy. Want to compete?" That little encouragement was all it took. Francis became a champion weight lifter, competing all over the US and making quite a name for himself in the sport. In fact, he got his painting up on the mural of famous Joliet sports figures that graces the side of one of the big train trestles in town. It was awesome! The whole family was so proud of him for that. As I mentioned earlier, my picture isn't up there. So in that sense, Francis is the more famous one in our family!

Weight lifting didn't provide a big living, of course, and running Rudy's Gym wasn't all that profitable either, even though it was a big success. So Francis did the typical Joliet thing and took a job at the power plant after high school. Sound familiar? Well, guess what? That job that was supposed to be so secure, the right thing to do to support your life and family, went away one day. He was laid off. I always wondered: *Had I stayed on at the power plant, would I have been laid off too?* It's strange to look at these things with the clarity of hindsight. Perhaps if I hadn't quit the power plant job, the job would have quit me.

Francis went bouncing around to any number of odd jobs after that: driving a Canfield's pop truck, working at Union Oil with our dad, eventually taking a security job at the mall. One day, at the age of thirty-one, he heard that the Joliet Police Department was testing for new recruits, and he pep-talked the other mall cops into going and taking that test together. They were all good guys. They were all smart. They all knew what they were doing. *Why couldn't they go and get jobs as real cops?* That was his thinking.

Of course, all of the other guys were younger than him, and there wound up being a thousand people who took that test in the greater Joliet area—that's 999 competitors for one of just a handful of open slots at the police academy! Most people would tell you not to bother, right? Especially at the old age of thirty-one.

Well, guess what? In part because Francis was older and had more experience in the world, he had lots of common sense to draw upon—and he wound up acing the test. He ended up number one on that list of one thousand guys. He enrolled at the police academy and threw himself into it. He loved it. The late start made him appreciate every minute of it and maybe even have more passion for it than some of the young recruits who hadn't figured out what they wanted out of life yet.

"If I'd have started as a kid, I'd have never made it," Francis once told me. I feel the exact same way about Notre Dame. There's no way I would have made it through that school without all of my experiences in the navy, at the power plant, and at Holy Cross that came before it. No way! Perhaps there's a good lesson in that.

Our parents never pressured any of us to go to college. We all chose it on our own. We all went because we wanted to go. And that made all the difference in the world. Francis has probably been through more years of schooling now as a cop than any of the rest of us. But he loves it. There's a purpose to that education. It's not just throwing money at school when you're not interested in what you're studying. That whole approach to four-year colleges, as some sort of an automatic (and very expensive) step in life, just doesn't make very much sense to me. I saw too many kids at Notre Dame who weren't passionate about it, who were wasting their parents' money by blowing off classes and partying all the time. What's the point of that? Doesn't that constant production of passionless kids in our education system hurt the country? Think about it. We're churning out thousands and thousands of kids every year who have no inspiration, no dream; all they have is just a bunch of meaningless education that leads nowhere, because they didn't choose to go after that education passionately, of their own free will.

Francis had never picked up a gun in his life before he went to the police academy (except for a shotgun when he went hunting a couple of times in his early twenties). He had never shot anything at a target or range before. Today? He's a first-rate sniper. The best of the best. The whole thing's astounding! Plus, he combined his weight-lifting abilities, Rudy's Gym, and his life on the police force to influence all kinds of troubled kids in Joliet—not only through law enforcement, but in getting kids passionate about taking care of their bodies and teaching them how to be strong and confident in life. The ripple effect of his pursuit of his passion, and his later-in-life switch in careers, is massive. In fact, I think it could probably make a movie in and of itself! It may not have the cache and majesty of Notre Dame, but it's still one heck of a story. There are lots of stories like that in families all across this country. We need to pay attention to those stories. We need to pay attention to that inspiration that's happening all around us. To learn from it, and feed off of it.

I may have made a movie. I may speak about my life story all over the country, but I can honestly say that Francis' story inspires me as much or more than I ever inspired him. It's awesome.

Of course, all of us siblings were inspired most by our parents. Watching them through the years, watching my dad reach retirement and follow through on his own dreams was a spectacular thing for all of us. He always told me, "Work now, play later," and I mostly rejected that philosophy—at least in my youth. But my dad followed that rule of his to a very successful end.

After my parents spent all of those pennies my mom had been saving to purchase a little cabin property on a lake in Wisconsin, they slowly but surely turned that place into the home of their dreams. My dad used his ever-resourceful hands to expand and completely remodel the main home and to build himself a brand-new garage from the ground up while adding a second cabin to house the kids and growing legions of grandkids who came up to visit. My strong little wisp of a mom was up there hammering nails and ripping walls apart right with him, while simultaneously turning the basement level into a museum-quality shrine to her family.

All fourteen of our First Communion portraits are placed on the wall at the bottom of the stairs . . . right next to all of our diplomas. It's quite a sight. The whole basement is chock full of photos and memorabilia from each of our big endeavors in life: trophies, awards, wedding photos, uniforms, medals, you name it! And of course, everything in that entire house has its place. My mom's sense of order never went away, even when there weren't any more kids around full-time.

My dad actually became more easy-going later in life. He didn't look so tense all the time. He smiled. He joked around. He was actually funny! Who knew? I think there's a pretty simple reason for the change: he was living his dream. He had worked hard to get there. Now, after all those years of struggle, he had produced an amazing array of successful kids, and he could take his time to kick back, play some golf, and watch all of those kids and grandkids play in the lake at the bottom of the hill that lay right outside his front door.

I also have to say, success is the best revenge, isn't it? Remember all those people who used to tease my mom and dad about their gigantic family? Who'd make fun of them for having so many kids? How many of those people would dream about having so much love around them in the later years of their lives? As the years went by, and my parents entered those years when a lot of older people start to feel lonely and neglected, they were surrounded by love. They would eventually have more than seventy grandchildren! All of them loved and adored them from the start, because they got to know them in the happiest phase of their lives. They saw only the best of them, because they were living their dream to its fullest.

If that didn't inspire me to keep going, to keep aiming high to fulfill my own dreams in life, no matter my age, I don't know what would.

I was so glad to have played a part in fulfilling a couple of their individual dreams too. Of course for my dad, seeing one of his sons play football for Notre Dame was an unimaginable high, and I did that way back in the '70s. My mom's dream was something else entirely, though: a dream that she expressed every day as she ironed our clothes.

About a year after *Rudy*'s release, when my speaking career was really on fire, I missed three speeches because of bad weather. I realized living in South Bend wasn't going to work for me anymore, and I sought out a place with an airport that rarely closed. My search led me to someplace that offered much more. A land where big dreamers come to play: Las Vegas. I wasn't a gambler, never had been. But after speaking at a conference at the Rio Hotel, I fell in love with the place. Where else on earth (besides Los Angeles, which I didn't like) had men and women proven that anything's possible, that dreams can be real in such a massive way as they had in Las Vegas? A city built from absolutely nothing in the middle of the desert! It was awesome.

Of course, Vegas is also one of the entertainment capitals of the world, and it was in that town where I was finally able to help fulfill my mom's old dream: I hooked her up with some professional musicians and producers and put her into a recording studio to record two CDs full of her favorite old songs. She sounded great! She was so happy, so thrilled to get into that studio environment and do the very thing she had admired so much in all of those old crooners she loved to listen to. We still have copies of those CDs around, and we play them for the grandkids whenever we get a chance. Knowing that grandma recorded a couple of albums is an inspiration in and of itself, which opens doors for the more musical members of our family and lets them know that they can accomplish that dream too. The same way my success, and Francis' success, has inspired some of those grandkids to go on to professional sports careers themselves. When you think about it, the cycle of inspiration never ends. One dream leads to another. I marvel at that every day.

Allowing one dream to lead to another was what finally opened up a window in my personal life as well. In all those years of struggling to make ends meet while pursuing my film, I found it difficult to make room for lasting relationships. Now? With a dream fulfilled and my life busier than ever, I somehow had room. I fell in love. I got married. And before long I was starting a family of my own. It all just seemed to fall into place. After all those years.

The way I see it, there are three cycles in life.

During the first cycle, you're a child. You dream. But all of a sudden, your parents and society and schools are telling you how things work, and how they're going to be, and you get confused by it all and the complexities of figuring out what you think you should be in life.

During the second cycle, it's all about what you do. You learn how to unravel all of that confusion as you go through struggles and eventually become the person you really want to be. This is the time when you wind up doing what you have to do, not necessarily what you want to do. It's when you take a job as an insurance salesman, or a construction worker, or waitress, and hopefully develop enough to see the path you really want to be on for the rest of your life and take the necessary steps to get there.

The third cycle is when you've gone through all of that and gathered the wisdom of that entire journey, from all of your experiences (good, bad, and indifferent), and you realize that it's time to help other people learn how to get through those first two cycles on their own. It's all about giving back.

That third cycle is what my speaking career has been about from the beginning. It's not about telling people what to do. I'm not a "motivational speaker" in that way. I can't stand the idea that someone tells you to take ten steps to success. *Well, what happens if I mess up step number nine? Does that mean I can't achieve that dream?* That kind of thinking can mess with people. Instead, what I want to do is inspire people by sharing my story, sharing my experiences, opening up their eyes through the story of my own struggles and successes so they can go out and find their own paths to whatever sort of success they're seeking in life. There isn't just one way to accomplish a goal. There wasn't just one path to get into Notre Dame. You have to find *your* way to get to whatever dreams you have!

People get sidetracked by "self-help" ideas at times. Lots of books tell you to write down your goals and get organized about them. Well, what if that just slows you down? What if you're not someone who responds to that whole idea? I didn't write down any of my goals, and I accomplished them and exceeded them. I tell kids, "Just do it." I know Nike likes to think they have a monopoly on that phrase from their famous advertising campaigns, but it's a universal truth. Just do it! Go get it done, whatever it is you need to do. To me, that makes more sense. If part of what you need to do is to write down your goals, then write down your goals. Figure it out for yourself. That's the message. I don't have the answers—you do! The answers are inside you. The answers are in those gut feelings, that little voice that God gives you to know right from wrong, and you have to respond to that gut, to those messages.

"Where's the Rudy in you?" is a phrase I use a lot. Remember, Rudy was a nickname for *all* of my brothers. Rudy, to me, isn't an individual thing. It's a symbolic name. Ever since the movie came out, the name "Rudy" symbolizes a certain drive, a certain "never give up" attitude. I'm not about pumping up my own ego when I refer to Rudy in a third-person way like that. It's about using that recognition, using the power of the Rudy name and what it symbolizes, to inspire people. Where's the Rudy in you? It's in there somewhere. Let's bring it out. I'm not saying I have all the answers. But *you* do—and you're gonna have to do the work and do what you need to do to get to those answers. That's it. That's all there is to it. Just do it.

I'm no self-help guru. I'm certainly not going to dictate how you go about your life, or tell you any changes you should or shouldn't make. I simply want to be a mentor. If you've seen the movie, if you've heard me speak, if you've listened to the message, you'll see that it's all up to you now. That's the message that comes through in my conversations with crowds of all shapes and sizes, from ten kids in a classroom to ten thousand people in a stadium.

What is remarkable to me, what has kept me going from airport to airport, speech to speech, day after day, week after week, for all these years is the fact that my message gets through. The *Rudy* message has changed people's lives. I see it, hear it, live it, breathe it, and have the amazing good fortune to experience it firsthand every day.

I couldn't possibly count the number of speeches I've given and appearances I've made after which an audience member, sometimes many audience members, approached me in tears. Sometimes they've been moved by my words. Sometimes they want to share a personal story about how they've been moved or changed by the movie. And every time, I'm humbled and motivated to keep going.

After a speech in Iowa a few years back, an autistic child and his father approached me, and the kid handed me a copy of *Rudy* to sign. The cover of the DVD was all worn out. "It's the only movie he watches," his father said to me, and then he started to cry. "For years, I couldn't talk to my son. He wouldn't communicate with his mom and me at all. But for some reason, when he watches *Rudy*, we can talk to him. And he talks to us. It's changed our lives. I can't thank you enough."

It's hard not to tear up myself when I hear something like that. How do you even respond? I don't understand it. How is it possible that the act of pursuing my dream could lead to the making of a movie that would allow that father and son to connect as never before? It's astounding. It's a miracle. There's no way to plan for it or predict it. Over time, I heard of more autistic kids opening up because of the movie too. Was it the story? The cinematography? That beautiful music? Who knows? But none of it would have happened if I hadn't gone after my dream of Notre Dame in the very beginning. How wild is that? How amazing is it that God could put me on a path that would lead to that sort of conclusion? It's unimaginable!

I remember meeting a pilot who wanted to fly for Federal Express. He kept applying, and they kept turning him down. He watched the movie over and over, and simply kept reapplying after every viewing until he got the job. That message of perseverance was what he needed to succeed.

I met a woman who always wanted to be a nurse, but life got in the way; she never went to school. She saw the movie and decided to go for it—at the age of thirty-eight. She was forty-eight when I met her, and celebrating ten years in the career of her dreams, happier than ever.

I met a young woman at an appearance who had attended one of my speeches a couple of months earlier. She was visibly pregnant, and she told me that she was planning to get an abortion until she heard me speak that first time. My speech had changed her mind and changed her life, and the tears streamed down her face as she described how happy she was because of it.

There have been a number of little kids who were fighting leukemia who watched *Rudy* as a way to help them stay motivated to keep up the fight as they went through chemo.

Ethan Zohn, the soccer player who won the TV reality show *Survivor* and who has publicly battled Hodgkin's disease, has given lots of credit to *Rudy* for helping him gather the strength he needed to get through multiple grueling sets of chemo and two stem-cell transplants on his way to becoming a "survivor" in real life. The stories are just endless!

I don't talk about abortion or the sanctity of life in my speeches. I don't give instructions for becoming a pilot or a nurse. I never imagined that a movie could help anyone in their battle against cancer. All I do is share my experience in the hopes of unlocking the potential that every one of those listeners has inside of them. There's magic in that. I'm so privileged to experience that. It's a gift.

The thing is, every one of us has stories to tell of our successes and achievements. Every one of us can give back in that third cycle of life. You don't need a stage and a sound system and a giant audience. You certainly don't need a movie to be made about your life. I encourage everyone I know to share his or her success stories with anyone who'll listen. Not just to share the end result—bragging won't help anyone—but to share the process. That's the key: tell them how you did it. Tell them how you achieved your success. Show them that wherever there's a will, there's a way. Open their eyes to the possibilities in their own lives. You never know whose life you'll change.

One of the most surprising stories for me took place over an eighteen-year span. Something I said eighteen years earlier had created an entire movement, and I wasn't even aware until I got a call asking me to go give a speech at an alternative school for inner-city high school kids.

The principal of the school had heard me deliver a speech shortly after the film's release, way back in 1993 or early 1994. He was eighteen years old at the time. He was thirty-six now, and he was actively fulfilling his dream to teach some of the toughest kids imaginable that they could be anybody they want to be.

That principal picked me up at the airport, and as we drove up to his school I looked at him and said, "You want me to speak in there? It looks like a prison! I can't go in there." I saw all of these tough-looking kids headed in through the front door, wearing their jeans down below their underwear, with head wraps and all kinds of gang-banger gear. "That's a losing situation," I said. "Those kids won't listen to me."

"Oh yes they will," he said.

"Why? Why would they listen to me?"

"Rudy, I'm not going to tell you. I want you to find out for yourself. As we walk through that door, they're gonna transform."

It didn't make sense to me, and I think I was more nervous heading into that school than I've been walking into any situation in my life. Yet as soon as we walked inside, I saw what he was talking about. Each and every kid was handed a uniform: A pair of khaki pants and a T-Shirt. The shirts had a phrase on them: "Rudy's Lessons." Every one of those kids had read a copy of a little paperback I wrote in 1999 called *Rudy's Insights*. The school had been using *Rudy* and my inspirational topics as a basis for their entire curriculum.

As soon as I walked into that auditorium, they started chanting,

"Ru-dy! Ru-dy! Ru-dy!" It was awesome. I fed off of that energy and gave one of the best speeches of my life. It was so powerful to see my message getting out there and reaching kids in even some of the toughest neighborhoods in America. Gang life had nearly swallowed their whole community. If it weren't for this school, these kids would have been walking the streets with guns in their pockets. Yet here they were, embracing a message of hope, a message of inspiration. Embracing me! An old, stocky guy from the Midwest! I was really floored. I couldn't thank that principal enough, even as he went out of his way to thank me for inspiring him eighteen years earlier.

I had been hoping that the *Rudy* message was getting through to kids for years. In 1997, my wife and I founded the Rudy Foundation, a nonprofit specifically aimed at supporting and recognizing folks who live in the spirit of *Rudy*. As part of that foundation, we also set up the Rudy Awards, aimed at high school and college kids who make an exceptional effort to do their personal best, overcome obstacles, stay on track to reach their dreams, and build the qualities of character, courage, contribution, and commitment in their everyday lives. The whole idea was to recognize the future Rudys of the world and to give them a boost. The awards are given out at schools all across the country now, and in recent years more than a million people have voted to select the winners. I'm as proud of that as anything else I've done in my career. I know those awards touch lives. More than that, I know the ripple effect of spotlighting these kids in their communities inspires others to follow the same set of principles. We all see so many of the super-talented individuals, the gifted athletes and academics, getting awarded over and over again all through our school years. When we stand up and recognize the little guys, the less-talented guys and gals with big hearts and big dreams, that sends a message. A message of hope.

And boy oh boy, do we need a message of hope more than ever in America today.

Life Lessons

Fame. Celebrity. Success. None of it makes a man immune to the highs and lows of life.

How many politicians have we seen fall from grace? How many star athletes and celebrities have we seen collapse right off of their pedestals? Life lessons keep coming at you no matter how successful or powerful you might be. Challenges, obstacles, roadblocks keep coming, no matter how old you are and how many obstacles you've already overcome to get to wherever you happened to have arrived in your life.

That I know firsthand.

The thing I also know—and this is part of the wisdom and clarity that comes with age and experience—is that it's all a part of God's plan. All of it. Every bit.

It's all about the journey. And that journey is ongoing, no matter how much you fool yourself into thinking that you've finally "made it."

God will make sure of that. Every time.

Is there any doubt in anyone's mind that America was slapped with a major wake-up call in the late 2000s? After years and years of running up debts we simply couldn't repay, after building an illusion of prosperity on a sandbox rather than a solid foundation, all of our markets came crashing down: the stock market, the housing market, the job market, the Main Street markets, the retirement market, the health-care market, the political market, the social market, the American Spirit market, the personal bank account market, even our personal self-esteem market. Almost everything that seemed to be going right in America suddenly went "poof," just like that, by the end of 2008.

How did that happen? How did we *let* that happen?

I think the simple answer is we, as a society and as a government, took our eyes off the ball. In America, we have always stood for something, but for far too many years, we've simply stood for the wrong things. We stood for expansion at any cost. We stood for the false notion of "bigger is better," at any cost. We stood for the false riches of brands and status, rather than real prosperity and happiness. We set up a system of what I like to call "funny money," where everyone was getting loans based on nothing to build things that didn't really need building, until suddenly the funny money ran out, and there was nothing left, and no one could repay those debts, and then no one could pay their bills. The Wall Street guys, the big banks, the perpetrators of much of the funny money disaster—they all got bailed out. They, in a sense, got rewarded for their bad behavior. And they continued to play like high rollers with America's future, while the little guy continued to struggle and fail.

People call it the Great Recession. I think a more accurate term is the Great Reset.

The thing is, hitting the reset button in life can be incredibly positive. How many times did I fail and hit the reset button in my own life during my journey to Notre Dame and beyond? Many! But my life improved after every failure. My attitude improved. My focus improved. And that's a lesson that America, as a whole, needs to remember. We've been through world wars. We've been through the Great Depression. We've always come back stronger, and I believe we'll come back stronger again. But we've got to get focused in order to do that. We have to honor our great soldiers of inspiration and empowerment. They gave us the ability to do and think and be, and to have and to use our freedom of speech. Are we mad? Are we angry? Of course! But it's time now to churn that anger into positive things instead of being destructive and tearing people down. We must focus on what we really want to stand up for.

For years, as the banks were handing out home loans and equity lines and credit cards with $100,000 limits, we simply bought into it as if it were free money. It wasn't. Now we're paying for it. And we'll be paying for a long time to come. We bought into the illusion of status, building bigger homes, bigger buildings, bigger stadiums. We're caught up in the need to be bigger and richer, at the cost of tradition and values. It's an empty shell. Where's the feeling? Where's the dream? Where's the passion that's driving us?

I'm not just flailing out wildly at America here. I'm no politician and I'm not blaming a party or a president, or taking a political stance, believe me. I'm angry about all of this and bothered by it deeply, because it happened to me, personally.

In the hullabaloo of the late 2000s, I took my eye off the ball. After so many years on the road, making a wonderful living giving speeches and feeding off of the energy that those audiences provided my spirit, I got a little lazy. Maybe I was just tired. Even rock stars will tell you the constant blur of airports and hotels starts to get to you after a while. And I'm no rock star! The long and short of it is, I found myself searching for quick fixes, for easy money, for ways to set myself up for retirement and a life of luxury that wouldn't require so many countless hours of nonstop effort and travel.

I had gotten married. I had two kids. There was a part of me that wanted to settle down with them. But there was also a part that saw lots and lots of people all around me getting very rich, very fast, by dabbling in the real estate market in our seemingly endless boomtown of Las Vegas—as well as lots of other crazy ventures in all kinds of start-ups and risky businesses—and the temptation of that big, easy money seemed too good to pass up. I used what equity I had to start expanding into those ventures myself.

Real estate came first. I had bought and sold condos back in South Bend, and I owned a nice house in one of the finest neighborhoods just outside Las Vegas at the time. So I took out some loans against that house, and I sunk some big money into building projects that I thought were "sure things." (There's a phrase to be wary of, always!) Well, guess what? I was just as foolish as everyone else in America who falsely assumed everything was a "sure thing" because the boom times had lasted for so long. It's amazing how quickly we forget about history. It's amazing how quickly we all forget that there are cycles to every economy. My timing was all wrong; the real estate bubble burst, and those sure things suddenly became burdensome debts instead of the wonderful, overflowing assets I had expected. The debts were so large that I couldn't keep up. Suddenly I was under water. All that money I had saved up from all those hours on the road went "poof"—just like the stock market, and all of those other markets in America.

It was around this same time when I started to hear people talk about tremendous profits being made all over the place in the sports drink and energy drink markets. So my ears perked up when a business idea came my way: a plan to create a first-class sports drink that would use the brand of "Rudy" and my inspirational message to grab the attention of sports enthusiasts everywhere. The plan would be to create this beverage, market it like crazy, and then sell it to a big conglomerate. After all, a little company called Vitamin Water had sold to Coca-Cola in 2007 for $4.1 billion. That's *billion* with a *B*!

"Sounds good to me!" I said.

It didn't go well. The company was floundering after a few months and desperately needed an infusion of cash. *How do you raise money, and fast?* With the addition of some new business partners, we went after an idea to make a public stock offering.

Again it didn't go well. My mind kept thinking of that capital *B*, and an easy-street life of living off those beverage profits.

At one point, I was named CEO of the company. I'll spare you the finer details of what happened behind the scenes, but the Securities and Exchange Commission (the SEC) eventually came knocking on my door.

They filed a complaint against me and my company. I told the SEC everything I knew. I was an open book.

I fell into the same obvious trap that the rest of the country had fallen into in all of those boom years: I shouldn't have been chasing the money. I should have been chasing the dream. I'm especially sorry that my chasing the money affected other people who believed in me as well. It was one of the most profound, simple, important lessons I would ever learn—and the consequences of that lesson would haunt me for years.

I've thought long and hard about this, and I think it's an important lesson for America. It stems from my personal journey and the power of the *Rudy* message. (Funny that I would learn a lesson from my own story, and my own movie, this late in life.)

Back when I had the dreams of going to Notre Dame, playing for the Fighting Irish, and making a movie about my life, those dreams led to great things. I found myself surrounded with great people who shared those dreams and helped me reach those dreams. When I dreamed of becoming a great public speaker, that developed into a very lucrative career for me. The money was a secondary effect of all those great dreams. Only now, when I dove into the realms of real estate and beverage companies, when all I was doing was dreaming about making money, did I find myself in real trouble.

When the SEC filed a civil complaint against me and my company, I fully accepted responsibility for what I had done. I was the CEO. It would take a couple of years to sort it all out, but finally, in 2011, we settled the case and I paid a hefty fine.

I also paid a hefty price in the press: headlines stating "SEC Sacks Rudy!" I had never really suffered any negative press attention before. This was a first. And a last. There wasn't much I could say, but this I know: I never, ever should have focused on the money.

We've got to stay focused on the correct dreams in life. Good dreams. Meaningful dreams. It's the only way forward. I was shocked and hurt to have to relearn that lesson so late in life. And yet, I'm glad to have learned it. It's a message I can now share with others, in my speeches, in my TV appearances, and even here, in this book. Perhaps God sees me as a messenger for that lesson, the same way I've been an unlikely messenger for so many powerful lessons in my life.

If that's the case, and if I can help even one other person in the world avoid getting into a similar bad situation, then I'm happy to have gone through that struggle. I'm happy to be that messenger.

⊏⊐

The year 2011 was not an easy one for me.

Remember my sister Carol? The one who was left behind at the grocery store when she was eight years old? The one my mom panicked over, throwing us all back in the car so she could race back to the store to find her? Well, Carol was now caring for my father pretty much full-time. He was aging, and my mom couldn't take care of him alone. There was something fitting and beautiful about that. I'm so thankful, all the time, for her service to my parents. They sacrificed everything for us, and I was encouraged to know they were surrounded with love.

But at the same time, I was suffering under the financial weight of the ever-struggling economy, dealing with some issues in my marriage, and still juggling a nonstop speaking-engagement schedule at a time in our country when I seriously questioned whether the *Rudy* message of hope and perseverance was even getting through anymore; it all seemed like too much.

And then my dad died.

I can honestly say that he died a happy man. As I've already mentioned, he was living his dream. He had his wife by his side at their dream cabin by the lake, and he was surrounded, constantly, by the love and admiration of the massive family that he and my mom had created.

But that doesn't make it any easier.

He was my greatest inspiration. He was the guy I wanted to make proud. He was the guy I so desperately wanted a hug from and who gave me the most meaningful hug in the world on one of the proudest days of his life. I loved him. And though he wasn't the type who would say it out loud, he loved me too. I knew that. Always.

I got some one-on-one time with him just a few days before he passed away. We hugged each other. We told each other, "I love you." I managed to say good-bye in my own way, and felt blessed to see him smile one last time. I loved seeing that smile on his face. That smile he worked so hard, for so long, to find.

It's interesting that even at the end, some of the old feelings from back in Joliet were still lingering inside of him. He asked one of my sisters one day, as he lay in his bed, "How many big shots we got?" My sister knew exactly what he meant by that. He was thinking of all those people at work who used to put his family down. The same ones who dismissed the notion that a Ruettiger could get into Notre Dame, let alone play for the Fighting Irish. She answered swiftly: "They're all big shots, Dad."

He smiled and replied, "Good."

In the last picture ever taken of him, as he lay there in his bedroom, I swear you can see an angel hovering above his bed. It's right there, clear as day to every one of us kids and all of his grandkids who have stared at that picture and marveled at it. Believe what you will. But my dad was a good man. And I fully believe that angel was there to take him up to heaven. I know that's where he is right now.

Hope

Things in life are never *all* bad. While there were plenty of tough times that year, there were some highlights. I was invited to a high school in the Bronx where Regis Philbin had gone to school. On the same day, *Yankees Magazine*, the official magazine of the New York Yankees, sent a reporter over to interview me for a feature. I happened to mention to that reporter that I had always wanted to go to Yankee Stadium. Imagine my surprise when he took me right over and introduced me to members of the Steinbrenner family and the groundskeepers, and let me walk down on that field for a picture; he basically opened the whole place up to me for a personal tour! It was like living a childhood dream, and I even got the chance to tell them of my wish to throw out a first pitch at a Yankees game someday. We'll see if that happens. Nevertheless, to this day they still play a clip from *Rudy* on the JumboTron during every seventh-inning stretch at that glorious ballpark. That was one inspiring day!

In between the bad times, I got invited to speak at major corporations all over this country. Everywhere I went, the sales teams were as fired up as ever to hear me speak, and they were eager to take my message and apply it to their business practices.

But with dad gone and the country still mired in this state of joblessness and hopelessness, I was definitely in a funk. That's a weird thing to be when you're "Rudy." People expect to see the fire and energy and excitement that goes with the symbolic nature of that name.

I think I just needed some kind of a sign. I needed a message. Some sort of inspiration to get me back on track. I hoped and prayed that inspiration might be found back where it all began: on the Notre Dame campus. I was invited back to South Bend to sign autographs and attend a couple of dinners and special events for the College Football Hall of Fame that summer, and I jumped at the chance. *Sure. Why not?* I thought. Maybe a walk around campus, a visit to the Grotto, a walk into the locker room, or the chance to step foot again in that tunnel and take a walk out onto the field at Notre Dame Stadium would do me some good.

I even set myself up with a room at St. Joe Hall. St. Joe's isn't a dormitory for Holy Cross students and seminarians now. It's the Parish House. But the rooms and the overall feel of the place are remarkably the same as they were back in 1972. Except for the fact that they gave me a room with a private bathroom, it was the same little space with a simple wooden desk, a lamp in the corner, that military-style metal-framed bed, a closet with a rickety old bureau stuffed in it, and no air-conditioning! I opened up the window and caught a breeze off of the lake. The trees had grown so tall that I could no longer look across the water to the Golden Dome. For that, I'd have to step outside and hop on one of those paths I used to travel every day.

The sound of my feet crunching on that gravel walk was so familiar in my ears, it took me right back to my youth. I headed west at first. I just wanted to get beyond the tree line to catch a view of the dome, and where I wound up standing was the very spot where I had taken Freddy to share my acceptance letter from Notre Dame. The very same spot where Sean Astin sat on a bench in my movie and opened his acceptance letter, bursting into tears of joy and relief when he finally realizes his goal of getting into the school of his dreams after four semesters of trying and failing.

We had moved a bench there temporarily just for the movie. But today, there's a stone bench permanently affixed to that spot. And there's something remarkable that I noticed as I took a seat there to gaze across the water. Staring straight ahead at the Golden Dome, noticing how beautifully its image was reflected in the water below, I caught a glimpse of another reflection off to the left. It was a reflection of the local power plant. I looked up at the dome and then turned my head just a few degrees left and noticed the smoke stacks and hulking presence of that concrete building rising into the sky. It blew me away. I had never noticed how close those two buildings were to each other. From that vantage point, the difference between the Golden Dome of Notre Dame and that power plant couldn't have been more than ten degrees apart. The simple turn of a head. The symbolism of it sunk in hard. The difference between my predestined life in a power plant and the glorious life I was so blessed to be living was only a few degrees apart. A matter of turning my head and grabbing a different perspective. I could look straight ahead and see both of those worlds represented in those two buildings, and I was so grateful in that moment for knowing that I had made that shift. I had changed my thoughts; I had changed my direction in life and chosen the Golden Dome.

It was a pretty good start to my days on campus, recapturing that sense of awe and wonder, the magic I always felt in that setting.

I found a part of it pretty quickly the first time I walked over to the Grotto too. The beauty of that spot and those glowing candles lit my soul for a moment. Then I walked up the steps and made my way into the Basilica, where I basked in the glow of the stained glass for a few moments before wandering over to climb the steps under the Golden Dome.

Inside, I couldn't believe who I ran into: LeShane Saddler. The former Notre Dame football player used to hang out at my condo, met his wife at our Thursday night hang-outs, and always participated in chalk talks with lots of enthusiasm and gusto. I couldn't believe it. He was happy to see me, and I was surprised to run into him in that setting. It turns out he works for the admissions department now. He took me back to his office and we wound up talking with some of the admissions folks, who were really glad to meet me. And they told me something that no one had told me before: that a vast number of applications and essays they receive from high school seniors all over America today mention *Rudy* as one of the reasons they're applying to Notre Dame. I couldn't believe it! I knew the Rudy Awards were going strong, of course, and that at least some students out there were getting the *Rudy* message, but were high school students really still watching that film in a way that was influencing their college decisions?

That's when LeShane revealed something really cool as well. After graduation, he had spent thirteen years as a high school teacher, teaching US history. And for each of those thirteen years, he had shown *Rudy* in his classroom. Sometimes, before he would screen it, his students would pipe up and say, "What does this football movie have to do with US history?"

He would tell them, "This movie isn't about football. This movie's about dreams, it's about perseverance, it's about heart, it's about endurance, it's about overcoming the odds, and that's a story that you're going to see repeated throughout the history of this country."

Man! That really fired me up.

At one point I made my way across campus and headed to the brand-new football facilities—an entire building dedicated to the football team's training and locker room that didn't exist when I was in school. It was kind of funny as I walked up toward the entrance. There were a few football players standing outside the door in their street clothes. Practice had just ended a short while ago, apparently, and they were hanging out chitchatting before heading wherever they had to go. As I approached the door, one of the bigger guys who completely towered over me said, "Can I help you? You can't go in there." I smiled at him and introduced myself, and in an instant his whole attitude changed. Clearly my legacy was still strong here. All of those other players standing around asked if they could take pictures with me, and they pulled out their cell phones. I asked if anyone would mind if I took a look around. I just wanted to see what they had done to the place, and that big guy who stopped me suddenly became my tour guide.

Lo and behold, just inside the doorway, in a spot that every one of those players would pass on the way in and out of that locker room every single day, there was a plaque on the wall commemorating *Rudy*.

The Notre Dame locker room today is probably finer than any locker room in the NFL. It's carpeted, with fine wood lockers and a red-velvet rope cordoning off the big "ND" on the floor, so no one accidentally steps on that mighty symbol. The training facilities were gorgeous and staffed to the hilt. The hallways were filled with statues and trophies and memorabilia. It was awesome. I hope those kids realize how fortunate they are! It didn't even smell like a locker room in there.

Outside once again, walking between the grand old buildings, my eyes were drawn up toward heaven and I started to feel that glory. I took a walk over to the stadium where someone from the grounds crew happened to be around to unlock the gate and let me take a walk inside. I went all the way up in the bleachers, toward the top, to that spot where I used to sit and look down on the field, dreaming of playing someday. I went down and walked into the tunnel, turning back to look at the field from the vantage point where I had once stood with all of the excitement in the world, raring to run out and lead my team onto that field; then I turned the other way to see Touchdown Jesus perfectly framed through the far end of the tunnel.

In that moment, I thought of my father. It was just outside of that tunnel where he had given me his first hug.

I could hardly believe he had given me his last just a few weeks earlier.

I didn't sleep well that night. The bed was uncomfortable. The room was too hot. My mind simply wouldn't turn off and relax. I tossed and turned, thinking about what was next for me. I had lots of speaking engagements lined up. I knew I would have a chance to move past some of the mistakes, and that I would find a way to recover financially as long as I stayed focused on my dream. But was the dream of continuing to spread the *Rudy* message even working? I hoped to spread the message far beyond the business world, far beyond the sports world, to kids from all walks of life. But whenever I looked around at young people today, addicted to video games, suffering from obesity and diabetes like never before in a society that has an impossibly hard time creating jobs, I couldn't help but wonder: Is there any hope left? Are these kids today getting the message they need in order to survive and thrive in life? Are they getting the wisdom and inspiration they need to help save our country?

I just needed a sign. Something to tell me I was still pointed in the right direction. That my dream was still worthwhile. That my dream was still having an impact.

I've said it before, and I'll say it again right here: sometimes when you're looking for something, asking for something, even praying for something, the answer falls right into your lap. As long as you're ready to receive it, God's gifts come when you least expect them.

I took a jog the next day and spent some more time wandering around campus—into the library, into the student center. Late that afternoon, I sat down to grab a coffee outside the Notre Dame bookstore. The sun was setting and that beautiful midwestern orange glow was starting to cast long shadows across the lush greenery and old stone buildings.

All of a sudden, a group of teenage-looking girls came running out of the bookstore's side doors.

"Are you Rudy?" one of them shouted. "Are you the real Rudy?! The man inside told us that you're Rudy Ruettiger."

I thought about denying it. I wasn't really in the mood for any kind of attention. I just wanted to enjoy my cup of coffee. But these girls were so excited for some reason, I said, "Yeah. I'm Rudy."

Well, you would have thought I was one of the Beatles in 1966. These girls started squealing and screaming. "Oh! I'm gonna cry. I'm gonna cry!" The reaction was all tears and giddiness. "Can I get a picture? . . . Can I give you a hug? . . . Mr. Ruettiger, I love your movie. It's my favorite!"

I didn't know what to say. "Thanks!" I said. "Here, sit down, sit down. What brings you girls to campus?"

There were about ten of them, ages thirteen to fifteen, and they were all there for a summer program on forensics. A science camp, basically, that was teaching them all of the principles the crime scene investigators use, just like on the TV show *CSI*.

They started asking all kinds of questions about the movie. They wanted to know what Sean Astin was like, and how we wound up casting him. "Did you know that Sean went back to college after we filmed *Rudy*?" I told them. They were all surprised by that. "Yeah, he had gone for a couple of years, but after the movie he went back and decided to finish his degree at UCLA." They all thought that was real cool.

They asked about Jon Favreau and Vince Vaughn, who had both turned into really big stars over the years, and I explained to them how fulfilling my own dream of making a movie helped give them their chance to break into Hollywood. They thought that was pretty cool too.

It was strange to me, but these girls knew all kinds of details about the film, as if it were fresh in their minds.

"The part where your friend died—how did that really affect you?" one girl asked.

"When you lose a close friend who you've mentored with, you realize how life is so short," I said. That's when they really started listening to me. I could feel their energy, and I started to tune in as they tuned in to me. A few more girls gathered around, and then some older girls in their late teens and early twenties who were camp counselors came over too.

The whole thing turned into a deep chat session.

One girl asked about the scene on the bench by the lake. "Did you cry 'cause you were so happy?"

"I did," I said.

"I cry too, when I'm happy," she said.

One girl hadn't seen the movie, but she knew all about it. "Oh! You're the one who couldn't play for three years, and then got to play, and made a tackle?" It was amazing that she knew the story without having seen the movie. How does that happen?

One girl said, "No offense, but I thought you were a lot older. I thought you had passed away."

We all had a good laugh at that one.

I asked the girls where they were from. One was from Detroit. Another from Carlyle, Pennsylvania. One was from Michigan City. One from just south of Chicago, near Joliet. It was wild. These girls were from all over the country! And they all knew *Rudy*. So I asked where they had seen the film. Some of them saw it in school. One girl said it was shown in health class, which I thought was interesting. Some saw it at home; their parents showed it to them. A couple of them owned the DVD. Some had watched it on Netflix. One of the eighteen-year-old girls said she had been watching it over and over since she was five years old. *Five!*

They all spoke about what an inspiration the story was, and I decided to share something that had happened to me just a few weeks earlier. I had gone to a Lakers game, and I was down on the floor before the game started and was introduced to basketball star Kobe Bryant. I didn't know if he'd even know who I was. But when I said my name, his eyes got real big. "Rudy? From the movie?" he said to me.

Turns out Kobe Bryant had watched *Rudy* when he was sixteen years old. He told me, right then and there, that the movie was what inspired him to get serious. *Rudy* is the reason he's in the NBA. He watched it over and over again through the years just to remind himself what was important. *Rudy* is the reason he's always the first guy at practice, working out longer and harder than everyone else, he said. He realized that if Rudy could make his dream come true, then a guy with his sort of talent had an obligation to work just as hard to get as far as he could in life. The girls loved that story!

"You've gotta go after your dreams, because you never know who you're going to influence," I said. I was really getting pumped up now. "When I was trying to get into Notre Dame and to play football, I never imagined I would meet Kobe Bryant, or that he would be influenced by me. Who could ever imagine that? Heck, I never imagined I would meet *you!* But we meet 'cause you do something; you fulfill a dream."

They all posed for cell phone pictures and started posting to their Facebook pages as I asked them to tell me what they thought the message of the movie was. This was sort of a test for me. I wanted to see if it was still getting through to this younger generation.

One girl responded without hesitation: "Keep going for your dreams."

Another personalized her response. "It made me be confident and see that I could do anything I want to if I try hard enough."

"Your movie reminds me of the slogan Notre Dame has," one of the older girls piped up. "*Play like a champion today.*"

At this point, I realized that these girls were searching for something, just as I was searching for something. There was something in the air as the sun set. Some of that Notre Dame magic had made its way to the bookstore patio.

The girl from Detroit spoke up again: "People where I live, they loved that movie because you tried and you did everything you could."

"Isn't that what America's all about?" I said.

One girl then looked right at me and said, "I love how you're as inspirational in real life as you are in the story."

Phew. That one got me. With everything I had been through that year, it was all I could do not to well up with tears. I decided to jump right back into the message: "Girls, you ever look in the mirror and say, 'I have a pimple today'?" They all laughed. "You ever look in the mirror and say, 'I'm not that good-looking'? Well, you know what God sees? God sees nothing but beauty. That's it. You're fooled by these goofy people giving you goofy thoughts.

"The truth is you *are* someone," I said. "The truth is, get rid of your goofy thoughts. The truth is, don't let someone influence what you want to do. You have that choice. That's the most powerful thing you have. No one is going to stop you from doing what you want to do but *you*, and that's the truth."

One of the youngest girls was sitting close to me this whole time. She was the quietest of the bunch, listening very intently. For some reason I turned to her right in that moment and said four words: "You're awesome, little lady."

She started crying. For some reason, right in that moment, she needed to hear those words. I don't know why. I can't presume why. This young girl needed that encouragement.

I nearly started blubbering too. This girl was about my daughter's age, and I know how hard it is for kids going through that awkward adolescent stuff, dealing with school and bullies and certain teachers who do the opposite of inspire and certain peers who do the opposite of inspire and even parents who do the opposite of inspire. I tried to pull myself together and keep talking without losing it.

"So, are you going to listen to someone who says to you, 'You can't do that'? Is that the guy you're going to listen to? Are you going to listen to someone who says, 'Here's why you *can't* do it,' or are you going to listen to someone who says, 'Sure, you'll find a way'? Because the fact is, you already have the answer. It's inside of you. What's the answer? *'Do it.'*"

The other girls noticed her crying, and a couple of them put their hands on her shoulders. I turned my attention back to her.

"Don't let people influence your thoughts. I know what you're going through, and you know what? You're gonna be a big winner. 'Cause you're fighting right now, aren't you?"

The girl nodded and cried harder. All the girls came in for a big group hug. The unconditional support they gave to each other in that moment was a beautiful thing. These girls had only known each other for a few days. It was remarkable.

Not every one of them would get it. Not every one of them would remember this experience a week or a month or a year from now. But there was more than one girl in that group who would remember that moment—the feeling of that moment—for the rest of their lives. I certainly knew I would.

Over an hour had passed since they first came up to me. It was almost dark. One of the counselors spoke up and said it was time for all the girls to be getting back. They all went, "*Awwwww,*" and came in for a great big group hug good-bye.

"We learned a lot of lessons here tonight," I said.

In some ways, I think I was saying it mostly to myself. That hour had been exactly the connection, the boost, the sign, and the answer I needed.

As the summer sun set down over Notre Dame, the school that forever changed my life, you know what I saw in the eyes of those girls? Inspiration. I saw a little sampling of our next generation, from all walks of life, from all across this country, who with or without my help were seeking out the message. Getting the message. Living the message.

The *Rudy* message. The message I have been so humbled by and have tried to do my part to deliver in any way I can for all these years.

And that gave me hope. More hope than I'd had in a long time.

As I said good-bye and walked across those sprawling green lawns, as the first stars of evening lit up in the sky and those familiar bells rang out from the Basilica, I was filled with the very same feeling I had the first time I ever stepped foot on that campus.

It felt like a new beginning. The beginning of something big.

I wasn't sure where that path would take me, but with every step I took, I was certain I was on the right path.

Acknowledgments

This book would not have been possible without the hard work, dedication, friendship, and support of the entire team that makes up my life—starting with my brothers and sisters, and of course, my mom and dad. Losing my father as I worked on these pages was not easy. But I know he's in heaven, smiling down on his great big family full of "big shots." My dad wore that Notre Dame ring I gave him until the day he died. I wear it now, in his honor—every day—while he wears the Notre Dame ring that I wore myself for nearly forty years.

I want to thank my beautiful, loving, and talented children, Jessica Noel and Daniel Joseph, who continue to inspire me to live my dream. My agent, Joel Kneedler at Alive Communications, and my editor, Debbie Wickwire at Thomas Nelson, who believed in me during the tough times. Don Stillman, whose introduction allowed this book to get off the ground. And Mark Dagostino, who had the passion and commitment to bring my full story to life through every twist and turn.

A big thank you to my assistant, Carol Cummings, for keeping all the facts and paperwork in order, and my attorney, Michael Eldridge, for handling all the law and order.

Thanks also to Thomas Hensey and the Rhino team. The Wolfington brothers, Ryan and Sean, who gave me their friendship and support. Tim Blenkiron, a true winner when I really needed one. My good friends Jerry Mowbray and Jon Jannotta. And especially to my lifelong Notre Dame family, teammates and friends.

My forever gratitude to the *Rudy* team, from Angelo Pizzo, David Anspaugh, Rob Fried, and Marc Platt to Sean Astin, Jon Favreau, and all of the others who believe in the message of never giving up . . . whose hard work and talents served as the spark that allowed me to begin sharing that message with the world.

Finally, thanks to God. All faith and courage comes from Him.

About the Authors

DANIEL "RUDY" RUETTIGER is the subject of the blockbuster film Rudy and a popular motivational speaker. His humble background and determination to pursue his dreams, no matter the challenge, has made him legendary and an inspiration to everyone from school children to businessmen and athletes, even presidents. He established the Rudy Foundation to help children around the world and the Rudy Awards for high school and university level athletes.

MARK DAGOSTINO is a *New York Times* best-selling coauthor and one of the most respected celebrity journalists in America. For ten years he was on staff in New York and Los Angeles as a correspondent, columnist, and senior writer for *People* magazine, interviewing personalities such as Shaquille O'Neill, Michael J. Fox, Christopher Reeve, Jennifer Lopez, and Donald Trump.